The Beauty of Aqua

Brian Beeler

Copyright © Brian Beeler 2020
This work is licensed under the Creative Commons Attribution-NonCommercial-NoDerivatives 4.0 International License. The noncommercial redistribution of this novel unchanged in any way, shape or form is both allowed and encouraged.

Printed in the United States of America
Second Edition, 2020
ISBN 978-0-692-19286-3

"There isn't anyone you couldn't learn to love once you've heard their story."

- Fred Rogers

CONTENTS

	Forward	
1	Today	1
2	1985	3
3	The offer	17
4	Welcome to Wonderland	43
5	City by the sea	67
6	The beauty of Aqua	97
7	Everything can be said in food	127
8	When two fire roosters fall in love	163
9	Unrest	185
10	Aqua Vitae	219
11	Last days	259
12	Exit	291
	Postscript: Places mentioned, Glossary, About the author et al	320

Forward

All Upton knows is his very limited view of the world which has limited his hope for happiness. Born in Canada and raised on Cape Cod he has given up on finding a better life and has settled for being a townie. He wants for little more than to ride his motorcycle and have a good meal; neither of which happens very often. But one day he meets a kindred spirit and they find that together they are greater than the sum of their parts. Together they find happiness and the strength to endure in their struggle for the same.

Set in 1985 "The Beauty of Aqua" is an exploration into what makes for a good life today and how we hope we will be remembered after we are no longer here. It is also an exploration into the foods of Central Vietnam and in particular the City of Đà Nẵng.

1

Today

The room is small and brightly lit from the late-morning sun. It is a traditional Vietnamese-family-altar-room. The only furniture in it is a waist-height credenza topped with a family-altar adorned with fruit, freshly prepared foods and a half-dozen photographs of departed loved ones all in light-blue backgrounds. Bright light streams in from the open windows highlighting the smoke from the burning incense. Its smell intermixed with those of the dishes of food and lemon blossoms from just outside the tightly packed room. There is a somber tone among the family members, some with tears in their eyes. They are performing a one-year-death-anniversary-ceremony. Sitting squarely on the altar are the portraits of an elderly man and woman also in front of light-blue backgrounds. Between those two photographs sits something unusual: a small statue of a rooster ablaze in a fiery red, orange and yellow.

2

1985

I wish I could've said I had better things to do but I didn't. There was no work on that cold, February Cape Cod morning or until next month at the marina which meant putting the finishing touches on a course syllabus I'd written and working on my motorcycle. While my fairly fresh computer science degree better suited me for the former task my heart was in the latter. At university my advisor liked my senior thesis and encouraged me to use it in creating a course but no local schools were interested, which likely meant no one would ever see it but me. I wasn't happy but I had a roof over my head, beer in the garage refrigerator and a nice motorcycle, when it ran. Welcome to life as a townie.

The Beauty of Aqua

There's a special joy in taking an old motorcycle that was destined for the scrapyard and bringing it back to life. Before me was an almost functional 1964 Honda CB77 Super Hawk. While not usually respected among "proper" motorcyclists because of its smaller engine it fit my definition of a motorcycle: two wheels, an engine and could remind me I was still alive. If a big motorcycle was a meat cleaver then the Super Hawk was a steak knife. It could handle both the open highway and tight backroads which fit my riding style.

When it was working I'd ride the backroads of the Lower Cape where some of what made Cape Cod famous still existed. The Cape was changing and not for the better. Those from the mainland, flush with cash, bought up whatever they could to either build a house that was clearly out of place in our community or turn it for a quick profit which caused many to leave for the mainland. We were caught in a diaspora that most refused to see. I didn't blame those for selling but the conditions that caused it because it was turning our small community into a place of weekend homes for the nouveau riche. Our quaint fishing village with its traditional cottages and gingerbread-style homes was now dotted with houses that clearly didn't fit. The Cape Cod I knew and loved was dying a slow and painful death.

About once a month a real estate agent would stop by and offer dad a small truckload of cash for our tiny, riverside home but each time he said no. I just didn't know how long he could do that.

1985

I was in the garage trying to reassemble one of my motorcycle's carburetors when there was a knock at the side door.

"Upton; you there?" It was Matt and close to quitting time so hopefully he stopped by the packie.

"Yeah; it's open."

"Hey Upton; brought you a four pack."

"Four pack?"

"You weren't my first stop."

Matt was an interesting character. Born and raised on the Cape, soon after high school he disappeared for a couple of years. Not that he would say but rumor had it he wound up in a monastery in Thailand and others thought he'd set up a cabin up north like Thoreau in Walden. Matt listened more than he talked. Wherever he went it changed him. While his parents were well-off he passed on owning much of anything. He had always been a good friend and was there for me when I needed one.

"What do you need Matt?"

"I got a stuck bolt on my motorcycle and need a breaker bar. Can I borrow yours?"

"Sure, it's on the wall. You know you could always get your own?"

"But then when would we share a beer?"

I laughed. "You got me there but a breaker bar is cheap."

"It's not about the money Upton: the less I own the freer I am. Remember the floods a few years ago?"

"How could I forget? It was hard to tell where my street ended and the river started."

"The houses in my neighborhood were flooded and we lost everything. Next door I saw the family pulling out piles of water-logged clothes and other valued possessions and they were devastated. I don't think they appreciated it."

"It?"

"The opportunity."

"How can losing everything you own be an opportunity?"

"It's an opportunity to do something different. Look at you with this motorcycle."

"It's almost fixed and will be running by spring."

"I don't doubt that Upton, it looks great. What I'm saying is what about the day you have to sell it?"

"Why would I sell it? I'll just take it with me wherever I go."

"What if you can't take it with you?"

"Then I won't go."

"And missing an opportunity in the exchange."

"Yeah, well, c'est la vie."

"Not 'such is the life' but more like the life you choose and since you only live once you should try to make good choices. You need to find what's important to you and then you'll see how much of your stuff is holding you back."

"So what's this 'life with less' done for you?"

"Besides freedom? I get to travel. Last summer I rode an old BSA motorcycle throughout the UK. The summer before I spent at a friend's cabin up in Northern Maine."

"I wondered where you went after we fixed your motorcycle. For me travel's a waste of time and money. I mean I still go back up north once in a while to visit friends from university but why would you go to India?"

Matt was surprised by my question. "What's wrong with India?"

"Nothings wrong with it but there's not a lot of indoor plumbing."

"That's true Upton but I don't travel for the toilets: I travel for the experiences."

Matt made a good point, I guess. I wouldn't know since I'd never really traveled.

It was six in the morning and there was frost on my bedroom window. Our home was typical for our Cape Cod community which meant little insulation and a lot of heat to keep it warm so mornings could get pretty cold. Thankfully our trusty husky "Diefenbaker" kept my feet warm during the night like he always did. I dozed on and off until I heard the sound of the furnace kicking over signaling I had a few more minutes of sleep before I had to get up.

Dad was in the kitchen. "Coffee son?"

"Sure; thanks dad. It's pretty cold this morning."

"We could be back in Newfoundland where it's really cold."

"No thanks. I was born there but I think my blood must of thinned-out living here."

"Don't let anyone hear you say that son. You'll always be a Newfie."

I chuckled. "What are you doing today?"

"Same as always. Heading to the marina to see what needs fixing."

"Need a hand? I'm tapped."

"Sorry son, you know it's just me 'til next month."

"I know, just thought I could earn a few dollars. I think I need a new carburetor for my motorcycle."

"What about the rest of it?" He asked half jokingly.

"The engine's rebuilt and turns beautifully, transmission is still tight from the last rebuild and the rims are aligned. All I need is a carburetor and I'll be finished."

"Famous last words." Then he paused for a second looking like he was caught in a moment of reflection and the smile left his face. "I'm selling the house and moving back to Newfoundland; Saint John's to be exact."

"What? Why?" I felt like I was just hit with a shovel from behind.

"From what I make on the sale I can retire instead of working for another few years and since your mother died I've had little interest in staying here."

"Any offers?"

"Too many and the last one was too big to turn down."

"So when do you close?"

"Not for awhile and construction doesn't begin until next spring. The buyer needs time to have new house plans drawn up and—"

1985

"—they're tearing the house down too?" Another whack from that same shovel.

"Times change Upton and there's nothing we can do to stop it. I'm sorry."

"What about me? What about my stuff?"

"Roy has plenty of space at the marina. Leave anything with him."

"I guess I need to think about moving. The Cape's too rich for me to stay."

"Sorry Upton. You're always welcome to stay with me. Saint John's is beautiful and on the water."

"Yeah; it's beautiful but it's not for me. I don't know where I want to go. So you taking much back to Canada?"

"No; Roy's buying my tools and I'll yard-sale the rest. I don't want to take much with me."

"What about mom and Beall's stuff?"

"What about it?"

"Are you just going to dump it?"

Dad paused and I could see the sadness in his eyes. "Yes Upton because I don't need to save something that's already in my heart."

"You still miss Beall."

"Every day Upton, every day."

"Me too dad; and mom?"

"Same but different. Unlike a child that's part of you like Beall was your mother and I were best friends first and husband and wife second which is rare. So yes; I still miss my friend."

"You could find someone else?"

"No, I can't. I still love your mother and always will."

Living in the same house with the memories of a lost wife and child must've been difficult so I didn't blame dad for wanting to leave. We'd hear a sound in the night that had a familiar tone to it reminding us of the person that died. For one, brief moment they were with us but in a jarring way. It's sad we can't remember those that have died in a place of comfort instead of fear and doubt.

This time next year my childhood home will be demolished and other than university it's the only place I can remember living. While I had a year to move that didn't matter: what I had known and been attached to would soon be gone.

To dad's credit he understood my lack of desire to move inland. Almost all his life had been lived by the sea and he too couldn't imagine living anyplace else. Occasionally he would ask me about using my degree to which I would reply "someday." He could see I was stuck in a deep and painful rut and if things didn't change I wouldn't change.

Well, the opportunity for change blew in like a bad storm. At least I had a year before I had to move.

Life on the ocean and life on the land are not the same. On land everything around you is seemingly in control. Governments set forth haphazard rules and regulations on how every inch within its territory should look. Traffic lights tell cars when to go, sidewalks are your preset paths from place to place and "open areas" consist of a few trees that are constantly being trimmed and regulated.

In contrast your neighbor the ocean is completely unmanageable. What one day fed your family with a bounty of seafood the next takes the lives of those that brought you that same bounty. What one day brought you the soft sounds of rolling waves the next could bring death and destruction. What one day is gentle the next becomes violent yet we find comfort in sitting on a beach and watching the waves because it reveals a truth buried deep within each of us: we are not in full control of our lives.

A seasoned fisherman understands this. He knows every time he goes out he might land the best catch of the year or so little as not to cover the trip's costs. He also knows that his life could possibly end in a few hours with his body never to be found yet he still goes out. Like the cowboys of the Old West, fishermen prefer to take their chances on the uncertainty of nature instead of the absurdity of the manmade society they left behind.

When it was tuna season every fisherman geared-up for the challenge. One good trip could bring in thousands of dollars making or breaking a fishing season.

Roy at the marina was a commercial fisherman for many years before hanging up that hat and resigning himself to a life mostly on the land. For a long time he'd run his boat whenever he could and sold carpet downtown at his father-in-law's store in the winter for the benefits. This was good as he had to take some time off to treat a minor case of cancer before returning back to the store and the sea. I could see his desire to return to fishing but I didn't agree with his choice to go back to work on land after regaining his health. He later became the marina manager when the old one retired giving him a place he enjoyed in both worlds.

Roy liked his job and was good at it. His days of getting underway had long passed but tuna season was different. Everyone knew that when the tuna were running so was Roy and he could only be found in one place: out at sea and last year I worked as his only crew. While others preferred to have a third crew member Roy only wanted one. He said it was easier to work with just one person instead of two but I suspected the real reason was it meant a bigger payday for him. It also meant a bigger payday for me.

Last August we were up in George's Bank with much of the night spent on autopilot allowing us to get some well-needed rest for the busy day ahead. I awoke to the morning sun shining into our small cabin while Roy continued to sleep. Walking outside I found nothing but gentle, rolling seas. I did a quick inspection of our boat and returned to the cabin to make a pot of coffee afterwards heading back up to the pilothouse. We were still many miles away from where we needed to be and there was nothing to do but to let "captain autopilot" continue his task until intervention was required.

Sitting in the pilot's chair I could see to the horizon in every direction and there was nothing here but us. Complete emptiness. Looking off the port side I then spotted two dolphins swimming beside our boat. I sipped my coffee while watching them and at that moment I had an experience that I had never had before: a complete absence of all my concerns for the past and future. I was at peace and felt like I had been transported to a far-off land. For that one, brief moment all I could see were those dolphins living in true freedom and that was intoxicating.

After we returned to port and our lives back on land I saw how unhappy I was with the life I was living but didn't know how to change it. I was stuck. I also saw the difference between me and Roy: if I ever got cancer I could never go back to working at a carpet store.

Knock. Knock. Knock.
"Hey Upton; you there? It's Matt."
"Yeah; it's open."
"Brought your breaker bar back. Thanks."
"No problem Matt. Glad to help."
"You good Upton?" Matt could see I wasn't after dad's news.
"No; dad's selling the house and moving back to Canada."
"Sorry to hear that Upton. When's he selling?"
"Not for awhile and we've got a year before we have to leave but they're tearing it down to build something 'bigger and newer'."
"Mainlanders?"

"Yeah so I have to start thinking about a new place to live but not for a while."

"Use this as an opportunity. Now is the time to sort through what you have and to decide what you need that way there's less to do when you move."

"Good idea Matt. I'll get around to it after I get my motorcycle on the road this spring."

"Don't wait Upton. Start today while you have the time. If you wait you might never get it done."

Welcome to the story of my life: not getting stuff done. I did well enough in school and university but there were times I didn't have the strength to do the simplest daily tasks. In "fight or flight" terms I usually made the third choice: freeze and feel worthless. I had to change. "You're right Matt. I'll start tomorrow."

"It's difficult to do but every day it gets a little easier. The hard part is that you have to do it every day, but it does get easier."

"OK. Thanks Matt. What are you doing tonight?"

"I'll be at the Squire having a beer with Jimmy and Tony. Join us?"

"Not tonight. I want to try to fix this carb and I'm making dinner for dad and me." I paused, "Hey Matt, where'd you go the first time you disappeared? If you don't want to say that's fine."

"I went away Upton. I kept in touch with my parents but otherwise I just went away."

"Why would you? Your family has money. You had nothing to worry about."

"Money is a tool but it comes at a price: the more you have the more you worry about it. I was expected to take over the family business and run it successfully. The weight of running a business my family worked so hard to build was too much for me so I left. I took some money from a trust my grandfather left for me and travelled. First to Spain then up through France to Norway. After that all I wanted was to see more. I headed to India for a few months, east through Nepal and Burma then finally to Thailand where I lived in a Buddhist monastery."

"Rumor had it you might've become a monk."

"The rumor was wrong. I lived and worked there but not as a monk, just as a normal person. When I came back to the States I headed up north and lived for awhile up by the White Mountains in New Hampshire. I learned what I needed to learn and came back to the Cape."

"What's that?"

"We need to remember and sometimes be reminded that our lives have value." Matt smiled because he knew what I needed. "I'll bring you a book."

"Another one?"

"Another one."

About a week later uncle François, dad's brother, called much too early in the morning.

"Hey uncle; you want to talk to dad?"

"Not this time. I have an offer for you."

The Beauty of Aqua

3

The offer

"I hear your father's selling the house."
"Yeah; c'est la vie. Thanks for the reminder."
"I have an offer for you."
"What is it?"
"Tell me first, you still writing that computer course you told me about?"
"Yeah and it's finished. Why?"
"The nonprofit group I work for has a contract for a computer science teacher at a small university for a year. Interested?"
"Not really. My motorcycle's almost running and you know I have no interest in living inland."
"Sorry, forgot to mention it's on the ocean."

"Really? I don't know."

"What I do know is that you're stuck Upton and if you don't do something different you'll be another townie for the rest of your life. Nothing wrong with being a townie but it's a bit limiting. I'm giving you a chance for something different. What do you have to lose?"

I had already lost my home, half my family and had little more than a few books and an old motorcycle that I liked to ride, when it ran. I had nothing that really mattered. Admission of that fact was both painful and liberating. I decided to bite. "Where's the job: East or West Coast?"

"East, very east. Or West depending on how you get there."

"Huh? Where is it?"

"Vietnam; Central Vietnam. The City of Danang."

"But the war."

"It's over but the country is still very rough."

"I know the war's over but—"

"—and there's motorcycles. Lots of motorcycles. Hondas and Russian Urals. I also heard they have some really good food."

I thought hard and, truth be told, I had no better place to go. I also wanted to be someplace with good food and that wasn't here.

"OK uncle: sold. What about the language?"

"French is the second language so that'll work in a pinch and you'll be assigned a government translator. Get your university records together and meet me up here in Montreal. I'll take you to the Vietnamese mission where

The offer

you'll get a visa. Bring your Canadian passport and leave your American one with your father. In fact forget you even have one. They're not very welcoming of Americans right now as you can imagine."

"Pas de problème avec mon passeport du Canada. C'est bien. Je suis Canadien!"

"Very funny. A Newfie with a good Boston accent and a bad Canadian-French one. They'll never understand you."

Ouch. "So when do I leave?"

"In four days. Get up here as soon as you can and I'll rush you through what we need to do. Bring one carry-on and one suitcase. Pack only what you really need."

"What about my job?"

"You're working? Thought it was just your father at the shop 'til March?"

"Yeah but he might need a hand. Besides I've got other things to do."

"Like drinking a few beers at the Squire with the boys? You'll be fine."

"Why so quick uncle?"

"My first and second picks had to drop out at the last minute."

"Wow. Glad to know I was your third."

"You weren't. No US Citizens were allowed to apply for the job but we're in a jam and you meet the requirements."

"I'm starting to wonder if this is for me."

"It is Upton: fish or cut bait?"

The Beauty of Aqua

I made my decision pretty quickly because I had few options and they were all poor choices. "Fish. I'll catch a bus to Boston and an overnight to Montreal. Meet me at the station?"

"We'll have some Molsons and poutine."

"Once again you know me all too well uncle. I miss poutine. What about Bar-B-Shed for barbecue?"

"Bien sûr neveu."

"See you soon uncle."

"Au revoir Upton."

I should've been excited but wasn't. I'd found change to be a force that many times was too difficult to face but uncle was right: I needed to do this or I'd be a townie for the rest of my life. Nothing wrong with being a townie but uncle was right again, it is a bit limiting. In just a week everything in my life was going to change and I was scared.

I needed to find dad. "Hey dad! You there?"

"In the kitchen."

I walked into the kitchen and it seemed not as familiar as before. This was the kitchen of my childhood, the kitchen where mom, dad, Beall and I would eat our meals. A place I cherished and after tomorrow I'd never see again. I felt lost in my own home because it was no longer mine.

"Uncle called me."

"He said he would."

"He found me a teaching job in a city on the ocean."

"Really? That's great Upton. East or West Coast?"

The offer

"East, very east. Or West depending on how you get there."

"Huh?"

"It's in Central Vietnam. The City of Danang."

"But the war?"

"It's over."

"I know that but life there must be really tough."

"I don't doubt that but I need to go. This time next year you and this house will be gone. I really don't want to stick around to see that and I don't know what to do. Uncle's offer isn't perfect but it's something different."

"Something different is good. I don't regret traveling when I was young. Go, be safe and remember you always have a place to stay with me."

"I know dad but it's time for me to be on my own."

"You'll be on your own but not alone. When you remember your family you're never alone."

"Thanks dad."

"So what about your stuff?"

Back to the business at hand. "I don't know."

"Grab some boxes from the packie and leave 'em at the marina. Roy will let you store whatever you have in the back of the boat barn while you're gone."

"Thanks again dad."

"You're welcome Upton." He paused, "I hope you can find some happiness son."

I should call Matt. "Hey Matt; you free?"

"I am. What do you need?"

"I'm moving sooner than expected and need a hand figuring out what to keep and not keep. Can you help?"

"Sure. I was going to swing by and drop off that book anyways. I'll be there in a bit. Take everything you own and bring it out to the garage. We'll sort it there."

"Everything?"

"You can't fix a problem you can't see, so yes, everything."

"Will do Matt. See you soon."

About an hour later there was a knock on the side door of the garage and it was Matt. "Door's open."

"Hey Upton; so you're moving sooner than expected?"

"Yeah; day after tomorrow."

"Why so fast?"

"I got a contract teaching job. The first two choices had to drop out so they offered it to me."

"Where is it?"

"Central Vietnam."

Matt smiled. "I thought you said travel was a waste of time?"

"I did and after thinking about what you said I figured I might be wrong."

"Good Upton. How long's the contract?"

"A year."

Matt smiled even more at that news. "Nice. Work in the East and make a paycheck from the West. You picked the winning ticket my friend."

"How do you figure that?"

"While experiences gathered while traveling abroad are good, living abroad is life-changing. You're required to adapt and change almost all your ideas about how life, a good life, should be lived."

"Any advice?"

"When you sit down with a family for dinner what they're eating might look strange but if they're eating it it's fine. Not eating what's in front of you is seen as disrespectful because food everywhere is a source of pride."

"I'll remember that. Anything else?"

"Live like a local."

"How? I don't speak the language."

"Live like a local means travel like the locals travel, eat what the locals eat and sleep like the locals sleep. In every city there's a few places that cater to tourists serving western food and acting like a western hotel. Avoid them like the plague."

"Why? It sounds like an oasis in the desert."

"They're the desert and the local life is the oasis. If you want some seafood are you going to the clam shack at the marina or one of the tourist traps on Main Street?"

"Marina clam shack, hand's down."

"Why?"

"Because it's authentic and not something dressed up for the tourists." I thought about what I just said. "I get it Matt. I understand. Thanks."

"It took me a lot longer to learn the same."

"So where do we start?"

"Think about what you need for one day like clothes and your passport. Then think about what you need for the next three or four days. With what's left ask yourself what you've recently used. If you use it often keep it and if it's been unused for awhile chances are you don't need it anymore. Give it to someone that can use it and don't just store it away. Save as little as possible."

"What if I need something I gave away?"

"Ask to borrow it. Bringing a four pack helps."

I laughed. It worked on me.

"When you respectfully borrow something from a friend you also get a chance to talk with them and many times you'll find they need something you have. You've spent time with a friend and both of you have solved a problem."

"Thanks Matt. I'd better get to work."

"Enjoy your travels Upton. You'll have a great time." With that Matt started to head out but stopped and pulled a book wrapped in newspaper from his heavy jacket pocket. He smiled and handed me the book. "Here's your book Upton."

"Thanks again Matt."

I spent the morning sorting and packing about a half-dozen boxes and then moved them and my motorcycle into the back of dad's truck. Here I thought I didn't have much but when everything was in front of me it seemed I did. At first choosing what I wanted to take with me, put in storage and give away was difficult but I thought about Matt's advice. Everything I looked at I could see a use for and wanted to keep but knew I couldn't. These things that once brought me some kind of joy now felt like a weight around my neck. As I continued I found the more I tossed the easier it became to choose what was really important.

The offer

What to take? Only the bare essentials: some clothes, my passport, the course materials and my university records. What else? My Bell RT helmet and riding jacket. Also a few of my favorite Grateful Dead and Bob Dylan bootleg cassette tapes and both books Matt gave me. Anything else? Yeah, some family photos.

I found that act was both difficult and rewarding at the same time and I felt happy for a change. Society says to be happy we need more possessions but this most recent act of culling showed me that I might be happier with less. Matt was right again. Everything was just happening much too fast.

When I finally finished loading everything I hopped in dad's truck and headed to the marina. As I started to leave I realized that I had just removed most of my life from the home I grew up in. I felt separated from a place that had almost always been my home. It wasn't long until I pulled into the marina and started looking for a parking spot out back when I heard Roy's bark. I got out and he walked over to my truck.

"Hey Upton; your dad called and told me you needed to store a couple of boxes with me."

"I've got a few and my motorcycle."

"Ever get it running?"

"Well, almost."

"Not a problem now. Where're you moving to?"

"Vietnam, for a year."

Roy paused, "Why are you going there?" I could hear the tension in his voice.

"A job. Why?"

The Beauty of Aqua

"It's hot there and I'm talking sweat right through your shirt before you get your morning soup hot." He said with more push in his voice than before.

"How would you know that?"

"I was a Machinist's Mate in the Coast Guard stationed just south of Saigon in '65 for a bit then I got moved over to the Point Marone west of there in An Thoi."

"I didn't know Roy. You never said anything."

"Because I didn't want to." I could tell he was recalling a painful memory.

"You saw combat?"

"Some but that was a long time ago when I was 'petty officer Parsons'."

"Sorry about that Roy."

"That's OK Upton. There were some good times too. The people were nice and the food was really good."

"Like what?"

"I didn't speak the language so I couldn't tell you. I'd just walked down the street and got something that looked and smelled good. You should do the same."

"You miss anything from there?"

Roy thought for a moment. "All the motorcycles and family meals. There's a lot more motorcycles than cars. So many when you're at a stop light you feel like a little fish in a big school. And once in a while I'd eat a meal with a local family. We'd sit on the floor next to a motorcycle yet the food could've been served at a fine restaurant. You'll never eat better Upton and eating good food like that every day is a life-well lived."

The offer

Roy had been a good friend of the family for a long time and was a good boss to work for. He also knew about my struggles.

"I'll try to remember that. Anything else?"

"The women there wear a special dress. Also don't know the name but when they wear it they're all beautiful."

"I think you needed more shore leave."

He laughed. "That was always true. What city you going to?"

"Danang. Been there?"

"No but they got a beach: China Beach. Suppose to be beautiful."

"Better than Nauset?"

"Like a lot of things you'll find there it's not that it's better or worse, it's different. Very different."

"Thanks for letting me leave my stuff here. I'll be back in a year to pick it up."

"Maybe. You might stay."

"I doubt it."

"Don't say that Upton. Once you fall in love with that country it'll never let you go. It becomes part of you like no other place in this world. It stole my heart and it will get yours."

"Think you'll ever go back?"

"I'd like to but doubt they'll be letting any Americans back in anytime soon." Roy paused in thought, "How'd you get in?"

"Canadian passport."

"That'll work. Better not talk about also being an American. I'm sure they're still a little pissed at us and to be honest I can't blame them."

"I was told I should be fine."

"You'll be fine Upton but remember to behave. They've been through a lot and don't need another westerner disrespecting them."

"Thanks Roy."

The Squire wasn't a place many tourists visited due to its usual sight of weather-worn and rather surly fishermen drinking and holding forth, like they like to do in their own boisterous ways. There were also a few US Coast Guardsmen from the nearby lifeboat station and Roy was at the bar nursing a beer probably thinking about the choices he'd made that brought him here on that night. The building was old with uneven floors littered with various wounds from its many years of use. Tourists say they like "going local" but really what they wanted was "faux local." Something new and different yet safe. The truth is new and different is rarely safe. That's what makes it so seductive and a bit scary.

There's Jimmy. "Hey Jimmy."

"Upton; beer?"

"Ordered at the bar and on its way."

"Good man. No one likes to drink alone." A poignant reminder of my impending trip and how I'd be without my friends. I took my seat.

The offer

"Where's Tony? He working tonight?"

"No; the Dreadnaught's closed tonight and he'll be here soon." Tony worked Down Cape first starting as a dishwasher but made his way up to running the grill which he really liked. He was a good guy that could tell a good story.

"What about Josh?"

"His place isn't closed so he's working." Josh was a talented chef and also like Tony loved good food. We three also had the same struggles.

No better time than the present to drop my news on Jimmy. "I'm leaving the Cape for a contract teaching job."

Jimmy looked at me with bewilderment. "You're leaving? I don't believe it. For good?"

"A year but dad's selling the house so maybe. Not like I can afford to live here anymore."

"Well, you can always crash on my couch if you come back as long as you help with the rent."

"Thanks Jimmy. It's appreciated."

"When are you out of here Upton?"

"Tomorrow."

Now he was surprised. "Why so fast?"

"The first two choices had to drop out at the last minute so it's my turn."

"Good job Upton. You came in third. You're a winner!"

"Funny man. Actually I wasn't even third but that doesn't matter because I'm the one going."

A pitcher of beer and four mugs arrived at our table. Matt was at the bar and chatting with a few friends when I caught his attention and waved him over. "Upton, Jimmy. What are you gentlemen doing tonight?"

"This." As I pointed to the pitcher of beer.

"May I join you?"

"Of course good sir." I said jokingly in a poor British accent. Matt took a seat. Four mugs of beer were poured: three for us and one for Tony who was on his way.

"Did you finish packing?"

"I did. Thanks for the advice Matt. One suitcase and one carry-on. A few boxes went into storage with my motorcycle. I appreciate the help."

"No problem Upton. I was stuck in the same hole and I just shared what helped me."

"Is that why you left? Because you were in a hole."

"Kind of but I had to leave and be challenged in everyday life just to see I was in a hole. The experiences I'd gained in my travels helped me climb out of it."

"You learned a lot traveling didn't you?"

"Quite a bit. Learning from travel is like drinking from a fire hydrant: you'll never come close to getting it all and that hydrant is about to hit you full-on. Learn to enjoy the challenge."

I'd like to say we continued our talk on other weighty subjects since I was leaving but we didn't. After that our conversation rarely strayed from the mundane. Even in the inevitable face of change all I wanted to do was to avoid talking about it.

The offer

Dad was up early and in the kitchen. The coffee was made and smelled welcoming.

"Coffee son?"

"Yeah; thanks Dad. Do you think they drink coffee in Vietnam?"

"I don't know but you're about to find out. You about ready to leave for the bus station?"

"That'd be great. Thanks dad."

"No problem. Nervous?"

"Yeah, a little." It was more than a little; it was a lot but I didn't want to let on.

"I'll miss you dad."

"I'll miss you too son. We'll talk on the phone."

"Maybe, maybe not. I don't know how good the phone service is over there."

"We'll write. Besides you'll be back in a year. You'll visit me first when you get back?"

"Bien sûr père."

"How did you ever survive four years in Montreal with that accent?"

Ouch. "You and uncle are always dinging me on my French."

"We were born in Montreal. It's our responsibility to protect the French language."

"I think the French would disagree."

"Yeah…" He said trailing off then changed the subject. "Anything I think you'll want and I don't take with me when I move I'll leave with Roy."

"Thanks dad. Take good care of Diefenbaker."

"I will. I think he'll be happy back in Canada."

"Thanks again. We should go."

The ride was taken in complete silence. Dad and I couldn't say a word. The AM radio, full of static, was ignored. When we arrived at the bus station we could barely speak.

"I love you son."

"I knew that dad. I love you too."

"I knew that son."

And with a hug I headed into the bus station. Two hours to Boston, wait around for a couple more and an overnight to Montreal. A good time to sleep.

It was nice to be back in Montreal. Yes, it was still winter and still cold but the barbecue and poutine were always warm and that was what mattered. Although far from the coast Montreal has always had a special charm about it to me. The mixture of high-culture and everyday, working folk led to its unique flavor and it was a good place to go to university. Also the food which was one unto itself. I was happy the ride was over and couldn't wait to get off the bus.

"Upton!"

"Uncle!"

"Welcome back to Montreal."

"Thanks. Looks like nothing's changed."

"Other than a few new buildings it's still the same."

"Let's eat. Bar-B-Shed awaits."

"Later. We need to get over to the Vietnamese

The offer

diplomatic mission and get you a visa. After that we'll eat."

"I've missed Montreal barbecue so much."

"You've always loved good food Upton. We'll eat in a bit. Give me your passport if you please." I handed him my passport. "I'm glad you even had one."

"Mom wanted to go to France as a family but that never happened."

"I'm sorry Upton. Now you'll get a chance to use it."

"How far to the mission?"

"Not far. Only about twenty klicks."

We soon arrived at the Vietnamese mission. It was on the second-floor of a strip mall and not what I expected. Uncle had me sign a few forms in the car. He took them, my passport and stuffed them into an envelope with $400 cash.

"That's a lot of money for a visa. Why so much?"

"It's mostly for 'coffee money'."

"What's 'coffee money'?"

"It's what the Vietnamese call small bribes."

"Really? That seems dishonest."

"I don't know what to say Upton. Yes, it's dishonest but if that person doesn't take a few bribes he isn't going to eat. Right now Vietnam is dirt poor and I don't blame our friend for doing something we'd probably do if the tables were turned."

"Point made uncle."

"C'est bien neveu. Let's go in. Don't say a word unless I tell you to."

I said nothing and everything went quickly. We headed back to uncle's car.

"So when do I leave?"

"First thing in the morning. You'll fly first to San Francisco then Hong Kong and finally Hanoi."

"Is that near where I'm working."

"No; Hanoi's up north. You'll meet your government minder there and then you'll head south to Danang."

"Government minder?"

"Oui; even as a Canadian they'll be watching you so behave yourself and say nothing about being a US citizen. One word and they can and will boot you."

I smiled. "You said boooot." He wasn't amused. We drove out to the street and my passport had its first entry.

Later that evening we found our way to Bar-Beq-Shed. It was a favorite for not only the quality of the barbecue but the quantity. Our small table was overflowing with plates of pork ribs, brisket, chicken thighs, rib-eye, poutine and beer. The ever-necessary ingredients for a great meal in this city.

Montreal barbecue is a proud, century-old tradition of creating specific cuts of meats with the proper proportions of fat, seasoned in their trademark mixture of salt, pepper, coriander and a few other spices then smoked for hours over local wood. In the darkest days of winter that was all I needed to find a bit of happiness in every bite. That and poutine.

Poutine is a gift from the heavens. While a simple poutine is made with only three ingredients: french fries, gravy and cheese curds the secret to a great poutine is the

The offer

care in which it's made. Ours that night started with a base of perfectly golden-brown fries, coated in a coarse salt, that snapped with a bit of resistance to reveal its warm and tender core. The gravy was made of rendered duck fat and was added to the top with goat cheese curds.

Completing our trifecta of joy was the beer which was, of course, Canadian and plenty of it because anything else would've been heresy. It was a meal of decadence that was fit for a medieval king.

"Hey uncle; you haven't said much about the job."

"Because there isn't much to say. You're going to a university and you'll be teaching computer science for a year. I don't know much past that."

"How'd you come across it?"

"The nonprofit I work for places English teachers throughout Asia but occasionally from time to time we receive a contract for others like computer science teachers. Your name came up from someone else so it made it possible for me to recommend you."

"Someone else?"

"Your university was asked for a list of qualified grads who could teach and your name found its way on it."

"What do you know about where I'm going?"

"Nothing."

"What about the computers?"

"Part of our contract is to supply the school with what's needed. The computers are on their way and should be there in about a month or so. Difficult to say."

"What happened to the guys you picked for the job?"

"They had to drop out. Couldn't get a visa."

"And I got one in a day with my 'immigration issue?' That doesn't sound legit."

"It doesn't matter Upton. We both know you needed this. You're not happy and staying on the Cape wasn't doing you any good. You were stuck and I got you unstuck. I have a friend with a similar problem and he also thinks this is what you need."

I became defensive. "Who's your friend you've been sharing my life with?"

"An old university friend I trust. He was a student and I was a teaching assistant in his class. Nice guy who also loves good food but has a dry sense of humor that can be a bit irritating. We've always kept in touch and he's been a good friend. He understands what you're going through and likes to help people make good choices over poor choices. Taking this job was a good choice."

"You sure uncle?"

"Oui mon neveu; I'm sure."

"I'm scared."

"Of course you are but in no time you won't and you'll be stronger."

"Thanks uncle. I will try to remember that. Any advice?"

"Oui; behave yourself and don't irritate anyone because they'll be watching you."

"That doesn't sound good."

"Tensions are still tight even though the war's over. There are some that are still bitter about being on the

The offer

losing side and sometimes they come and cause more harm than good. They'll be watching you to make sure you're not one of those troublemakers."

"Can I still drink the beer?"

Uncle laughed. "Oui; beer is fine. Just be careful not to drink too much. Most everyone you'll meet will be nice to you but a few won't so keep a sober head."

"I'll behave myself."

"I know nephew otherwise I wouldn't have given you the job. You're going to be challenged a lot over the next year but you'll be fine."

"You travelled when you were young didn't you?"

"Oui mon neveu; I was in Paris with your father after the war working for the Canadian Government to help them rebuild the city."

"Paris looks beautiful."

"It wasn't then, it was a total mess. Le régime de Vichy was a client state of the Nazis, had just fallen and a few of its leaders were being 'removed'."

"Removed?"

"What I mean is one day they disappeared and all that was left of them were the memories of their misdeeds. After the war the country was awash in firearms and the Russian-made Chekhov was the preferred tool for those removals. One day those that hurt France so badly were here and the next they were ghosts. Those people collaborated with the Nazis and that collaboration cost the lives of over 70,000 Jews from France. Your grandmother, Anne Kursinski, was Jewish and if she'd stayed in France instead of coming to Canada we might of been in that group of 70,000." I could clearly see the sadness on his face. "Excusez-moi neveu. The past is the past and there's no changing it. We can only learn from our mistakes and move forward. After the war Paris was on very hard times but there was a real sense of optimism. A sense that tomorrow would be a better day. The people of France had been to hell and back but could still see a brighter future and I gained a new respect for them. They were always kind to me and your father notwithstanding their complaints about our Canadian dialect. My old university friend use to do the same."

I smiled because I could see the moment in his eyes when he was thinking about his time in Paris. Being around those that had suffered so much yet still had optimism had clearly been a good influence on him.

"What did you do there?"

"Your father helped restart seafood imports to the local markets and I had just started working for the Ministry of Foreign Affairs."

"That's a bit vague."

"Because it's meant to be. I helped coordinate between the Canadian and Free French Governments. Nothing nefarious but the past should stay in the past."

"Are you still working for the Federal Government?"

"Oui mon neveu; same as always and part-time with the nonprofit that got you your job. I can retire in a few years and maybe I'll join your father in Saint John's."

"He'd like that. You two have always been close and I'd sleep better knowing he wasn't alone. While I'm gone would you keep an eye on him? He's never been alone

The offer

before and I worry about him."

"He's got Diefenbaker."

"That's true and both will be happy to be back here."

"Your father and I are family so we are never alone just like you'll never be alone when you remember your family. I'm sure he'll be spending a lot of time with me here in Montreal."

"I worry he's going to miss working."

"Your father loves turning a wrench and he's good at it but he's ready to let it go. I'd watch him work and it was like watching a Buddhist monk in meditation. Every move had a purpose and every bit of his attention was on the job at hand. He took joy in seeing the fruits of his labors in the boats he fixed which is something I think we all want."

"He was always gently reminding me that if I wasn't doing what I enjoyed I'd never be happy and I wasn't."

"Your father understands what happiness is and has lit the path he found with the hope others would find their way too. He's also been good at that."

"About the job; why am I leaving so quickly?"

"We received a 'use or lose' grant for the position and the computers. That's why we're in a rush to get you where you're going. It's a new world nephew and while the demand for English teachers is always growing we think the need for computer science teachers could be fairly big. 'Give a man a fish and you feed him for a day. Teach him how to fish and you feed him for a lifetime.' Vietnam wants to move forward now that the war's over and your job is to help them rebuild for a better future."

"Sounds like a big job."

"That's why like your father you need to pay careful attention to your work."

"OK uncle. Is that quote from the bible?"

"Non neveu; Lao Tzu, the founder of Taoism. You'll soon find that there are many common lessons between the East and the West."

"Anything else I need to know?"

"Don't get romantic with anyone. You're there for a year and then you'll be gone."

"I'll try to remember that."

"One last thing: if anyone asks where you've been living tell them you were with me in Montreal."

"Again, doesn't sound legit."

"Let me worry about that. Just don't irritate anyone."

We finished our dinner and headed to uncle's house for the night and a quick sleep. This time tomorrow I'll be long gone.

The next morning uncle dropped me off at the airport. "You have everything Upton?"

"Yeah uncle."

"A little gift for you." He handed me a can of maple syrup. I laughed and put it in my carry-on bag.

"I guess you can't get that in Vietnam."

"No you can't nephew."

"Thanks uncle."

Uncle François looked at the clock on the wall. "It is time for you to leave."

The offer

"See you again uncle"

"Bon voyage Upton." He turned to leave then looked back. "Remember your uncle will be looking out for you." With that he was gone.

I was now more alone than I had ever been before but it wasn't as bad as I thought it would be. Tickets in hand I walked down the jetway and on to my plane. All I could do was sleep.

The Beauty of Aqua

4

Welcome to Wonderland

It was late at night when my plane finally landed and we were waiting on the tarmac for an unknown reason. After some time a truck with a boarding ramp arrived; something I hadn't seen since I was a small child. There was an announcement in what I guessed was Vietnamese and everyone rushed to get their bags from the overhead bin and leave. I started to get up but the flight attendant gestured with her hands for me to remain seated. My fellow passengers quickly filtered out through the forward cabin door and when the last one left two police officers boarded the plane, then gestured for me to follow them. Not what I wanted to see. Welcome to Vietnam.

The Beauty of Aqua

As I walked through the cabin door I was hit with a mild breeze and not what I expected for February. We walked down the boarding ramp and an old US Army JEEP bearing a Vietnamese license plate pulled up next to us, stopped and the driver got out. Even though he was wearing a suit, a well-tailored one at that, the two police officers next to me snap to attention and saluted. He approached us.

"Upton?"

"That's me. How'd you guess?"

"You are the only westerner on the plane."

I sheepishly replied, "Oh yeah."

"These are my credentials." The man showed me his identification card and it looked like Navajo.

"Welcome to Việt Nam. My name is Nguyễn Sinh Dũng. You may call me 'anh Dũng.' I am with the Ministry of Foreign Affairs and will be your liaison while you are here in my country. Follow me if you please."

We got into his JEEP and without another word we drove to the terminal then passed through immigrations. While I was expecting a long, drawn out process I was surprised to see it only took a few minutes. Anh Dũng seemed to carry some weight around here. We worked our way out to the airport terminal exit.

"You are from Montreal cháu Upton?"

"I was living there but I'm originally from Newfoundland, it's east of Quebec."

"A Newfie? Est-ce que tu parles français?"

"Je parle en français."

"And not well cháu." Anh Dũng said with a slight smile.

"How do you know about Newfoundland?"

"I went to Sir George Williams University in Montreal in the 1950s. Difficult cold in the winter but everything else was pleasant. Very good barbecue. It is where I studied English and Political Science."

"What a coincidence. I went to McGill."

"I know that cháu Upton and it is not a coincidence. The position required the teacher be educated in the Province du Quebec and a Canadian citizen. That is why I am your liaison. It was part of your background check." He could see the concerned look on my face. Clearly he knew a bit about me and hopefully not about how I was also a US citizen. We made our way out of the airport.

"My government is most interested in helping you teach and to make sure you stay out of trouble. We should retrieve your bags and I will take you to your hotel downtown in the Old Quarter. Early tomorrow morning we will board a train to Đà Nẵng."

"What about the computers?"

"They should arrive in one month, maybe longer. Difficult to say."

We retrieved my suitcase and walked through the airport terminal exit where I was met with another pleasant breeze but this time with the smell of something good. Ahead of us were parked a collection of very strange cars and a few trucks.

Anh Dũng's car was a well-worn, dark-green Russian UAZ with the only other color a fire-red, hammer-and-sickle badge on the front grill. I tossed my bags in the back and got in.

"Where's the seatbelt?"

"No seatbelts cháu: this is Việt Nam."

It was very late when we left for the hotel. While Hà Nội was one of the country's largest cities it was quite dark.

"Don't you have street lights?"

"We have some very nice street lights but there is little electricity so we can not often use them."

"I didn't know." Because I didn't know much.

We continued our drive in the dark night and little could be seen.

"I will pick you up at five in the morning and we will go to the train station. I would suggest that you not leave your hotel without me because it is not a good time to be an American in Hà Nội."

"I'm Canadian."

"Yes cháu. I do not know what I was thinking."

Does he know? We spoke little after that.

Hà Nội at night with few lights was haunting. The eclectic collection of buildings cast odd-shaped shadows onto the street only interrupted by the occasional pedestrian with the city still returning to normal after the recent Lunar New Year celebrations. We arrived at the hotel conveniently near the train station. Due to the darkness little of the Old Quarter could be seen but the smell of barbecue hung heavy and sweet in the late, evening air. We soon arrived at my hotel and stopped.

"Barbecue this late?"

Welcome to Wonderland

"Yes cháu Upton; Vietnamese people like barbecue and it is common to smell it late at night. We like to sit on our front steps, drink beer and have barbecue."

"That's legal? Back home someone would've called the police and made us move the party to the backyard."

"Việt Nam is different. In the West the act of drinking beer and having barbecue on your front steps is seen as antisocial and that you should only do these things in private. In Việt Nam we see doing these acts in public good for our community because our neighbors know they are welcome to join us."

Drinking beer and eating barbecue on my front steps late at night with my neighbors? That I was looking forward to.

"Follow me cháu Upton if you please. Let us go inside and get you to your room."

We left his UAZ and anh Dũng picked up my carry-on bag while I grabbed my oversized suitcase.

"Merci monsieur."

"What did you say?"

"Thank you."

"Oh; that is what I thought you said."

Bang! Bang! Bang!

I heard a loud knock at my door.

"Hold on. I'm coming."

It was five in the morning and I was still in a daze from the combination of lack of sleep, jet lag and hunger yet still managed to open the door.

The Beauty of Aqua

"Bonjour cháu Upton. Please meet me downstairs in fifteen minutes if you please. Someone will be waiting outside of your room to bring your bags downstairs."

"Oui monsieur; je serai là dans quinze minutes."

"What did you say?"

"I'll be there in ten minutes."

"Oh; that is what I thought you said."

I got cleaned up and dressed within a few minutes. Opening my door I found a police officer waiting outside and was surprised when he pointed to my bags. Nodding yes he carried them out.

The dark alley outside the hotel was lit by the first light of the morning. To the west the sky was still dark but to the east you could see the faintest of light acting as an announcement that the morning was finally here. Hà Nội still looked like a ghost town and everything was still very dark but I could see this pleasantly varying array of yellow-orange and light, blue-green narrow storefronts and a very narrow street with a few people walking from here to there. Women were pushing bicycles while balancing baskets of fruit and flowers. There was a pleasant snap in the air and the smell of something good which was seductive.

We loaded up Anh Dũng's UAZ with my bags and quickly headed to the train station. As we passed a small lake I caught the fleeting sight of the tail section of a US Air Force plane.

"What's that?" As I pointed back to the wreckage.

"It is an American plane that was shot down during the American War. After the war ended we decided it was something better remembered than forgotten."

"Isn't it painful to look at?"

"Yes cháu Upton; it is. That is why it is there. It is better to remember the pains of life than hide them away."

We pulled up to the train station. Against a light-gray building read in large, red letters: "Ga Hà Nội" and I quickly checked my Vietnamese-English dictionary.

"Hanoi Chicken?"

Anh Dũng laughed for the first time. "No em; 'ga' is short for 'nhà ga' or train station and is from the French word 'gare' for station. 'Gà' is chicken. You should look carefully at the tone marks."

"'Ga' and 'gà' sound the same."

Anh Dũng rolled his eyes and we headed inside.

"I'm starving. Any place around here I can get something to eat and a cup of coffee?"

"Yes cháu; we have many choices for both."

"That's a relief. How's the coffee here?" I had train station coffee before and it wasn't very good so I weighed my options between taking my chances on something local or trying to find a packet of instant coffee somewhere around here. Not that I liked instant but at least it was a familiar taste. Anh Dũng saw that moment as an opportunity to shed a little light onto this westerner's ignorance and said with confidence.

"Our coffee is the best in the world."

My local pride kicked in. "Better than Timmies?"

"Vietnamese coffee is different. Follow me if you please.

We walked over to an old, metal cart surrounded by a couple of small, plastic tables with matching stools and took our seats. Anh Dũng called out "Em ơi! Hai cà phê sữa đá Sài Gòn!"

"What's 'em'?"

"'Em' is a pronoun and how an older person addresses a younger man or woman."

"What does 'ơi' mean?"

"'Ơi' means 'ơi'."

"Huh?"

"My apologies cháu Upton. I forgot you do not use that expression in Canada. It is a way to get someone's attention."

I could see the woman preparing our coffees as she poured into each glass some coffee with the consistency of thinned-out motor oil over a mixture of ice and something white. We were soon served.

"Iced coffee? Looks good."

I looked at my glass. This was coffee but still looked foreign.

"Is this your first Vietnamese coffee?"

"My first Vietnamese anything."

Anh Dũng smiled. "You are in for a special treat. Drink cháu."

I took my first sip and what I tasted was an epiphany. Inside that glass was a simple concoction of only three ingredients: Vietnamese-grown coffee, sweetened condensed milk and crushed ice. The flavor of the coffee was strong but not bitter. I could also taste notes of cocoa and butter which was a pleasant surprise and I could've drank the entire glass in one shot. I was happy.

"You should drink slower cháu Upton. Vietnamese coffee is very strong. You like no?"

"Oui; c'est très bien."

"What did you say?"

"It's very good."

"Oh; that is what I thought you said."

He both knew what I said and what I meant which, by the smile on his face, pleased him. We sat quietly and enjoyed our coffees until I broke our silence.

"Anh Dũng; why'd you go to school in Canada?"

"I wanted to study English in an English speaking country. I received a scholarship and was very happy to go to Montreal as I also spoke the French language which was a great benefit."

"And they understood you in Montreal?" I said with a friendly jab.

"Yes cháu Upton; I was a foreigner in a foreign land but I quickly adapted to the Canadian-French dialect and when I walked into a shop and spoke French almost every time it brought a smile to the shopkeeper's face. Those in Montreal and I love the French language and that gave us a common bond. I was by myself but with my language skills I soon became part of their community."

"How'd you get the scholarship?"

"Good fortune. I was a good student, worked hard and my teacher had a friend in Canada that told her about a scholarship for students from my country. I applied and was chosen."

"Sounds more like skill and not luck."

"That is a western thought: if you work hard you will succeed and if you do not succeed then you only have yourself to blame. This is not true because there are many factors that control our lives in which we have no control over. Just because I succeeded where others failed does not make me better than them. Just because I failed where others have succeeded does not make them better than me. Everyone is unique but no one is special, some are just more fortunate than others. There were other students that were better than me but I was the one chosen. It was by chance that I am here today and I try to appreciate my good fortune." Anh Dũng paused, "The Vietnamese people work very hard every day yet have little to show for their efforts while some westerners have gained great wealth for little work compared to my fellow countrymen. Are we to blame for our poverty? For the most part no because much of our daily efforts for the last thirty years went into fighting instead of farming, digging up bombs instead of building new homes and burying our dead instead of celebrating them in life." Anh Dũng paused again then his attitude improved. "The past is the past and there is no changing it. We are now building a new Việt Nam and someday we will be much stronger. That is where you come in."

"Me?"

"Yes cháu; you are here to help us build a new foundation for my country."

For a moment I saw Việt Nam like France after WWII. The country was poor and battered but something amazing grew from the ashes.

"I'm sorry that this country has suffered so much and I'll do my best to help."

"I know that cháu Upton else you would not be here. You came highly recommended."

"My uncle helped but thanks. Funny, you were living in Montreal when he was there too. Maybe you met?"

"No cháu; we have not met. Montreal is a big city."

"Do you miss Montreal anh Dũng?"

"Yes cháu Upton; while I do not miss the very cold weather there are a few things I miss like Montreal barbecue, poutine and Canadian beer, Molson."

"Same here but the cold wasn't too bad."

"Says the Newfie."

"You got me there. Anything else you miss?"

"Yes cháu; one thing that I have not had for many years."

"What's that?"

"Maple syrup. It is a taste only to that part of the world and can not be found here."

I smiled, removed the can of maple syrup uncle gave me from my carry-on bag and handed it to anh Dũng. "Here anh Dũng. It was a gift from my uncle but you may have it."

He smiled back. "Thank you cháu Upton. That is kind of you."

"No problem. I had some the other day and you haven't had any in years. Please and enjoy."

"It is interesting how the simplest foods can bring us the greatest joy. Merci beaucoup cháu."

The Beauty of Aqua

We soon finished our coffees and started our way to our train.

"The train will soon leave. We should buy some food to take with us." He smiled. "You will have your first meal in my country. We will start with something simple: xôi, sticky rice. Very good for train rides."

Anh Dũng walked over to an older woman serving sticky rice and soon returned with four banana leaves and a paper bag serving as containers.

"These are yours; xôi and xôi gà. One is plain and one is with chicken. We can eat them on the train."

"Not with a train station?"

Anh Dũng again laughed out loud. "Humor is good."

"How long's the ride anh Dũng?"

"About fifteen hours, maybe longer."

"Really? What about food?"

"There are street food carts at each station."

"Train station food?"

Anh Dũng once again saw an opportunity to educate me. "Yes cháu Upton; the food you get at Vietnamese railway stations is much better than what you would find in the West. You will enjoy it."

That was a completely new idea to me: good food at a train station.

"Here cháu." He opened the bag and handed me the contents "This is called bánh bao."

"More food?"

"This is for something now and the sticky rice is for later."

In my hand was a glistening, white bun and what I tasted was another epiphany. Inside of that simple, soft, white bun was a mixture of barbecue pork, cabbage, spring onion and ginger. Also something salty that was quite good and quite seductive. Every salt, sugar, fat and starch was in perfect harmony.

"You like no?"

"It's barbecue. What's there not to like?"

"I am pleased you enjoy it. If you open your mind to new and different foods I promise you my country will not disappoint."

We found our train and settled into our sleeper car.

"There are a few words you should learn like 'vâng' for yes and 'không' for 'no.' In the South they say 'dạ' for yes but that is incorrect and the Hà Nội dialect is the correct one."

"'Vâng' and 'dạ' for yes?"

Anh Dũng again rolled his eyes. "That is close enough cháu."

"So the dialect of the South is kinda treated like the Canadian-French dialect?"

"Vâng cháu."

"I think I'll use 'dạ'."

"Then I will not only be able to assist you with your French but also with your Vietnamese."

Anh Dũng's French was impeccable. It was clear that he was not only well-educated but more than willing to share that education with others. While he was correct that I was not using the more common Metropolitan dialect or accent that didn't matter to me. I was using the dialect of my family. My parents and some of my grandparents were born in Montreal and the City of Quebec and the Canadian-French dialect was their mother tongue. It was the dialect where I could still hear them say "I love you." and "You will be fine." While not the Metropolitan dialect it was the dialect in my heart, that's where it would always be and I suspected the people of Việt Nam felt the same about the dialect spoken in their family.

"Việt Nam is a polite society where one is expected to say 'please', 'thank you' and 'I am sorry.' Please is 'xin' short for 'xin vui lòng', thank you is 'cảm ơn' and 'I am sorry' is 'xin lỗi'."

"Thank—cảm ơn."

Anh Dũng smiled. "You are welcome cháu. There a few other words you need to know so you may show respect. An older man is addressed as 'anh', an older woman 'chị', someone younger than you is 'em', someone much younger than you is 'cháu' and a child is 'con.' There are more but these are the ones you need to remember for now. Do you understand?"

"Not really. Can't I just use 'you' and 'I'?"

"You could but it is not considered polite because when you meet someone and use the proper pronoun you acknowledge your place and their place in our community. When you say 'anh' and 'chị' to an older person you show respect to them."

"Very different from English."

"Vâng em; in English you can address an older person, younger person or child as 'you' and to us that is disrespectful."

"I will try to remember that."

"Once you see yourself as part of a community here and not just an individual you will remember."

"I don't see myself as part of any community. I had to leave the village where I grew up and I'll most likely never live there again."

"You are now part of our community cháu Upton. Although you do not speak our language every interaction you have with your neighbors will bring you closer together or further apart. If you show respect for what your community respects you will become part of it. Once your community sees your respect for our customs they will open their homes and hearts to you. The Vietnamese are very welcoming people. Finally you combine the two like in 'cảm ơn em' and 'xin lỗi anh'."

I gave it a try. "Cảm ơn chị."

Anh Dũng laughed at my mistake. "I am a man. You should say 'cảm ơn anh'."

"Xin lỗi anh Dũng."

"Không có gì cháu."

"What's 'không có gì?"

"Nothing. It is similar to 'You are welcome'."

"Cảm ơn anh"

"Không có gì cháu."

The lesson was over but anh Dũng said on the long ride down he'd also teach me a few numbers and the currency. He settled into his sleeping berth. "We should rest. I hope you have something to read."

I thought about the book Matt gave me, decided now was better than ever to read it and removed the book that was wrapped in newspaper from my suitcase. I opened it and read the note:

"Upton, Every life has a story. Write them down here. Matt."

Unlike the last journal book this one was blank.

"Cháu Upton; it is a long ride. We should sleep."

Sleeping wasn't a problem because of the time difference. I was out like a light for a few hours until the train slowed. The sign above the station house read "Ga Vinh." Anh Dũng was reading in his sleeping berth.

"Are we there?"

"Không cháu but we should go and buy some food."

We weren't the only ones with that thought. When the train stopped there was a mad rush to the doors and the herd headed straight to the nearby food carts. We left our sleeper car and pushed our way through the crowd to a stall near the old, yellow-orange station house. Anh Dũng spoke to the woman behind the food cart. "Bốn gỏi đu đủ." We then rushed back to the train with our catch.

"This is a green papaya salad. It is made with green papaya, carrots and dried beef."

"Salad is nice but what about the rest of the meal?"

"This is the meal. Salads in Việt Nam are very different from the West."

"I'm not much of a salad guy."

"Try it if you please. It is very good."

Anh Dũng was so right. All my life I had thought a salad was made with iceberg lettuce, tomato wedges and if you were lucky a few unpeeled cucumber slices unceremoniously topped with a dressing that was engineered to mask all other flavors. It was never a meal, just a way to say you ate something healthy before the main course. Gỏi đu đủ completely departed from the thought that salads were simple and boring. Its mixture of green papaya and carrot at its base offered substance where iceberg lettuce failed. The beef jerky and light-vinegar based dressing with bird's eye chilis added a kick that I couldn't have foreseen.

"You like cháu Upton?"

"This is amazing. I never imagined a salad like this before."

Anh Dũng smiled as he was very proud of his country and her foods. "Keep an open mind to our food and it will continue to amaze you many more times."

Matt's advice about eating like a local rang true. In my first day in Việt Nam I had been totally drawn in by the mystique of her food and her food carts opening my eyes to Vietnamese cuisine.

Anh Dũng pulled out a couple of beers from a bag and I read the label. "Bia Hà Nội?"

"You pronounced 'bia' very well."

While born in Newfoundland and raised on Cape Cod I had the all too familiar Boston accent and beer in Việt Nam and beer in Boston were pronounced exactly the same. At least I wouldn't go thirsty. I couldn't say water but I had "bia" down pat. He handed me one. "Cảm ơn anh."

The Beauty of Aqua

"Cháu Upton. You have an interesting accent. Is that how they speak in Newfoundland?"

The answer was no. One hundred percent, without a doubt or exception no, but hiding my Boston accent was about as easy as walking across Boston Common on New Year's Eve, drunk and in the snow. And yes, that's a very specific example. I needed to remember my "r"s and not to say "wicked" or as uncle said I'll get the "boooot."

"Kinda?"

"Interesting. Cảm ơn cháu."

His question served as a reminder to be careful when speaking with others. We enjoyed our meal and beer then settled in for the long train ride ahead. Nothing to do but sleep.

It was about eight at night, dark out and we stopped again. The sign above the station read "Ga Huế." There was an announcement on the speaker and Anh Dũng smiled.

"What was that?"

"The train will be delayed for three hours."

"And that makes you happy? Hanging around a train station for three hours isn't a reason to smile."

"I am smiling because we have time to go into town and eat."

"Do you think of anything else besides food and my French accent?"

"There are many good French speakers in Việt Nam and especially here in Huế City. They can help you fix the flaws in your speech but that is not important right now. It is time to go eat bún bò Huế."

"What's bún bò Huế?"

"You have not heard of this dish? Do you not have any Vietnamese restaurants in your village?"

"We have a Chinese restaurant?"

Anh Dũng was not at all amused with my linking of these two cuisines. "Mon Dieu. Follow me if you please."

We stepped off the train and anh Dũng walked over to two police officers standing nearby. He opened his wallet to show them his identification, they inspected it, snapped to attention, saluted and after a few words with them returned. "Our automobile is waiting. Follow me if you please." We walked out of the station.

If Hà Nội was a ghost town at night Huế City was a ghost town from a hundred years ago. Long rows of five-meter-wide houses with large, open sections dotted the landscape. It was clear the war had been here and its signature could be seen all around us. We walked over to a Vietnamese Government, standard-issue, dark-green UAZ, again with its tell-tale fire-red, hammer-and-sickle front badge, and got in.

"Where're we going?"

"Chợ Đông Ba. Đông Ba Market to my favorite shop for bún bò Huế."

We left the station where I saw many of the buildings had either been demolished or were being rebuilt.

"When I was young I saw on television the battle that happened here. There was so much destruction but being here I see what happened differently."

"How cháu Upton?"

"It becomes personal. It's no longer looking at what happened through the words of a reporter and the lens of a cameraman. I can see what happened for myself."

"What do you see cháu?"

"With every lost home I see a family that was also lost. I see lives that are no longer remembered. I see what a reporter and a cameraman could never show which is what really happened. There must be a lot of unhappiness here."

"Happiness is fleeting and the people of Huế City understand that thought. For hundreds of years this was the imperial capital of my country. It had the best universities and was the heart of Vietnamese Buddhism. The greatest minds and the most creative artists were here. Ten years ago it laid in ruins and food was in short supply. Many fathers, mothers, brothers and sisters were now dead and there was no emperor. Their empire was lost but they survived in part because of the lessons of their ancestors and their traditions. As with education and art the best foods could also be found here.

As the story is told the emperors not only expected to have the finest homes and the most beautiful wives, sometimes over a hundred, but also the finest foods. Some would even demand that they not be served the same dish twice which required the royal chefs to become very creative. Some of the finest and best known dishes come from here but there are many more that are only known to the people of this city. The food of the Vietnamese people is one of our most enduring traditions which brings us happiness with every bite.

The weather has also had a great effect on Huế City because it rains here more often than many other places. During the heaviest of rains all you can do is patiently wait for drier weather and over hundreds of years that has shaped the culture and her people. When I visit here I also feel more patient."

We continued our way to the market. Ahead of us was cầu Tràng Tiền, the Tràng Tiền bridge. Its outline was accented with red, yellow, blue and white spotlights which reflected off the water below.

"Why's that bridge lit with colored lights? It's beautiful."

"You answered your own question: because it is beautiful."

While the landscape was somewhat dark from the lack of electricity I could see a few colored-lanterns around us intermixed with the results of war and each felt like it was lit in the hope for a better tomorrow.

"We're eating at a market? No restaurants open this late?"

"There are many places to eat. The restaurants do not always have the best meals just because they have their own walls and roof. Like street food the vendors in the markets also make very good meals."

"Back at the marina in my village there was a small seafood restaurant. Someplace only the people who appreciated good seafood would go and it was better than any other place in town."

"Same-same Việt Nam." Anh Dũng explained that people would rent stalls to sell produce, meat and run mini-restaurants. What I thought I'd see was something like Faneuil Hall in Boston. In reality it was much, much more primitive but very functional. Vendors were setup along a few long rows separated with discarded pieces of plywood. The meat and produce vendors were long gone and some had been replaced with tiny food stall after tiny food stall. Each had a few plastic or wooden stools and a counter for customers connected to the main meal prep area. Behind was a large stock pot heated by charcoal. The smells promised you everything in exchange for your soul. It was intoxicating and for a moment I had the amazement of a small child. I stopped to smell the rich scent in the air.

"Cháu Upton; are you fine?"

"I'm OK. It's the smell. I've never smelled anything so seductive."

"Do you still want to go to a restaurant? I know a place that serves western food."

"A friend of mine back home told me to never go to places like that. I want to eat here."

"Your friend gave you good advice. Follow me if you please." Anh Dũng looked like he was on a mission. We passed stall after stall with every imaginable food but only his favorite shop would do. We walked over, sat down and anh Dũng ordered for us. Our meals quickly arrived and without a word he began to eat. He was happy.

I was presented with a bowl of soup in a fire-engine-red tinted broth, a bed of rice noodles laid below and above were large pieces of bamboo shoot, tomato wedges, spring onion, mushrooms, beef shank and black tofu.

"Anh Dũng; black tofu?"

"Không cháu: huyết. Le sang animal."

"Animal blood? Do I eat it?"

He was amused by my questioning of such a treat. "Try cháu, it is very good."

It was my third epiphany that day. It had a gentle taste and was mildly flavored. Something I never thought of eating before brought me comfort. The same could be said for that bowl of soup. We soon finished our meal and returned to our train.

"How long to Đà Nẵng?"

"Two hours, maybe longer."

Last chance to get some sleep before I get to my new city.

The Beauty of Aqua

5

City by the sea

It was dark except for the few lights on at the train station. The sign above the station house read "Ga Đà Nẵng." Anh Dũng knocked on the side of my sleeper berth.

"Time to go cháu Upton."

"We're here?" I was barely awake as I slept well on the ride from Huế City.

"Vâng cháu; I will take you to your house. Get up now if you please."

"Yeah; une minute s'il vous plaît."

"What did you say?" He couldn't be serious.

"One minute please."

"Oh; that is what I thought you said."

I grabbed my bags from underneath the bottom bunk and we left our sleeper car. As we stepped off the train

The Beauty of Aqua

two police officers started walking towards us and it was clear we were on their radar. They walked right past me to anh Dũng, stopped and saluted then picked up our bags. We headed into the station then out to the street.

"There're police officers carrying our suitcases."

"Vietnamese people are very hospitable."

"The police in the West don't carry our bags."

"Same-same Việt Nam."

I was too tired to question his circular logic. While drowsy from the jet lag and train ride anh Dũng's wit was fully functional. All I wanted to do was to get to my house and sleep. We were met with another well-worn, dark-green UAZ with a driver outside of the station which took us to my new home. Leaving the train station we talked along the way.

"Where am I going to live?"

"I have rented you a room in a house near your university and my government will pay for your rent, meals at the house, laundry and a bicycle for you to use."

"A bicycle?"

"Vâng cháu; a bicycle is a vehicle with two wheels and propelled by pedals. Bi-cy-cle."

"I know what a bicycle is and I traded mine at fifteen for a motorcycle. Any chance of me getting one of those?"

"Không cháu Upton; it takes time to adjust to life in Việt Nam and even longer to her traffic. It is safer if you use a bicycle for now."

We pulled up to what would be my home for the next year. The brightly painted light-blue, concrete house with white-painted trim was five-meters wide and three stories tall not including the rooftop garden. A white-painted, rot-iron fence and gate separated it from the sidewalk. There were two well-worn, metal, bi-fold doors on the first floor and equally worn, teak wood, french doors that faced the balconies on the second and third-floors which overlooked our peaceful street. Like Hà Nội there were still a few multi-colored lights flashing in the cool, night air that were left over from the recent Lunar New Year celebrations which cast the street in a pleasant glow. An older woman walked by and for a moment stopped to stare at me. I was a foreigner in a foreign land.

"Chị Phương is the owner of the home where you will be staying and your room is on the second-floor. She will cook your meals and take care of your laundry. I am sorry em but she speaks no English and little French."

"Pas de problème monsieur."

"Good luck with that cháu." And I suspected that would never stop until I took him up on his advice to improve my French.

On the day-long train ride down anh Dũng shared with me a few stories from his life. It seemed he had my best interests in mind and expressed the same with his somewhat dry sense of humor.

"Thanks for everything anh Dũng. I appreciate it."

"And thank you cháu Upton for bringing me the maple syrup."

Anh Dũng spoke a few words with chị Phương, handed her an envelope and left.

The Beauty of Aqua

She was waiting to show me my new home. We started to walk inside when she stopped and pointed to my feet. Seeing a few pairs of shoes outside the front door I joined in by taking off mine when I was then offered a pair of house slippers.

Next to the front door was a twenty-liter bottle of water with a few well-worn, drinking glasses and the light-blue, front room was lit with cool-fluorescent tubes, high on the walls and ceiling, and contained two solid-wood couches with paper-thin cushions. I could see the kitchen in the back of the house and an old Honda Super Cub parked next to the staircase. There were a few times I would've liked to have worked on my motorcycle in the warmth of my family's living room but I doubt dad would've approved.

Chị Phương pointed to the concrete staircase and we headed up. Still stiff from the train ride carrying both my bags up a flight of stairs was a bit of a struggle.

She walked me over to the bedroom in the front of the house, turned on the overhead light and opened the french doors to my balcony. Turning around she pointed to an electric hot-water kettle, the mosquito netting above the bed and made her exit.

"Bonne nuit cháu."

"Bonne nuit madame."

Welcome to my first night in the City of Đà Nẵng. My floor had three rooms, one of which sat unused behind my bedroom. My new place in this world was spacious and sparsely furnished with a full-size bed, dresser, clothes-rack, nightstand with an electric hot-water kettle sitting on top, desk and chair and with the only lights on the ceiling. I walked over to my balcony to quietly absorbed the night air when I saw my peaceful community for the first time. The street lights with their orange-yellow glow accented the similarly colored buildings.

Across from me were a group of older men sitting on little, plastic stools drinking beer in the cool yet comfortable night air. A few motorcycles could be heard in the distance but here it was quiet with just the men across the street saying "Một, hai, ba, vô!" before downing a glass of beer. Anh Dũng had taught me the numbers one through ten and I recognized that they were saying "One, two, three!" I was a bit jealous because it reminded me of my wayward days back on Cape Cod and thought if I brought over a case of beer they'd let me join in. They dressed like fishermen, looked like fishermen and certainly drank like fisherman. It didn't matter that we didn't speak the same language because we spoke the language of fishing and had an appreciation of the sea; plus I'd be bringing the beer.

There was an ensuite bathroom connected to the bedroom, while typical for Việt Nam, was different from my part of the world. Turning on the bathroom light I saw scurrying across the floor the biggest cockroach I'd ever seen. I shouldn't have been surprised, this being a tropical climate, but it was still a shock. It was a "wet" bathroom meaning everything got wet which seemed like that might be an inconvenience but later showed its advantages. If the bathroom was strange then the mosquito netting was completely foreign. Since the balcony doors didn't have screens it was there to keep the bugs away and it would at least keep that cockroach out.

Then it hit me: I had never been so alone in my life.

It was about 4:30 in the morning and I was still mixed up from the jet lag when I heard a rooster. Then another. How could such a small animal make so much noise? Was I near a farm? Then about a half-hour later a loudspeaker on the street started loudly playing bizarre music and what sounded like an exercise routine. I dragged myself to my balcony to find a very strange world before me. All those different sights, sounds and smells hit me like a firehose which was exhilarating and seducing at the same time. My balcony overlooked a small street and the street markers at the corner read "đường Lê Lai" and "đường Nguyễn Thị Minh Khai." That's where I live.

Starving I went downstairs looking for something to eat and saw some rice porridge and fish on the kitchen table. Chị Phương approached and asked, "Cháu Upton ăn cháo không?"

An invitation for breakfast. I sat and was served; first the rice porridge then the fish. On the table was a small bowl of amber liquid seasoned with tiny chili peppers. She held a spoonful over my bowl and paused for a signal from me in which to add it or not. I nodded yes and that was one of the best choices I ever made.

City by the sea

What awaited me was a taste of paradise. The amber liquid was "nước mắm" or Vietnamese fish sauce and it was the best salty flavor I had ever tasted. This treasured nectar had a wonderful mixture of garlic, sugar and chilis which permeated through every bite of the rice porridge and accented the fish. While very different from anything I had in the past this dish was comforting and to chị Phương's surprise and joy I devoured the bowl in front of me. She smiled and offered more which I happily accepted. After my second bowl I remembered Matt's advice about how eating what was in front of you was a sign of respect. She was pleased to see this foreigner enjoying her cooking so much.

Cháo or rice porridge plays a huge role in Vietnamese life. It is comfort food much like macaroni and cheese is to those in the West and is eaten with many meals or alone when one is not well. For me it was no doubt served as a gentle introduction to the local fare. It's a simple soup made of rice and water. While obviously bland by itself with the introduction of nước mắm it is transformed into something magical where the rice porridge becomes a vehicle to deliver the rich, salty flavor of the nước mắm with every bite.

After breakfast all I wanted to do was explore this strange, new world. I thanked chị Phương for breakfast and headed towards the front door.

It was the first time I'd seen this city in the daylight and it was stunning. The houses and shops along the grey, cobblestone sidewalks were only five meters wide and painted the same varying shades of yellow-orange or like mine a combination of different blues reminiscent of the sea. This city was shockingly beautiful. Some contained family shops like small markets, motorcycle repair or something similar to the ubiquitous food shop like the one across from me.

I turned right on đường Lê Lai to the traffic filled street ahead. While fairly quiet here đường Nguyễn Thị Minh Khai ahead was not with shops everywhere. Lots of people on bicycles packed the street but they always kept moving. To a westerner the traffic looked like nothing but stress but that frustration couldn't be seen here with everyone patiently moving forward like a school of fish.

With a map courtesy of anh Dũng I headed south about a half-dozen blocks to find my university. It was a collection of older concrete, five-story buildings but a couple had recently been built. The students were well-groomed and sharply dressed in school uniforms with men in simple, white-collared shirts and women wearing the traditional, student áo dài, also all in white, which they seemed to wear with a patriotic pride. Where one of America's most popular symbols of independence was a gun held in a clenched fist Việt Nam had the graceful áo dài which also stood for tradition, liberty and happiness.

A couple of blocks south of there was a large market with a sign above its entrance: "Chợ Han." While closer to Faneuil Hall in Boston than Đông Ba Market in Huế City it wasn't by much. The large, two-story concrete building held over a hundred tiny, open stalls on its two floors and had everything imaginable. I wandered aimlessly from crowded aisle to crowded aisle on the first floor seeing everything from freshly caught fish to a rainbow of colorful fruits and vegetables to rice and flour and a section with an array of religious objects. The smells of sandalwood and jasmine from those stalls were intoxicating which drew me in. The walls were tightly packed with golden statues to unknown patron saints, red signs with Chinese characters and bundle after bundle of fragrant incense wrapped in red strips of recycled cloth. I thought it'd be nice to bring something to chị Phương so I bought one of the bundles of sandalwood incense in front of me with some of my advance salary I'd received from anh Dũng on the trip down.

With incense in hand I started to leave when I heard the haunting lyrics of a familiar song echoing throughout the market:

"Mirrors on the ceiling, the pink champagne on ice. And she said, 'We are all just prisoners here, of our own device'."

I was hearing "Hotel California" and had to find its source. On the second-floor were a collection of stalls filled with various types of clothing, tailors and a very small selection of electronics laid out like a Middle Eastern bazaar.

The source of the music was a nice and gently used Japanese boombox with a price tag in Vietnamese currency. I'd seen similar ones in the West sell for about $200 and suspected the shop owner would also want a premium because of its rarity. I thought about my dozen or so prized Grateful Dead and Bob Dylan bootlegs I'd brought with me and nothing to play them on. After Matt helped me minimize my life making such a purchase seemed unwise but I knew it was of good quality, would be well-used and shared with chị Phương which I'm sure she'd appreciate.

The shop owner approached and said something I didn't understand. I'd left my US Passport with dad but brought US currency with me and hoped he might accept the same. Removing my wallet the shop owner saw my very small stack of $100 bills and quickly held up four fingers. We all need to make a living but that was too steep for this New England Yankee. Replying with three, which was still well over the original selling price, he accepted with a handshake. I handed over three crisp hundreds and he placed my new acquisition along with the Eagle's album I'd heard in a reused paper bag as the original packaging was long gone. Now I could listen to my favorite music and I was pleased.

On my way out I noticed something tasty. Near the front entrance there were large, clear bags with all types of dried seafood and the one with tiny shrimp caught my eye, or more correctly my nose. I communicated with the stall owner by pointing to the shrimp and a small pile of bags by the side then held up one finger. The woman quickly filled my order and handed me my bag.

"Năm trăm." I thought she said, "five" so I took my best guess handing her a 500đ note which seemed correct.

"Cảm ơn cháu."

"Không có gì chị."

I took advantage of a pedicab parked out front and with my map showed the driver the way back to my home. Chị Phương was there and I greeted her with the incense and shrimp I had purchased which she thanked me for. With the help of pantomime I told her the boombox would be in my room and she could use it when she wished.

"Cảm ơn cháu Upton."

"Không có gì chị Phương."

It was close to eleven and I needed to continue my explorations with the hope of finding something tasty to eat for lunch and it was my first time going to a food cart without anh Dũng.

A block north from đường Lê Lai was đường Ba Đình which was quieter than đường Nguyễn Thị Minh Khai with its mixture of homes and fewer shops. Along the north side of the street was a yellow-orange wall where food carts were serving lunch and the tree canopy from above offered some welcomed shade. The sun at this latitude was more intense than back on Cape Cod but its warmth felt nice on that winter morning. A common thread was seeing house after house with their front doors open to the world and as I walked by each home I could see a slice of life every five meters. There were women caring for infants and sewing clothes, men repairing fishing nets and a few elderly couples sitting and enjoying a glass of coffee.

Back in the West we knew some of our neighbors but rarely spoke to them. Like most westerners we would come home from the day's work, get out of our car, check the mailbox and quickly head inside to lock ourselves in for the night secure in our suburban isolation.

The smells from the food carts were inviting and seductive at the same time and no large street signs were needed to advertise what was being offered. I could see a cart selling sandwiches at the end of the street, walked down and liked what I saw. The woman behind the cart said something I didn't understand.

"Parlez-vous français madam?" She waved her hands like a jazz singer from the 1930's showing she didn't. I pointed to the sandwich she was making and held up my index finger. She smiled and continued on in her work quickly filling my request. I had successfully managed to feed myself without anyone's help; except for the woman who made my sandwich. Being able to accomplish that task and having the pronunciation for "bia" down pat I knew I wouldn't starve or remain permanently sober. She handed me my sandwich then pointed to a few little, plastic stools set up around her cart so I sat and ate. Similar to other street food vendors what she was selling was brightly painted on the side of her metal cart. Her's said "bánh mì que." My sandwich was a crispy, string baguette filled with a meat pâté, chili and aioli sauce. That first bite was another culinary epiphany. The thin ribbon of spicy pâté and sauce was in perfect balance to the bread yielding satisfaction with every bite. Sitting on that simple stool on a street corner eating this common sandwich I felt like a king. I finished and started my walk back home.

"Cảm ơn chị."

"Không có chi cháu."

I turned the corner and headed south back to my home soon arriving at two street markers that read "đường Lê Lợi" and "đường Lê Lai" and turned right. Vietnamese is confusing. My street had its charm with a healthy 50/50 mix of shops and homes when one shop soon caught my eye. There were the prerequisite little, plastic tables and stools but no sign showing what they were offering. An older woman with a sweet smile behind her steel cart was serving soup. The smell was so very seductive. All the seats were filled and the diners ate without a word of conversation. Further down the street I could see my house and returned home. The combination of the morning's rice porridge, bánh mì que and jet lag created the ideal conditions for a late morning nap.

I woke from my nap to a warm, sweet breeze from the south and the sounds of life on that first day in Đà Nẵng. Laying there in my post-nap bliss I had no desire to go anywhere because I was at peace. Living so close to the street brings the world into your home and reminds you that you're not alone. I'd seen more that morning than I'd ever seen before. Every step revealed a glimpse of life that I never could of imagined before and I knew I'd never be the same again. There was so much life in this city all on display every five meters. If this was what one day in Đà Nẵng did to you I had no idea who I'd be in a year. My peaceful, post-nap time was interrupted by a call from below.

"Cháu Upton. Are you there?"

I slowly rose and drifted over to my balcony to see anh Dũng below. He was dressed comfortably, yet professionally, and stood next to a well-worn, light-green and white Honda Super Cub with an equally worn red license plate. "Hello anh Dũng."

"Bonjour cháu Upton. Would you like to drink some coffee?"

"Sounds good. I'll be right there." Heading downstairs I remembered to switch out of my house slippers and into my street shoes on the front steps where anh Dũng was waiting for me.

"Good morning cháu. Did you sleep well last night?"

"The bed was really hard but otherwise I did. Thanks."

"Beds in the West are much softer than ours but our beds make sleeping in the hot, summer months more comfortable. Any other concerns cháu?"

"How about using a hose to wash yourself down instead of using toilet paper?"

He laughed. "Vâng cháu; that is Việt Nam but also many other places in the world. Toilet paper is much more expensive than water. Anything else cháu?"

"There's a rooster that woke me up before dawn. How about that?"

"He will soon not be a problem. We should go and drink coffee."

"More of that iced coffee we had in Hà Nội? Yes please." After trying Vietnamese coffee I couldn't say no.

We walked down my street towards đường Lê Lợi and stopped at a small, corner cafe in a family home named "Cafe 47", functionally named for its house number on our street. Outside were a collection of simple, wooden stools with matching tables and umbrellas where we sat. A small dog from inside the cafe came out wanting me to pet her. Anh Dũng ordered for both of us and our cà phê sữa đá Sài Gòn soon arrived. We sat drinking our coffees in view of the world and he could see I was once again enjoying my cool drink.

"You like our coffee better than Tim Horton's?"

"It's not better, it's different. I'm sure it's good when it's hot out."

Anh Dũng seemed pleased with my response in not making a judgement. "Vâng em; this drink is best in the summer months."

"Speaking of summer how hot does it get?"

"During the day it is about 30°C, sometimes 35°C. Warmer than Montreal." That was an understatement.

"That's hot. How about an air conditioner?"

"Không cháu; even if we could find one it would be very expensive and because of power outages it would not work many nights. It is better for you to adjust to sleeping in the warm weather."

I could hear Matt's advice to "sleep like a local." "How do you sleep in weather that hot?"

"By napping during the day. The Vietnamese people like to get up early in the morning and nap during the hottest part of the day. Afterwards we are refreshed and return to work when the weather is cooler."

"No problem with getting up early thanks to that rooster."

The Beauty of Aqua

Anh Dũng smiled at my naivety. "We keep chickens and roosters so we have food to eat. Do not worry about him. He will soon be someone's meal."

"And another will replace him."

"Vâng cháu but then they will also eat him."

"And the great circle of life continues. Any word on the computers?"

"Không cháu but they should be in Hà Nội soon. I will tell your translator when they arrive."

"Oh yeah; what about my translator?"

"Soon cháu. It will be worth your wait. I am sending you my best one."

"No rush anyways without the computers."

We enjoyed our coffees and our view of the street.

"Anh Dũng, were you in the war?" I could tell by his pause that he had.

"Vâng cháu; I fought in the American War."

"'American War'? I guess you wouldn't call it the Vietnam War since it happened here."

"It was the American War because that was who did the most fighting in my country." Anh Dũng played his cards close to his chest but this time let his hand slip a bit while he paused thinking about the past.

"If you don't want to talk about it that's fine."

"No problem cháu. I want to talk about the war to others so they may learn from our suffering. What did you want to know?"

"Where were you?"

"I was in Hà Nội then my home city of Hải Phòng for a few years soon after there was much bombing."

"What did you do?"

"I was a liaison between my government and another then I worked for my uncle. Nothing nefarious but the past is the past."

He paused then changed the topic. "Cháu Upton, why did you want to come to Việt Nam?"

"Not sure, it happened by chance. My father is selling the home I grew up in and moving to Saint John's in Newfoundland. I guess I needed a change."

"No mother?"

"No; she died from cancer."

"I am very sorry cháu Upton. Cancer is bad. Here in Đà Nẵng there is more cancer than Hà Nội or Hồ Chí Minh City and we do not know why. No siblings?"

"One, a younger brother. He drowned in a pond in my village soon after my mother died."

"There is much sadness in your life."

Without a pause I replied, "There is."

He showed concern for me. "When I feel that way I think of my mother and father and how all they wanted was for me to have a better life than they did. They worked very hard to educate me and made it possible for me to live the good life I do today."

"Nice thought anh Dũng. I will try to remember that." He reminded me of my uncle which was comforting.

"No problem cháu. Saint John's is very beautiful. Why not live with your father?"

"He offered but I felt I needed to be on my own."

"Maybe fate or something else brought you here?"

"Maybe. I don't really believe in fate but being here only a day has made me rethink a lot of what I believe in and don't so that might change. I know I've changed."

"How cháu?"

"I'm not sure but something's happening. How I see the world has been challenged and I need to keep watching. I'll let you know when I find out."

"Maybe you found some happiness here?"

I thought about his question. "I think so but I'll let you know after I have something to eat."

"I have a friend in my life that finds our best foods can bring happiness every day and I think you have found the same."

"I have. Like every new sight is special so isn't the food. I could be happy eating it for a long time."

"Like my friend I am happy for you both."

"Speaking of food are you hungry?"

"Vâng cháu."

Soon I learned any invitation to eat was almost always accepted as it was a chance to spend time with friends.

"Do you have a place in mind cháu Upton?"

"Yeah; there's a sandwich cart one street over. They make this delicious sandwich with just pâté, hot and aioli sauce. It's wicked good. I had one earlier while walking around but could go for another."

"'Wicked'? Is that an expression from Newfoundland?"

Think, think, think. "Kinda?" At least I didn't say "pissah." I needed to be more careful.

Anh Dũng smiled. "Cảm ơn cháu." With that we started our walk to retrieve our meal while continuing our conversation. "The sandwich you speak of is called bánh mì que. The breadstick bread is unique to this sandwich. This bánh mì is not too spicy for you?"

"Not at all. The food is much spicier than back West which is really nice with every bite giving a pleasant burn. You must of missed that in Montreal."

"The food in Montreal is very good but it is not spicy." Anh Dũng enjoyed the same foods I did in the West but loved with a patriotic fervor the food of his country as it was a great source of pride and joy to him and every other Vietnamese person.

"Have you tried our fish sauce yet?"

"I tasted it for the first time this morning at chị Phương's house and fell in love. She made it with some garlic, sugar and chilis. That first taste changed how I thought about food."

Anh Dũng smiled again. "Nước mắm is very important to us. When chị Phương saw that you enjoyed what she made I am sure it made her very happy. I do not know of another westerner that has had such a reaction and found so much joy in our fish sauce."

"It's now part of me." Chị Phương's nước mắm was that good.

"Do you miss western food anh Dũng?"

"I missed maple syrup but thanks to your uncle that is no longer a problem. There are times I long for Montreal barbecue. When I was at university I enjoyed that, poutine and Molsens with my friends which I miss."

"Yeah, same here. I like Molson too."

"You should try bia hơi. There is a shop selling it around the corner."

I paused to check my watch and it was a little after two in the afternoon. "Isn't it a little early to start drinking?"

"No problem cháu because it is the weekend and many people are not working." Anh Dũng paused, "And this is Việt Nam." Anh Dũng didn't hit me as a drinker, he was too smart for that, but someone that appreciated a cold beer on a warm day.

"Bia hơi is freshly brewed beer that has less alcohol than Canadian beers and adding ice makes it even less strong."

"You add ice to your beer?" Ice in beer to me was like the mosquito netting: completely foreign.

"Vâng cháu; you will like it."

I could hear Matt's advice to "live like a local" and decided not to fight the tide. "I guess it's five in the evening somewhere."

Anh Dũng smiled. "Vâng em; it is nighttime in Canada."

My comment no doubt reminded him of his university days back in Montreal. We stopped by the bánh mì que cart and anh Dũng ordered our sandwiches. He and the woman behind the cart spoke a few words and we continued our walk.

"The woman that made our bánh mì said she was happy to see you again."

"She remembered me?"

"I believe you are the only westerner that has ever been to her cart. To see you return the same day means you enjoyed what she made and that made her happy. There is great happiness in seeing what you create enjoyed by those that consume it."

Anh Dũng and I continued on to an alley off of đường Ba Đình and took our seats.

"Em ơi! Hai bia hơi."

"Dạ anh; hai bia."

"Dạ em."

I smiled. "You said 'dạ' not 'vâng'."

"Vâng cháu. 'When in Rome, do as the Romans do.' I am in Đà Nẵng, a city I respect, so I show my respect by speaking as they do."

"I wish I had that option with my French."

"I do too cháu, I do too. If you wish I will find someone to help you improve your French language."

"Again with my French? Mon Dieu."

"What did you say?" I smiled. I got the joke.

"What I could use is a Vietnamese teacher. I don't even understand the alphabet."

"Your translator is a very patient teacher and will teach you well."

We sat on little, plastic stools eating bánh mì que and drinking fresh beer on the sidewalk by the alley. The sun shined, a warm breeze blew in from the south and the beauty of this place was truly revealing itself to me. I could see what Roy back home enjoyed about this country.

"You married anh Dũng?"

"Vâng cháu; for many years."

"What's your wife's name?"

"Dung."

"That's your name."

"Không cháu; my name is Dũng and my wife's name is Dung. Different names."

"Sounds the same to me. Must of been confusing for your kids." Anh Dũng laughed and I guessed I was right.

"In time you will be able to hear the difference."

"I'm only here for a year."

"It should not take that long."

If someone told me about a week ago that I'd be sitting at a sidewalk table in Việt Nam, eating a sandwich and having a beer I wouldn't have believed them but here I was and would be here for the next year. Anh Dũng finished his bánh mì que and bia hơi and stood up.

"I must leave now to take my train back to Huế City. This was enjoyable cháu."

"Thanks—cảm ơn anh" I paused, "How do you say 'thank you very much'?"

"Cảm ơn nhiều."

"Cảm ơn nhiều anh."

"Very good cháu. Hẹn gặp lại cháu."

"What?"

"See you again."

"Cảm ơn anh. Hẹn gặp lại anh."

"Very good cháu. You are learning quickly. I know you will make the same progress in your French with the correct teacher."

"You're just like my uncle about my French. You'd like him; he's a good guy."

"I am sure I would like him if I ever had met him."

"You mean '… if I ever met him'."

"Vâng cháu; I do not know what I was thinking. Hẹn gặp lại cháu."

With that anh Dũng left heading towards đường Nguyễn Thị Minh Khai leaving me to enjoy the rest of the afternoon and my fresh beer.

It was still mostly dark and I was woken up by a rooster for the first time in about a week. I enjoyed my respite from those early morning wake up calls probably as much as the family who ate my previous avian alarm clock enjoyed their meal. Soon the morning exercise program was broadcast over the speakers from the local Communist Party meeting hall across from me. I nodded off for a few more minutes before finally rising.

I'd been caught in a very comfortable limbo for the last few weeks waiting for the computers to be delivered and being assigned a translator. Mornings started with soup, either bún bò Huế or bánh canh, with both shops on my short street. The women that made these two wonderful dishes always had a smile on their face when they saw me visit them because they knew I enjoyed what they made so well and wanted more. Yesterday was chị Giang's bún bò Huế so that morning it was chị Linh's bánh canh. I headed downstairs where I saw chị Phương in the kitchen and tried my best to greet her properly on that morning.

"Chào buổi sáng chị Phương."

She smiled. "Chào buổi sáng cháu Upton."

I pointed to the street.

"Em đi ăn sáng. Hẹn gặp lại chị."

"Hẹn gặp lại cháu."

My Vietnamese vocabulary now consisted of about a dozen poorly pronounced words, mostly foods, and the ability to poorly construct a couple very simple sentences. Very poorly but just enough to order a meal and ask for the toilet. While chị Phương sometimes giggled at what I said I could tell she appreciated my efforts to learn her language.

I walked out to the street and saw chị Giang looking my way to see if I was eating there today. I pointed down the street and said, "Em đi ăn sáng bánh canh chị Linh."

Chị Giang also giggled. Another one that both appreciated my attempts at the Vietnamese language and found amusement in my poor execution of the same.

Chị Linh's house and her bánh canh could be found close to đường Lê Lợi. During meal times her first floor main room also served as her restaurant with space for about a dozen diners able to get in before she quickly ran out of her soup of dreams. She started serving about six-thirty in the morning every day and ran out about an hour later. I'd noticed something interesting about her soup that unlike in the West the flavors and textures would quickly change over the hour it sat warming over its charcoal-heated fire. I would vary the times I ate their to

City by the sea

experience the differences. I walked up to her home and sat down. "Chào buổi sáng chị Linh."

"Chào buổi sáng cháu." Without another word she prepared my soup and today I was in for a treat. I looked over to see her adding some eel which, no doubt, was caught that morning right down the street. Even though I grew up in a fishing village I now ate more fish than I ever did and here I tried to have at least a little bit every day. I hadn't had anyone to talk to since I'd been here but that didn't matter because food this good should be eaten in silence.

Back in the West breakfast for me was the all too typical cereal or oatmeal with my beloved maple syrup: nutritious but boring. Never anything to get excited about but Việt Nam was very different with spicy and enjoyable meals instead.

Bánh canh is a soup made with thick rice noodles unlike its better known cousin bún bò Huế and both were satisfying in different ways. Where bún bò Huế was exciting bánh canh was calming. My bowl was filled to the brim with a thick broth and thick rice noodles and topped with a piece of eel and a few slices of Vietnamese ham. For the time it took to eat my meal nothing else existed but that wonderful bowl of soup. After finishing I sat back in my seat and quietly appreciated that last, glorious bite.

After breakfast I headed a few houses down to Cafe 47 for my morning coffee. This quaint cafe was run by a very nice, retired couple with their two dogs "bún" and "mì" named after two types of noodles. Even the dogs were named after food in this food obsessed country. Mì was the mother and bún the son. While bún could be seen running up and down the street chasing off the local rat population mì was much friendlier and would come up to me wanting to be petted. Back in the West dogs would never be allowed to roam free through a cafe which was truly the patrons loss. I took my usual seat by the street, saw the mother and waved.

"Chào buổi sáng chị. Cà phê xin." She knew I wanted the iced Sài Gòn version but couldn't say it.

"Dạ cháu; chào buổi sáng."

She headed to the back of the cafe to make my regular order as I enjoyed the street life that unfolded before me. Children were walking to school dressed in their standard-issue red, white and blue school uniforms each with a sewn-in name tag also showing their school, grade and class. I was told that this name tag custom was also found at the university where I'd be teaching which would make working with my students much easier.

My coffee soon arrived. "Cảm ơn chị."

"Không có chi cháu. Kính mời." An invitation to enjoy my coffee which I always did.

Cafe 47 was a place for locals and it was run that way. They knew one sub-par glass of coffee served to a neighbor could result in a boycott from the entire street which the cafe owners easily avoided by always making it right.

Four blocks to the east was the Hàn River. On par with my recently formed routine I'd walk down and watch the last of the morning's catch brought to shore, reminding me of my life back in the West, and would read a book. A few hours before this spot by the river was busy with fisherman in long, wooden boats, painted varying shades of neon-blue, bringing in the morning catch with the women handling sales of the same. That was the norm throughout the country. While both men and women labored it was the women that handled the money. After seeing a couple of heated card games from my balcony I could see the wisdom of that decision.

All those along the shore, save one, offered welcoming smiles to me every morning as I sat and enjoyed my view of the Hàn River but no matter where I sat one man, about my age and reeking of alcohol, had the habit of dragging his wet net over to and across my spot. As a visitor and especially with my "immigration issue" hanging over my head like the sword of Damocles I thought it would be best to give this fisherman as wide of a berth as possible and to stay away from him.

The busy morning was now gone and replaced with just the sounds of a single boat offloading its final catch and a woman waiting on the shore with her basket in hand. After a quick unloading they were gone and I had that shady spot on the banks of the Hàn River to myself. A warm breeze blew in from the south which was comforting. I sat and read in peace.

The street behind me quieted down as lunch approached which meant it was time to go if I wanted to get something to eat. Việt Nam was one of the few nations left in the world that still practiced the art of the midday nap causing almost everything to shut down from about noon to about two in the afternoon when life slowly reawoke.

At first I wasn't able to nap so I tried, in vain, to go about my life as before. I quickly found this didn't work and had to adapt. Napping was difficult to do but every day it got a little easier. The hard part was I had to do it every day but it did get easier.

I walked back to đường Lê Lợi to buy a couple of my beloved bánh mì que. With no more than a greeting the woman behind the cart quickly made my sandwiches per my preference of extra aioli sauce. With my lunch securely in hand I returned home. I quickly adjusted to and welcomed spicy food. Where a well-crafted Italian sandwich would bring pleasure a spicy bánh mì que also brought joy from its large fire. If you didn't sweat during a meal it wouldn't be remembered and a meal remembered was a meal enjoyed.

I sat on my balcony and ate my bánh mì que with a bia Larue, in a glass with ice, I'd grabbed from the kitchen. I rarely had a beer with lunch but "When in Rome do as the Romans." and it was five in the evening somewhere. Across the street chị Giang had finished cleaning up from lunch. She and her husband, a fisherman, were enjoying a meal together. Time to nap.

I awoke in the afternoon and like every other day before again found myself alone as I waited to hear from anh Dũng about the arrival of the computers and a translator. As my habit for the last month or so I could be found on my balcony reading. Below were the sights and sounds of life and as the day progressed above me was the early twilight that bathed my city in a cool, pleasant light. I'd been reading Camus' "Le Mythe de Sisyphe" and "Writings and Drawings" by Bob Dylan. Back on Cape Cod I was unhappy and wasn't sure why.

A Grateful Dead bootleg of "Me and my uncle" played softly in the background, thanks to my recently acquired boombox, from a show I saw at the Cape Cod Coliseum back in '79. It was my first show and my first real taste of the counterculture world. While much of the philosophy of the 1960's had receded like a wave that had just peaked and returned to the sea, it made way for our "hyper-capitalism" world of today. I could see the downside of this thought in the unrealistic rise in home prices in my village which, in turn, priced most of the young people like me out of the market and out of the place we were raised.

I soon heard a familiar voice from the street. "Cháu ơi!"

I looked down to see anh Dũng. "Xin chào anh Dũng. You want a beer?"

"Không cám ơn cháu Upton. I must leave to take my train back to Huế City."

"What brings you here?"

"I came to tell you that your computers should arrive soon. Are you ready to start teaching?"

"Dạ anh; I'm ready to go."

"I must leave now and will send you your translator very soon."

"Cảm ơn anh Dũng."

"Không sao cháu. Hẹn gặp lại."

"Không sao?"

"No problem."

"Cảm ơn anh. Hẹn gặp lại."

"Your Vietnamese is getting better. Very good cháu."

"After that I'll work on my French."

Anh Dũng laughed, mounted his Super Cub and drove away.

6

The beauty of Aqua

"Cháu ơi!"

It was chị Phương calling and she must of made lunch early today.

I headed downstairs and walked into the kitchen to see her talking to another woman about my age. She was slender, a bit shorter than me at about five and a half feet tall, wearing wire-rimmed glasses and a well-tailored, light-blue, modern áo dài, with shorter front and rear panels than the traditional form, with silken, white pants. She radiated with a special beauty not only on physical appearances but the way she held herself, with poise and grace. In her right hand was a tattered, leather briefcase that looked older than her and a nón lá, the traditional Vietnamese bamboo, conical hat. Just outside the main room was her bicycle which looked equally worn.

The Beauty of Aqua

"Hello?" I asked quietly.

She turned her attention to me and with a gentle smile asked, "Anh Upton?"

"Yes em." She was beautiful.

"Anh Dũng sent me and I am your translator. I would have been here sooner but have been in Huế City."

"Not a problem since the computers aren't here yet. What's your name?"

"Thủy."

"Thuy?" I mispronounced it. She giggled and explained to me my mispronunciation sounded like the word for something not nice. "Anh xin lỗi em."

Thủy's eyes opened and she smiled. "You speak Vietnamese?"

"Không em; I know enough not to starve but I want to learn. Anh Dũng said you could teach me."

This question seemed to please her. "Dạ anh; không sao. Are you hungry?"

"Always." Everyone in Đà Nẵng was always hungry and I just joined them.

"There is a western restaurant downtown that makes bánh pizza. Do you like bánh pizza?"

"Yeah but what's wrong with the food carts here? We've got really good bún bò Huế and some amazing bánh canh just on this street and one over there's even more. Did you want to eat bánh pizza em Thủy?" She had an uneasy look on her face. "You OK?"

"I am fine anh Upton. I do not want bánh pizza but that is what many westerners that come here want to eat."

"I eat on the street. Do you like street food em Thủy?"

Thủy warmly smiled. "Dạ anh; I like street food." It seemed she also preferred street food over bánh pizza.

"Would you like to have a bowl of soup together?"

A calm smile came across Thủy's face. "Dạ anh; I would like that very much."

Thủy spoke a few more words to chị Phương and respectfully said goodbye. "Hẹn gặp lại chị."

We left my home and walked out into the warmth of the late, morning sun with the smell of incense and something tasty in the air. "We should go over to the food carts on đường Ba Đình."

"Dạ anh; I know those food carts well."

"Really em?"

"I live close to you."

"Good em. Then we can dine together. I know it's not your job but maybe you could teach me about the food? It's all I've had since I've been here and still barely know what I'm eating."

"Dạ anh; I will teach you about our food and I will show you my favorite places."

"Are you sure?"

She smiled. "Dạ anh; I am sure."

"Cảm ơn em Thủy."

We walked along đường Lê Lai on that warm day. Tiny spotlights of sunshine rained down through the overhead tree canopy onto the gray, cobblestone sidewalk in front of us. The air was pleasant and there was a sweet breeze from the south. While đường Nguyễn Thị Minh

The Beauty of Aqua

Khai up ahead was again crowded with bicycles and a few motorcycles it was quiet here.

"How'd you get into translating?"

"I did well in school and after the war the government needed translators so that was what I studied at university. I also wanted to show visitors what I love so much about my city."

"You're from Đà Nẵng?"

"Không anh; I was born in Hội An, a small fishing village nearby, but now live in Đà Nẵng with my family."

"I also grew up in a fishing village and before I came here fixed boats."

"You were not a teacher?"

"I was fixing boats while looking for a place to teach. Truth was I didn't want to leave living by the ocean."

"Thankfully Đà Nẵng is on the ocean and it is growing quickly. Do you like our beach?"

"Haven't seen it yet. Anh Dũng said I shouldn't travel far without a translator."

"I think my—anh Dũng worries about you too much. Since your translator is here I will show you our beach this afternoon. Bãi biển Mỹ Khê is one of the most beautiful beaches in the world. Have you heard of it?"

"Không em but I don't get out much." I was ignorant.

"No problem anh. During the war the Americans called it 'China Beach'." China Beach was well-known in the US and returning servicemen talked about it like it was paradise although I suspected anything would've looked that good after what they'd been through.

"My friend told me about it. He said it's beautiful."

The beauty of Aqua

"Your friend has been to Đà Nẵng?"

"Không em; Roy's been to Sài Gòn but not here."

"Too bad anh. Sài Gòn is nice but Đà Nẵng is better."

"You really love your city don't you em Thủy?"

"Very much anh Upton. It is a special city."

"How do you figure that?"

"Đà Nẵng is almost two thousand years old and for many centuries ships from all over the world came here to trade." She stopped walking, shifted her posture towards me, stared right into my eyes and with a firm voice said, "When the French came and tried to take our land for themselves they were removed. When the Americans came and tried the same they were also removed. These acts were done while we were at a great disadvantage. We did the impossible and that is what makes us special."

I was reminded of uncle François recounting how those that had so badly hurt the people of France during WWII were also "removed" but at the point of Chekhov pistols. The Vietnamese people have an all too long history of being invaded but every time those invaders were removed much like the Americans did to the British during the American Revolution.

"How did the people of Đà Nẵng liberate themselves some many times?"

"With the help of our ancestors."

"You mean your grandparents also fought?" More of my ignorance was showing.

"No anh; with the lessons from our ancestors we removed those that wanted to take our city for themselves. We remember them every day in a special place in our homes and with the memories of their lives we found the strength to endure in our struggle for liberation."

We rounded the corner to đường Ba Đình and saw the street vendors were well-underway in preparing for lunch. Their metal carts with what they were serving was brightly painted on their side: "bún bò", "bánh canh", "xôi gà." Many had fifty-liter stock pots heated with a combination of charcoal and wood and all those smells came together in a symphony I'd heard many times before announcing that lunch would soon be ready. We turned into an alley off the street where a group of vendors were setup. The smells of what they were serving for lunch intertwined with those from a local bakery. We sat and Thủy ordered our lunch. She removed a pair of chopsticks from a metal basket on our table and carefully wiped them with a small piece of paper serving as a napkin. When finished she then wrapped the tips in the same paper placing them in front of me. She cleaned a pair for herself and did the same with our spoons. The smell of fresh bread wafted over us.

"You smell bread?"

"Dạ anh; there is a very good bakery here. The woman that runs it is well-known for her bread for bánh mì."

"I found a cart down the street that makes bánh mì que. It's wicked good." Crap.

"Dạ anh; I know that cart well. The bánh mì que there is very good and the bread they use comes from this bakery." Thủy looked over to the bakery and saw a woman standing on the second-floor balcony. She motioned to me to also look. "There is the woman that owns the bakery." An older and very beautiful woman stood on the balcony. She gazed towards the horizon and from her smile appeared not to have a care in the world. "She is beautiful, loves her city and is successful. I hope to be like her and someday I will."

The woman making our meal spoke a few words to Thủy. "She said that you have eaten at every cart on her street and she is happy to see you again."

"How would she know em?"

"This is Việt Nam. We talk to our neighbors and you are the only westerner that has ever visited any of them."

"So what do you like to eat em Thủy?"

"Everything anh."

"Like what?"

"All Vietnamese food." She smiled because that was her love which made me happy.

We turned our attention to our soup when it arrived and we stopped talking. The street became quieter and more peaceful. I watched Thủy carefully construct that first bite exactly with the preferred amounts of each ingredient and I was mesmerized. The calm look she had when she ate was one of bliss. Then it happened again and again with every bite. I knew that feeling because I too felt the same. It was clear food was her passion and she was caught in the celebration of it. We became lost in our soup. After we finished we sat silently to savor that last, glorious, bite together. Then I spoke, "Once again

The Beauty of Aqua

that was wonderful. What's it called? I've had it a dozen times but never knew."

"Phở 'không người lái'. Phở with no pilot. Phở is the most important dish to the people of Việt Nam and is from the North like my grandfather. This version is common and is made with vegetables."

"Why the name?"

"It was named after America's pilotless planes that killed many people during the war. Because of food shortages during the American War this soup was made with no meat, a simple broth and any vegetables that could be found. Let me ask the woman what is in it." Thủy and the woman spoke for a moment. "She said it has fish, cabbage, water spinach, radish and rice noodles. Fish is very important to the people of Đà Nẵng so we try to eat even just a little bit every day."

"I noticed that there wasn't a lot of meat. I thought with the war over things would've been better." My ignorance showed itself for a third time that morning.

"We are in thời bao cấp or the time of subsidy." Thủy paused in thought. This was personal to her. "As you can see the war has hurt my country very much. Because of this many times there are some foods we can not find. We are told to only use government coupons to buy food but we are flexible so we also have street food carts like those around us. Sometimes all we have is water spinach and rice. While it is hard we endure. I like to think that when we add our fish sauce to any dish it becomes better; it becomes Vietnamese."

"I didn't know that the food shortages were that bad."

"We have little anh Upton which helps us appreciate what we have. There is an old Vietnamese thought: 'The less items you carry the easier your travels.' We try to have few possessions which helps us find happiness. While many people lost almost everything in the war those that only had a few items found it easier to adapt to life as it had become."

"I think I know what you're saying. Before I left to come here I had to give away most of my possessions and put the rest in storage with my friend Roy. At first I worried about what to keep and what to give away but the more I gave away the easier it became to give away even more. In the end I only had a few boxes and my motorcycle."

Thủy smiled. "That is Vietnamese of you. You should feel at home soon."

"I already do even though I can't speak the language but I've seen how important your traditions are and I try to respect them." Feeling at home in Đà Nẵng came easy.

"That respect is the most important. You have a motorcycle anh?"

I smiled. "Dạ em; I do. An old '64 Honda CB77 Super Hawk that I rebuilt myself."

"Good anh. My family has a Super Cub. Honda makes good motorcycles."

"You're the first woman I've known that could ride."

"Really anh? Women in the West do not ride motorcycles?"

"Very few."

"That is sad. I always feel free when I ride." Only a fellow rider would've said that.

"I know that exact feeling. I'd ride to the beach and watch the waves."

She smiled when I shared that thought. "Dạ anh."

It was comforting to share my good memories with another rider.

"I should get a motorcycle while I'm here."

"Motorcycles are very expensive. There is a young man on your street that rents them. You could talk to him." Thủy paused, "I think you should wait before riding. Traffic here is very 'Vietnamese'."

She was concerned about me taking to the roads and rightfully so. Traffic in Việt Nam could be best described as a boiling pot of chaos and it appeared there were few traffic rules. I'd already seen a motorcycle with a family of four and another overloaded with bamboo baskets of fish from the nearby Hàn River.

"I think you're right. Thanks for the advice."

"No problem anh. I want you to be safe so you can teach." Thủy had been briefed on her job with me and understood that my tiny contribution could have large rewards in the future. Education had always been valued here but now it was of critical importance to the future of this city. A couple of the buildings at the university were new, ready for her students to learn and help rebuild this country.

"I saw some new buildings at the university and more going up everywhere. Is Đà Nẵng growing?"

The beauty of Aqua

"Dạ anh; my city is growing quickly. Everyday there are people from the countryside coming here to work and live. We are fortunate to be both on the ocean and have good land. Someday Đà Nẵng will look like Tokyo or Seoul."

"Tokyo or Seoul? Đà Nẵng is quaint but those cities are big and modern."

"Today Đà Nẵng is disadvantaged but someday soon it will not. We will build something that will amaze everyone who sees it."

"You sound sure that will happen."

"Because I am anh. The American War hurt my country and Đà Nẵng was not spared from that damage but the past is the past. All we want is to move forward, build a better future for our country and we are very optimistic."

"At the end of WWII my father and uncle lived in Paris and saw a great optimism in her people. It was badly damaged but she rebuilt and is more beautiful today than ever but Đà Nẵng isn't Paris."

"Dạ anh; Đà Nẵng has better food."

"I think the people of Paris would disagree."

"Their disagreement still would not change the fact that the food of Đà Nẵng is better because we are better connected to it. Almost everything we eat comes from within a few kilometers, purchased from a local shop or market and every child is taught how to make at least one important dish to their family. This way we are not only better connected to it we can pass our recipes on to our descendants."

The Beauty of Aqua

"Won't the food change when the city becomes like Tokyo or Seoul?"

"It will not because while buildings come and go, our food traditions and our recipes live in our hearts. With love we teach our children what our parents lovingly taught us. We honor our ancestors every time we make these special dishes."

"Honor your ancestors?"

"Dạ anh; honoring and remembering our ancestors is very important to the Vietnamese people. So important that every Vietnamese family has a place in their home to remember their ancestors. Every day we leave fresh fruit and light incense on our family alter. On important days, like the anniversary of their death, we honor their memory by making and then leaving dishes of their favorite foods in that special place. After a short time we remove the food and share it at our next meal."

"You celebrate the day they died?"

"Not celebrate: remember."

"OK em Thủy, remember. That seems morbid." This surprised Thủy.

"Why would you think that?"

"Because my mother died when I was young and when I think about that day all I can think about was how miserable it was."

Thủy's expression now mirrored mine. I tried not to show my pain but she could see it. "I am very sorry anh Upton. How do you remember her?"

"With sadness from the loss."

The beauty of Aqua

"I meant how do you remember her life? Everything that was good."

"I try to remember her life and the good times but her loss will always overshadow them. Having a place in my home just to remember her would be a place of sadness."

"This place in our homes is a place of comfort because we try to remember the good our ancestors brought to us and not how they died. All they suffered through and how they want us to persevere. We do not only remember their last days with us but their entire lives. In Việt Nam we believe that it is important to keep the memories of our ancestors close to our home and our hearts."

"I don't understand how remembering the day a person died can be a good day."

"If you stay here long enough you will. You will see how that place in our homes to our ancestors is not only a place of comfort but a place that gives us hope for the future. Our ancestors would want us to make our community a better place and that is what we will do."

Where real optimism was in short supply in the West, the City of Đà Nẵng was swimming in it and Thủy was an example of that optimistic pride. She was born and lived much of her life in an active war zone and saw the ravages of that conflict first-hand and in a way most westerners thankfully couldn't imagine yet all she could think of was how great her city would be in the future. To Thủy Đà Nẵng was "a city upon a hill" and that its light couldn't be hidden. Someday she saw its light, its culture and its food shining on the world. As a westerner I found this level of optimism in one's country and pride in her food to be… foreign.

"Do you really want Đà Nẵng to grow so big? Won't that change the city you love?"

"I want my city to grow because it is better for our people and our community. I will be sad to see what I love disappear but that is the fate of everything including us. There will be new people and they will find new things to love about my great city."

Someone once joked that there were only three sounds in the City of Đà Nẵng: roosters, motorcycles and construction. Đà Nẵng was growing quickly but in a way different from what would be expected in the West. After WWII many in the US started moving out of their cities and to the newly built suburbs with their well-manicured lawns and a car in every driveway. In exchange they accepted a banal and isolated life. A life away from the streets they and their families once lived. Where they knew the local shopkeepers and who had what they needed. Where their ancestors' memories lived.

By contrast Đà Nẵng simply expanded what had served them so well in the past. Instead of living in isolation like so many in the American suburbs, life as it had been known continued. Many buildings had three floors. The first would house a cafe, small restaurant, store or bicycle and motorcycle repair shop. The second and third were the family's personal living space. Instead of having to drive to find something the people of Đà Nẵng could simply walk out their front door and most likely find what they needed within a few blocks. This way of city life was very different to me but I soon saw its wisdom.

"Em Thủy; I've noticed you don't use contractions when you speak. Didn't you learn about them in school?"

"Dạ anh; I learned about them but I decided a long time ago not to use them. I 'don't' like their informality."

"Agreed that they create an air of informality but that's the point, to be informal."

"I am a person of few words and have found that not only as a translator but in life I must speak simply and clearly to be correctly heard. Using contractions would lessen the importance of what I am saying which would be my fault. When I speak I must make sure my words are understood."

Thủy was diminutive in stature yet like others of her ilk had a backbone of steel and she was going to be heard correctly.

"Anh Upton; what does your name mean?"

"My name has no meaning; it was my great-grandfather's. He was a well-known writer but had an awkward name."

"In Việt Nam names represent beauty, such as a bird or flower, qualities and characteristics that the parents wish for their child, such as wisdom or intelligence, or what their child has brought to them like 'blessing'."

"What's 'Thủy' mean?"

"My name is one of the five elements in the Vietnamese zodiac. It means water but a better translation would be the Latin word 'aqua.' It means intelligence, flexibility, softness but also difficulties keeping commitments. It is also a reminder of my love of the sea that I find very beautiful."

I smiled. "I also love the ocean and also see its beauty. I guess that happens to those that are born and live by the sea. It becomes part of you."

"Dạ anh; not living by the sea is like not living close to your best friend."

"I miss the ocean."

"I will take you there this afternoon and show you our beach."

"I'd like that. Cảm ơn em Thủy." I paused, "May I ask when were you born?"

"You should be careful when asking a Vietnamese woman her age but I will tell you: month one—January of 1958. When were you born anh Upton?"

"May 1957; month five. We're about the same age."

"Fire roosters." She seemed pleased with this news.

"Fire rooster? Is that with rice or noodles?"

Thủy laughed. "Không anh; it is our Vietnamese zodiac sign. We are both fire roosters."

"What's that mean?"

"It means we are both passionate about many things and sometimes not careful about following those passions." Thủy looked down and smiled. It seemed that sharing the same zodiac symbol meant something important to her. The Vietnamese zodiac governs many important decisions in one's life like their profession or choice of spouse. A good match according to this tradition brought the hope for a good future.

Vietnamese women handle themselves with dignity, poise and grace which is alluring. While she was attractive our relationship was suppose to be formal and I should heed uncle's advice as both Thủy and I were well-aware of the rules.

We left our table in the alley and made our way back out to đường Ba Đình.

"It is almost time to nap. You should go home anh Upton and sleep."

"That sounds good. The beach this afternoon?"

"Dạ anh; this afternoon."

"Anh ơi!"

My nap had long ended but I refused to get up and interrupt my relaxed state because there was no need to do so. Napping in Việt Nam is truly a wonderful tradition and sadly one that's been lost on much of the western world. Lunch is around noon and afterwards a nap for an hour or so. Everything goes quiet in the city. Even the banks and government offices close with workers napping at their desks. The result is a fresh start for the afternoon and more energy for the night. I dressed and walked out to my balcony. Looking down I saw Thủy.

"Hello anh Upton. Would you still like to see our beach?"

"Dạ em; that'd be nice. I'll be right down." I went downstairs, greeted chị Phương in the kitchen and headed to the street.

Outside was Thủy with her 1960's Honda Super Cub. While well-worn it also looked well-maintained and she was ready to go.

"Please sit on the rear and we will go."

I instinctually backed up and voiced my objection. "No, no, no; men don't ride on the back."

Thủy looked bewildered. "What do you mean men do not ride on the back of a motorcycle? There is plenty of room for you. You are small."

Ouch. "I'm a bit taller than you." While on the short side in the West I was a perfect fit for Việt Nam so technically I wasn't short. I voiced my concern. "In the West men don't ride on the back of a motorcycle with a woman driving."

"Why not anh?"

"Because... we don't. It's not 'manly'."

"You are not in the West, you are in Việt Nam and here in Việt Nam it is better for the person with more experience and a driver's license to drive."

"More experience? I've been riding since I was fifteen."

"Dạ anh; that is nice. I started when I was thirteen and I am the one with the driver's license so please get on." I could hear Matt's voice telling me to "live like a local."

"One minute. I need to grab my jacket and helmet."

"Where did you get a helmet?"

"Brought it with me. I've had it for years."

I quickly headed back inside and grabbed my riding jacket and trusty Bell RT helmet. While covered in dust

The beauty of Aqua

like everything else I owned the helmet's bright-red paint still shined. I headed back out.

Thủy smiled. "Nice jacket and helmet anh Upton. You look like a motorcycle racer. The color is very Vietnamese. Maybe we should paint a yellow star on the side?" The helmet's color did bare a resemblance to the red in the Vietnamese flag. "Now please get on the back and we will go." With that I got on the back of her Super Cub for this new experience of riding pillion with a woman up front. I soon found that Thủy could drive well but she seemed a little too hard on the small engine underneath us as she rarely let up on the throttle.

I had to speak up to be heard. "Aren't we going a little fast?" My hint for Thủy to back off the throttle a bit because the engine didn't sound like it could keep up for much longer.

She leaned back and loudly said, "No problem anh. Honda makes good motorcycles."

I couldn't disagree with her but the machine below us was long gone from the factory and many kilometers away. In the end my concerns would've made no difference because Thủy, like me with my Super Hawk, knew when to ride it hard and when not to by knowing the unique sounds of the engine so I had to trust her judgement.

Riding "pillion", or in the back, is very different from being behind the handlebars. When you're up front you have time to prepare for a necessary sharp turn or quick braking but in pillion you must trust the driver to not only make the best choices but be able to compensate for your extra weight in extreme conditions. I could already tell Thủy could handle a motorcycle and trusted her.

We soon left the rabbit warren of homes that made up our neighborhood in Hải Châu District finding our way over to the east side of Sơn Trà Peninsula. Where quận Hải Châu was dense quận Sơn Trà, once you got past the banks of the Hàn River, was rural with a few houses here and there and an occasional, large concrete structure that had been constructed by the US military during the American War.

We pulled to the side of the road, jumped over a small berm and headed onto the beach. While the road out to the beach was good there was little there except a few buildings with shops, a small collection of wooden fishing boats on the beach and a few signs translated into Russian. We stopped and dismounted. Thủy took off her helmet, flipped it over and placed it underneath the kickstand to keep the motorcycle from tipping over in the soft sand.

"It was good to be back on a motorcycle em Thủy."

"Dạ anh; when I ride on my motorcycle I feel free."

We leaned against her Super Cub and looked to the East Vietnamese Sea as the sun was setting to the west over the Hàn River. The setting sun lit the few clouds in the sky in a fiery red, orange and yellow. The beach was the most beautiful beach I'd ever seen. Much like Nauset Beach back on Cape Cod except to the north was the beauty of Sơn Trà Mountain with the clouds encompassing its top. The sand was soft and the waves made a pleasant sound. I felt a great sense of ease there like nothing else mattered but that moment. Not counting the coconut vendor a ways down the beach we were by ourselves.

"This is why I stay in Đà Nẵng. Việt Nam has many beautiful places but this is my home."

"I can see why em Thủy. This is like my favorite beach back home."

She looked across to the East Vietnamese Sea and to the clouds in rapture above. One lone fishing boat sat in the water painted a matted, gray-brown with her nets cast off to her port side. Thủy gently said, "The sky is beautiful."

"Dạ em; the color of the clouds look like a fire rooster."

"Dạ anh; it does." My comment seemed to have struck a chord with Thủy. She then looked towards the mountains to the north. "That is Sơn Trà Mountain. The road around it is one of the most beautiful motorcycle rides in Việt Nam."

There's a sense of peace one feels when riding a motorcycle in rural places. You're part of the world and not locked in a box shielded from it. Be it through rows of corn fields in Iowa or a beach road on Cape Cod the feeling is the same: you are alive. I could see the start of the road Thủy spoke of and it looked like what could be the best ride of my life.

"How long is it? Anything interesting up there?"

"About thirty kilometers with many hills. It is very beautiful and there are monkeys."

"Monkeys?"

"Dạ anh Upton; there are monkeys but they will not bother you."

"Is it crowded?"

"No anh; I have ridden there many times and have never seen anyone else."

Now I knew that ride around Sơn Trà Mountain would be the best of my life. Like everything else I saw in Việt Nam it was beyond my imagination just a short time ago.

Thủy picked her helmet up off the ground and dusted the sand off the side. It was similar in style and red like mine but had a large, black print of a famous portrait. I knew who it was but didn't think she did.

"Who's that on your helmet?"

"Chú Che."

"Did you just sneeze?"

She smiled. "No anh; I said 'chú Che.' He was a hero in the 'Revolución Cubana' of 1953. Ernesto 'Che' Guevara, uncle Che. Did you not learn about him in school?"

Thủy's English pronunciation was outstanding which must of been very difficult to properly develop while learning with little access to westerners and she could roll her r's like a native Spanish speaker. I was impressed and suspected her knowledge of that time was also on par. It was interesting to see how one man's hero was another man's enemy.

"Dạ em; just our history teachers didn't use the word 'hero'."

"I am sorry anh. Your history books only showed you one side and it was the wrong one."

I thought back to Cape Cod when dad and I were talking about traveling before I left. How seeing a place first-hand was always better than seeing it through the words or lens of another. While good for reference it's not for perspective. Growing up during the Vietnam War I heard a lot of ugly words about the Vietnamese people and my last month here had proven them all wrong. I couldn't say how either side felt about the war but to me, at that moment, I felt like I was in America after her Revolution. The people here wanted a better life for their children and those to come and that had to be respected.

"We should go anh."

I smiled. "Em Thủy, you drive well."

She tightened up her chin strap and returned the smile. "Cảm ơn anh. I have many small roads in my village that you would enjoy riding on. Maybe someday you will visit there."

There's a camaraderie among motorcyclists that's easy to explain. Instead of driving a four-wheeled "cage" like most with all its barriers from almost every thinkable danger, motorcyclists instead opt for two wheels with very little protection. While the automobile driver, with their air conditioning on full and the radio playing a banal pop song, drives through the landscape we are part of it. When we ride we can feel the different gusts of wind around us and every bump in the road. We have to think differently to survive and we respect the same in others. We, in a sense, are a community with its own language like a simple tap on the helmet to warn other riders the police were nearby. And that difference sometimes also caused us to "color outside the lines." Thủy and I had this bond. We were part of the same community.

"Are you hungry anh Upton?"

Back in the West I stuck to the standard "three square meals" but after being here for a short time I'd adapted to the local style of four or so small meals throughout the day which allowed me to try a large variety of different foods. I was curious to what Thủy had in mind.

"Dạ em Thủy."

"Good anh. There is a cart near my home that makes my grandfather's favorite soup very well."

Thủy mounted-up her Super Cub and tapped on the seat. "Please get on and we will go."

I "hopped" on as instructed and we left. Riding pillion would still take time to get use to but all I could do was try. Having an adept driver behind the handlebars made a big difference.

We returned to our ward of Thạch Thang in quận Hải Châu and parked our Super Cub by a cart with "bún ốc" brightly painted along the side with the prerequisite fifty-liter pot of something good brewing beside the chef. We sat, Thủy ordered for us and we were quickly served. Before me was a bowl of rice noodles in a fragrant, golden broth topped with spring onion, chilies and an unknown meat.

"Excuse me em Thủy."

The beauty of Aqua

I pointed to the mystery before me.

"What's this?"

"Ốc." I had just caught her before she became lost in her soup. "Snail. It is very good." With that she was gone.

I'd heard dad talk about eating snails and a few fisherman also did the same but that was definitely not the norm. I looked down and thought they looked... appetizing. I'd taken risks on trying new foods here and every time was rewarded with a great meal. I too dived in and like Thủy also became lost in that wonderful soup. We ate in silence and soon finished.

"Wow, just wow." I sat back in my little, plastic stool and again felt like a king. "That was one of the best meals of my life."

Thủy smiled with approval. "Like my grandfather this soup is from the North and was a favorite of his as a child. He was from Hải Phòng. When I eat here I think of him. I am very happy you liked it so much."

"It's past like em. The snail had a sweet taste and pleasant chew and the broth had a touch of shrimp. It was wonderful." I again slouched back in my seat to enjoy those last moments of bliss from my meal. Thủy was pleasantly intrigued by my enjoyment of our soup.

"You like Vietnamese food anh Upton?"

"After my first week here it's all I'll ever want to eat again."

The author Graham Greene wrote "They say you come to Vietnam and you understand a lot in a few minutes, but the rest has got to be lived." I quickly understood that a life without this wonderful food was not a happy life and I could care less for anything else.

"My grandfather would approve of that."

"Vâng em."

"We say 'dạ' in Đà Nẵng not 'vâng'."

"I'm sorry em. Sometimes 'vâng' just sounds better."

"Like the joy you find in our food my grandfather would also agree but you should still say 'dạ.' If not people will think you are from the North."

"I'd take it as a compliment if anyone thought I was from here."

For a second Thủy saw something in me that I didn't: living here had already started to change me. "I do not doubt that anh but you should still say 'dạ'."

"Dạ em."

Thủy smiled with approval. We once again mounted-up her trusty Super Cub, me on the back, and I was safely returned to my home for the night.

It was Saturday night and I was by myself as Thủy had been away for the last few days wrapping up her work in Huế City. I was reading on my balcony when I heard an unexpected voice from below.

"Anh ơi!"

It was Thủy. I looked down to see her below. She was wearing a short, light-yellow áo dài with blue and red flowers embroidered along the front and once again radiated.

"You're back?"

"How could I be here if I was not back?"

"Không em; I meant you're finished in Huế City?"

"Dạ anh; anh Dũng told me the computers will be here soon and I should come back and help you get ready. Do you want to eat cao lầu Hội An?" This was a new dish to me but Thủy already knew my answer. Every meal we ate together was always enjoyed. She would lead me from cart to cart around the city like a puppy dog and I happily followed. We'd eat in silence and afterwards, without a word, we'd sit quietly appreciating that last, seductive bite. Vietnamese food had quickly become my drug of choice and Thủy happily became my dealer. I headed downstairs locking the front door and gate behind me and we started our walk down đường Lê Lai.

"How are you em Thủy?"

"I am fine. Thank you anh Upton. I would like to take you to a special cart not far from my home. The woman makes cao lầu Hội An."

"Sounds good. What is it?"

"It is a special dish from my village in Hội An. It was my grandmother's favorite when she was a child and it is very good."

"Everything you've shown me has been very good."

She smiled with appreciation.

On the way to have our cao lầu Hội An we walked by the alley next to Thủy's house where I was surprised to see an old man standing in the shadows. It looked like he was wearing a brown men's áo dài with white pants, had a white cloth wrapped in a circle around the top of his head and he was holding a cane.

"Do you know him?" I motioned to the alley but the old man was gone.

"No anh; what did he look like?" I described the man and his outfit which caused Thủy to become nervous.

"What he was wearing is what older men wear when they are going to a funeral. Someone must of died."

"Where do you think he went?"

"Back in the shadows anh. We should go."

We quickly arrived at the cao lầu Hội An cart a few doors down from Thủy's home. Thủy and the woman cooking our meal chatted for a moment showing their familiarity. She returned with two bowls of soup.

Cao lầu Hội An is a speciality of Thủy's home village of Hội An and can immediately be identified by its thick and chewy, yellow rice noodles which were originally colored by minerals from a local water supply but now are colored with turmeric. Our soup was served with fresh greens, dried pork skins and a spicy broth. It also had a few pieces of pork which was a real treat.

"She had pork?"

"Dạ anh; she will be closing soon and she was kind enough to give us the last of her pig meat instead of bringing it to her home."

Nothing goes to waste in Việt Nam. If it can be saved or reused it is. If a piece of wood is too far gone to be used for its original purpose it's broken down into scrap pieces. When it's too far gone for that task it's then burnt as fuel for our meals. When you have little you make sure you get the best use of what you have. It was a refreshing change from my part of the world where most everything was disposed of for petty reasons never to be thought of again or until the day when our landfills become too full.

After our last bites from our silent meal we sat back in our chairs and said nothing. That was our custom. While some were quick to get up after eating we were not. We'd sit without saying a word to each other and savor what we just had. In those moments Thủy and I appreciated each other's company. The only thing that could make Vietnamese food better was being able to share it with someone who also appreciated the same.

"You like anh Upton?"

I sat up slowly, opened my eyes and smiled. "Dạ em; another great meal."

Thủy smiled with approval. "That makes me happy."

We paid for our meal and started our short walk back to Thủy's home when she stopped by the same alley we'd stopped at earlier. "You OK em Thủy?"

"I thought I saw the old man you told me about."

I looked but saw nothing. "I guess he went back into the shadows."

Thủy again had a nervousness about her. "I will go home now and you should do the same."

"Will you be OK?" I was concerned.

"Dạ anh; good night." With that she quickly unlocked the gate and front door to her home and even quicker locked the same behind her. I returned home.

I wasn't sure what I saw that night but I think Thủy saw something more.

The Beauty of Aqua

The next day Thủy spent at the university filling in for an absent teacher which left me with another day of reading on my balcony. I thought I should of been spending some of that time visiting a few tourist sites in the city before my teaching duties started but I was quite content to sit in my regular place high above my street. The late winter weather was gentle and the air sweet. I couldn't have asked for a better day to do nothing but read.

It was getting late and being on my own I decided to finish the night by having some phở in the alley around the corner by the bakery. Thankfully the cart was still open so I ordered and patiently waited. The smell of fresh bread once again hung over me like a fog and was comforting. I looked up to the second-floor balcony of the home that housed the bakery to see the same woman as before.

She was an older woman, about fifty years old, and very beautiful. Dressed in an aqua-blue, silk áo dài she stood there with both dignity and grace as she looked over her city. She had the smile of the Mona Lisa and looked like she didn't have a worry in the world. She looked happy which made me happy.

My phở arrived and before I started to eat I turned to the balcony to take one last look at that very beautiful woman but she was gone.

7

Everything can be said in food

I like getting paid not to teach, for now. I had been in Việt Nam for over a month without computers which was fine for me, leaving plenty of time to sit and read on my balcony, but left Thủy with a problem. If she wasn't working for me she had to go back to the local Foreign Affairs office and again start taking out high-profile tourists around the city on day-trips while we waited and, from a recounting of a recent tour, I could see why she disliked that task.

A typical morning would start off with her going to the one high-end, western-style hotel in the city promptly at five in the morning to patiently wait, sometimes for hours, for her western guests. When they finally came down she would take them on the same "dog and pony show" throughout the city. She saw the importance in showing them these places but it quickly became repetitive.

When it was time for lunch she would tempt them with the finest restaurants and street food Đà Nẵng had to offer but they universally turned her down for the hotel's restaurant which they falsely perceived to be their only safe place to eat and as their guide she was obligated to join them. They saw that third-rate, faux-western restaurant as an oasis and the rest of the city as a desert.

Thủy could eat anything cut or cooked properly but one. In a discussion about local restaurants in my village I recounted how my father and I would like to share a pizza made by a nice Greek family-restaurant and how the warm mozzarella was thick and fragrant. I could then see her starting to retch at the very thought of this delicacy from my childhood. Thủy couldn't eat cheese and even the thought of it made her sick. This was not good as the hotel's restaurant, to the guests' pleasure, coated everything in this vile substance. While Thủy would order off a poorly executed, local menu it made her sad that her guests had traded away a chance at a great culinary experience for a poor copy of the familiar; and to be so close to cheese.

She could still be my translator if she showed me around the city which she happily did. After two days we'd filled our scorecard with the required Foreign Ministry stops and were free to go where ever we wished and we did. From street food cart to street food cart all around the City of Đà Nẵng we ate three or four wonderful meals a day, all in silence. She showed me the best foods she knew and took the time to explain every dish and its history. When she did she radiated with pride because she loved her city and its foods and I was always happy to listen. Our shared passions for motorcycles and the same, great foods quickly brought us together as close friends.

I expected to have the day to myself as Thủy was asked that morning to fill in for an absent instructor teaching a first-year class of translators but I heard her familiar voice on that comfortable, early evening.

"Anh ơi!"

I leaned over my balcony rail to see Thủy below. While students were required to wear the same functional, white uniform every day teachers were not and many times their traditional áo dài was brightly colored and accented with bright, floral patterns making them the most beautiful teachers in the world. Thủy was no exception as she was wearing a well-tailored, bright-yellow áo dài with a green stem of pink and purple lotus flowers brightly embroidered along the front which was reflected in the few puddles left from the recent rain and the fresh scent of that rain hung sweet in the air. She looked beautiful but it wasn't my place to say so. "You look very nice."

"Cảm ơn anh. I brought you a letter from anh Dũng. Please come down."

"I'll be right there." With that I headed downstairs locking the front door and gate behind me like anh Dũng always told me to do. He was just looking out for me.

"Xin chào anh. Anh khỏe không?" She spoke slowly and clearly for my benefit.

"Chào em. Anh khỏe. Em khỏe không?"

Then she did her best to keep from giggling at me. Thủy had been helping me learn a few more Vietnamese words and phrases and improve my pronunciation. Sadly bits of my Boston accent still bled through my poor pronunciation but she was always a patient teacher. I could see that she would help anyone wishing to learn more about her country and its culture.

"Em khỏe. Cảm ơn anh. Here is the letter from anh Dũng." While the letter was in Vietnamese there was a pick list I recognized and it was what we'd been waiting for.

"The computers are here?"

"Dạ anh; the letter says they have arrived in Hà Nội. You will need to go and sign the paperwork to have them sent here."

"Em đi Hà Nội không? I'll need a translator."

"I would like to go but it would not be appropriate for me to travel so far alone with you so I will ask another to take my place." She paused thinking about possibly losing this opportunity to travel. "If my mother came with us that would be fine."

"Will she want to go?"

"Like my grandfather her family once lived in the North and she always enjoys seeing Hà Nội. My father's sister cô Dung may also join us. Did you have the street food when you were there?"

Everything can be said in food

"Once at the train station but otherwise no. When I got there we went right to my hotel and the next morning left very early."

"The street food in Hà Nội is very good." And with a confident smile said. "Almost as good as Đà Nẵng." There was her local pride shining through again and this discussion of street food started to make me hungry.

"Em ăn mì Quảng không?"

She smiled. "Dạ anh; em thích mì Quảng." When it came to food Thủy spoke from her heart.

I returned her smile. "I knew that em."

We headed over to the alley by the bakery off of đường Ba Đình to a mì Quảng cart and ordered. As our custom we ate in silence then sat for a bit to savor that last, glorious bite when I spoke.

"I knew after my first week here my life had changed. I couldn't speak or read the language but everything that I needed to know about this place could be said in the food. You can't come here and not be changed. I don't think I could live without it. It's become part of me."

Thủy was not completely surprised by my admission. "You no longer like western food?"

"Không em; I just don't want it. What could be better than a bowl of mì Quảng?"

Thủy smiled as this was also a favorite of hers. "Dạ anh; I like many foods but mì Quảng is also special to me." She smiled with good memories. "Someday maybe I will make you a dish my grandmother taught me, mì Quảng cá lóc. It is mì Quảng with fish and is very good. So mì Quảng is your favorite?"

"I don't have a favorite dish but it's the one I fell in love with. I've liked everything I've eaten but if I could choose my last meal mì Quảng would be it."

"Really anh? Not a dish from your village?"

"Nope. Not once I had mì Quảng."

Over the last couple of months I'd eaten over twenty different dishes, not including varieties of the same, and enjoyed them all, but mì Quảng was different because it was an eclectic bowl of pure happiness and I was in love with this beautiful creation from the Province of Quảng Nam. As phở is to Hà Nội, mì Quảng is to Đà Nẵng.

Phở started life in the North and for most of its life that's where it stayed but because of the war and soon after the Vietnamese diaspora to the West phở became known worldwide. Please don't get me wrong, I'll never turn down a good bowl of phở bò but my heart belongs to another.

A bowl of mì Quảng starts its life as a simple broth of fried garlic and tomatoes. Then pork belly is marinated in salt, pepper, shallots, turmeric and, of course, nước mắm. Shrimp is quickly caramelized in a hot pan with sugar and more nước mắm. After an appropriate time for the pork to marinate it's pan-fried and added to the simmering stock pot with the shrimp where salt and even more nước mắm is added.

Unlike in the West where the ingredients get much of their flavors from the stock, the opposite is true with most of the flavors staying with the tasty bits in mì Quảng. The stock is also much stronger than its better known cousin from the North. Something the people of

Đà Nẵng would say was true about both their beloved dish and their children.

Imagine you're sitting on a little, plastic stool at your favorite mì Quảng food cart in the city patiently waiting for your bowl of soup on this peaceful, winter night. You look over to see the woman behind the cart adding a handful of broad rice noodles to your bowl then she scoops in the warm and fragrant pork and shrimp. She stirs her charcoal-heated pot a bit to clear a path for her ladle to go deep in the pot to get the warmest stock, which she does with skill, and pours it into your bowl. Finally it's topped with a slice of hard-boiled duck egg, spring onion and crushed peanuts.

She hands you your bowl of warm soup and a plate of cool salad greens. Holding the bowl close to your face you breath in this soup of the gods. You smell garlic and, of course, nước mắm. The vapors warm your face and comforts you on this cool, late night. You put it down and prepare for your taste of heaven. The magic happens when you mix the fresh greens into your bowl. Everything is coated and warmed in the strong and fragrant broth yielding a very pleasant variety of textures and flavors. You take your first bite and forget time exists. Welcome to an everyday bowl of mì Quảng in the City of Đà Nẵng.

Life is not complete without once experiencing that special dish in that special city and this is why to me it's the best food ever served in a bowl. Maybe that's why in part I fell in love with my city by the sea. I knew after my first bowl of mì Quảng my life had once again changed.

We finished our meal and sat in silence enjoying the memories of that sensual soup.

"Anh và em đi uống cà phê không?"

"Dạ anh; em uống cà phê."

With that we walked down to Cafe 47 on that quiet night. The days were now a bit warmer then when I'd first arrived and it was pleasant. The sun was down and a warm breeze blew in from the south. We arrived and without a word we were served our regular coffees.

"Hà Nội was the first place I tried Vietnamese coffee. I could taste hints of cocoa and butter. It was so different and so unexpected. It made me happy."

"There is a special coffee in Hà Nội, cà phê trứng, which I would like you to try. It is very good."

"Special em?"

"Dạ anh; it is whipped egg yolk and sugar poured over hot coffee. I always get that when I am there. Hà Nội is very cold and this coffee is good on those days."

"How cold?"

"Very cold. Many days it is only 15°C."

I could top that. "Dạ em; that's pretty cold. Where I was born it gets down to -5°C with a good meter of snow on the ground."

"Dạ không cảm ơn anh. How do you drive your motorcycle?"

I laughed. "You don't. During those winter days there's little to do but work and stay home."

"No cafe like this or food carts?"

"Không em; not a lot of fresh vegetables either."

"I can see why you like our food so much." She paused, "I would be sad if I lived there."

We sat and watched some children playing badminton in the street seemingly without a care in the world. As usual the shop owner's dog "mì" came up wanting to be petted.

"Em thích Hà Nội không?"

"Em thích Hà Nội. Đà Nẵng is in my heart but Hà Nội is beautiful with many old buildings and parks and it is the capital of my country."

In the US every child knows where their capital is but few know about the struggles that made it possible. We learn the names and dates of important events but they are abstract to us where here it was experienced. 1945 for the people of Việt Nam was like 1776 for those in America. The people of Việt Nam fought for sovereign rule and Thủy saw some of those painful changes happen.

She finished her coffee and stood up. "Cảm ơn anh. I enjoyed our coffee but I must go home now."

"Are we all set for our trip to Hà Nội tomorrow?"

"Dạ anh; không sao. We will take the train early in the morning and get there late at night."

I'd done this trip before going the other way and it wasn't a lot of fun.

"What kind of seats did you get us?"

"Hard seats anh."

My heart sank thinking about sitting on a bouncing park bench for twelve hours.

Thủy smiled. "Không anh; soft bed."

"Not funny em."

"Anh Dũng thought it was funny." It was probably his idea.

"Chúc ngủ ngon em."

She smiled. "Your Vietnamese is getting better. Good night anh." It wasn't but Thủy was very kind. With that she left me to sit and enjoy that pleasant night.

After the long train ride to Hà Nội and finding a taxi to take the three of us to our hotel we settled in for the night. The hotel was in the Old Quarter near the place I stayed before. It was simple and well-cared for with the owners living on the top floor. The next day I woke up to a knock on my door from Thủy.

"Anh ơi! Please meet me and my mother downstairs. I called anh Dũng and he will meet us at the restaurant."

I spoke through the closed door. "Không sao em."

"Hẹn sớm gặp lại anh."

I dressed and walked through the hotel lobby to see Thủy and her mother waiting on the sidewalk. "Xin chào buổi sáng chị. Chào buổi sáng em."

Both Thủy and her mother smiled from my display of good manners and not my pronunciation. "Xin chào buổi sáng anh. Very good anh. Please follow us."

Alleys in Đà Nẵng were narrow but in Hà Nội there was barely enough room for two motorcycles to squeeze through these ancient alleyways plus, adding to the congestion, were the throngs of morning shoppers. Like the traffic on the street no one was getting frustrated with the wait and they accepted it with patience. We soon arrived at our destination for breakfast with anh Dũng waiting with food on the table.

"Xin chào buổi sáng anh Dũng."

"Very good cháu Upton. How is your French coming?" He wasn't going to let that go.

"C'est bon monsieur."

"What did you say?"

"You understood me."

He smiled. "Maybe cháu. Sit and have bún chả if you please."

Bún chả is a treat born in Hà Nội like bún thịt nướng except served with a clear broth where bún thịt nướng is served dry. First in your bowl you add a warm and light broth made from water, vinegar, sugar, of course, and nước mắm then add pieces of grilled pork and nem nướng, grilled pork sausage. Then from a second shared bowl you add some lightly pickled sweet and sour slices of kohlrabi and fanciful cuts of carrot. Finally in goes the rice noodles for a quick bath and you're ready to get lost in this special dish. Like mì Quảng in Đà Nẵng a complete life must include having this great dish in the great city of Hà Nội.

We ate with joy and without a word. Anh Dũng and I finished and we sat back in our chairs watching the morning traffic full of bicycles before us. He also felt like a king.

"That was so good anh Dũng. How's the bún chả in Đà Nẵng?"

The Beauty of Aqua

"There is good bún chả there but the best is here because this is where it is from. To most Vietnamese people Hà Nội is the most important city in the country because of its history and it is their capital. It has some of the best foods, attracts the best minds and has the most beautiful women." I was surprised by anh Dũng's next question. "Em Thủy has a special beauty doesn't she?"

I thought this might be a test. "She does but I think the only ones that get to see that special beauty are the fortunate few to know her well."

I could've said more but I didn't. Looking over anh Dũng's shoulder I saw Thủy was watching us and by the displeased look on her face also listening.

Anh Dũng thought about my answer and might of suspected I was holding back. "Cháu Upton, when you are riding a motorcycle along a cliffside road do you know the safest place to be?"

"Không anh; where?"

"As far from the side of the cliff as possible. Please remember that advice when you are with my—cháu Thủy. Vietnamese women have a natural and somewhat subconscious talent to allure men. Falling in love with one is like falling off a cliff. It would be best for you to drive slowly and as far from the side of that cliff as possible."

"I will try to remember that."

As a motorcyclist I saw the wisdom in his words; I just didn't know if I could follow them. Again looking over anh Dũng's shoulder I noticed Thủy and her mother standing up to leave.

"Here are the papers for you to sign. Sign where you see your name if you please."

I signed the paperwork on the table. "Everything there? No missing boxes?"

"Không cháu; I want you to be successful so I made sure everything was there. If you are we will expand your program to Huế City." Anh Dũng stood up. "Please be successful cháu. My people are depending on you."

"Dạ anh; I'll do my best."

"You are in the North and you should say 'vâng' otherwise people might think you are from the South."

"I'd take it as a compliment if anyone thought I was from here."

Anh Dũng smiled. "I do not doubt that cháu but you should still say 'vâng' when you are in Hà Nội." He paused and looked at me. "I see a change in you cháu Upton. I think there is less sadness in your life. Am I correct?"

"Vâng anh." Anh Dũng was looking out for me like my uncle would and that was welcomed.

"Well said my friend. My people can teach you much about happiness. I hope you are here long enough to learn. Hẹn gặp lại cháu Upton."

"Hẹn gặp lại anh Dũng."

With that anh Dũng left and I sat by myself and enjoyed the Hà Nội street life unfolding before me. Like Thủy my heart was in Đà Nẵng but Hà Nội felt and looked like Paris of old and a place I'd be happy visiting many, many more times. Our one day here was much too short but we needed to return to Đà Nẵng.

The Beauty of Aqua

Do you smell that? The smell of roasted pork wafted up from the street and into my room. It was seven in the morning and there was roasted pork right outside my balcony. I laid in bed and allowed that enticing smell to entertain me until I couldn't take it any longer, got up and headed across the street to chị Giang's house.

Since it was Saturday I suspected she was making something special and I wasn't disappointed. Not that I had any complaints about her usual fare but a little bit of variety was nice, especially from such a talented cook.

Today she was making bún thịt nướng: roasted pork with nước chấm: a dipping sauce made with water, lime, sugar and, of course, nước mắm. Pork was a rare treat and I was going to avail myself of it. As I walked out my door she waved me down. "Cháu ơi! Bún thịt nướng!"

"Dạ chị. Cháu ăn bún thịt nướng. Cảm ơn chị."

With that my reservation at one of the best places I'd ever eaten was made. As I walked over chị Giang prepared my plate without breaking her stride. She was an older woman but in very good shape. I think she did yoga. Within a few moments after sitting down she brought over my plate. This was a special treat.

Bún thịt nướng is also from the North like its brother bún chả except this is part salad, part rice noodles topped with pickled carrots and daikon radish, slices of cool cucumber and a few slices of grilled pork from chị Giang's sidewalk charcoal grill.

The bún thịt nướng was everything I expected but I was in the mood for something more and thought I should bring Thủy along. I found my way to her home where she was wearing a casual, matching top and bottom with bright-floral-patterns silk-screened all over. It looked both nice and comfortable. She was outside washing down the front steps.

"Em ơi! Em ăn sáng không?"

She thought for a moment. "Không anh."

"Would you like to eat sticky rice and chicken?"

"Dạ anh; em thích xôi gà."

I smiled. "I knew that em."

She returned my smile and we started our way down to đường Nguyễn Thị Minh Khai to a nearby shop, "Xôi gà Bà Hồng."

"Our we all set for our trip to Huế City?"

"Dạ anh; thank you for being my pig."

I smiled. "Phrasing em. The expression is 'Thank you for being my guinea pig'."

"Dạ anh; thank you for being my guinea pig. You will be very helpful to my class."

Thủy occasionally would be called to lecture in Huế City about translating technical terminology as this was her forte. She was both very intelligent and highly skilled. I was to give a pseudo-lecture with technical terms where Thủy would stop me to explain them. Lecture and stop, lecture and stop, lecture and stop for three hours which was hard on both of us. I was her guinea pig but I didn't mind as it was for a good cause: teaching English translation students eager to learn.

The Beauty of Aqua

We soon arrived for our sticky rice. It was a clean place set up along the sidewalk with sturdy chrome tables and chairs. Between us and a street full of bicycles was the woman making our meal. Next to her was an aluminum pot full of sticky rice and a charcoal grill with chicken. Thủy ordered for us, we were served and ate in silence.

Sticky rice is somewhat of a foreign concept in the West where we think a mistake was made. In the East this is not true with this particular very short-grain blend of high-gluten rice. What is yielded is a gentle mixture of rice lumped together that becomes the perfect vehicle for flavors. A few strips of chicken and a touch of nước mắm turns this simple rice meal into something magic.

After we finished we sat for a moment to bask in the morning sunshine. Its light poured over us adding to the joy we already felt from that simple meal. We were both in paradise and Đà Nẵng at the same time.

"Anh và em đi uống cà phê không?"

"Dạ em."

We returned to and peacefully walked down đường Lê Lai that pleasant morning. Drops of sunlight again poured through the tree canopy above and we were still basking in the joy from our simple meal. Continuing on in silence to Cafe 47 where, thanks to the cafe owner's attentive eye, our usual coffees were sitting at our usual table for us to enjoy. We sat quietly and looked out to the street.

"I'm lost em Thủy."

"Không anh; look at the sign." She pointed to the street markers a few meters away. "See anh: đường Lê Lợi and đường Lê Lai. We are here."

I smiled. "I meant I'm lost in life."

"How anh?"

"Because I am in love and I'm afraid I'll lose her."

"You met a woman? I think you are going too fast."

"Not a woman; here." I paused, "Look at this place. It's alive. People are walking around. Front doors open to see the outside world. Great food on every street corner. This place in the time I've been here has changed me over and over again. This place stole my heart and she can have it."

Thủy quietly absorbed with pride what I was saying because she saw the same joy in her city. "I can see it on you. I can see you are changing."

"How em?"

"I will tell you someday." She smiled and sipped on her coffee. "You know I love my country very much and I see the same beauty in her too. Thank you for your love of my home and thank you for respecting us."

"To do any less would be unthinkable."

"I think you should think less about the future and enjoy today. Maybe you need a bowl of soup?"

I laughed to myself. Good food was a path to happiness but I was full. "Không cảm ơn em. I ate bún thịt nướng before our xôi gà."

She smiled and then confessed. "Em ăn mì Quảng rồi."

The sun shined down on us as we sat quietly in that small patch of paradise enjoying our coffees together. She in deed saw a change in me but it was one I couldn't yet comprehend.

Thủy and I stepped off the train in the morning sunlight at the station in Huế City. A thick mix of light and dark clouds hung low over the nearby mountains and it was becoming hotter and stickier with the change of seasons. There was also the pungent smell of nước mắm in the air which was always a good omen. Thủy bolted for the train station exit. It was clear she had a plan in mind.

"Anh ơi! Please follow me. We will take a taxi and eat before our class this afternoon."

"Where are we going?"

She smiled. "Anh Dũng told me that there was a western restaurant I should take you to." Then she giggled. "Không anh; we will eat where we always eat: on the street and in the markets." It seemed her boss' humor was part of her.

I smiled thinking about all those great meals we had together.

"Anh Dũng said you liked chợ Đông Ba so that is where we are going. We will eat bún bò Huế at my favorite food stall. You will have to tell me if you like his better than mine."

"I'd feel bad telling you that."

"Being tactful is important in life but we are good friends talking about the same foods we enjoy and there will be no hurt feelings when we are honest with each other about that. I want to feel the same joy you felt when you had that other dish. In Việt Nam you do not have to stay with one favorite food cart for your entire life but you are free to explore, try all you see and share your experiences with your friends." She paused, "You should know that the same is not true with Vietnamese women."

"I will try to remember that."

We took a taxi to chợ Đông Ba and quickly headed through the maze of stalls. Like anh Dũng she knew exactly where she was going: to her favorite bún bò Huế stall.

Having bún bò Huế in Huế City is like having clam chowder in Boston, pizza in New York City or lobster in Maine. This was one of the most important dishes to Việt Nam and I was again about to have it in the place it was born.

"This was where anh Dũng brought me."

"Really anh? Let me ask the woman if she remembers you."

Thủy and the woman behind the stall spoke. "She remembers you, how much you enjoyed her food and it made her happy."

We watched our meal being made with joyful anticipation. The woman quickly grabbed our bowls and laid them out on the well-worn, wooden board in front of her. Without a pause she placed a handful of thin rice noodles in each bowl then bits of beef and pork, chunks of blood pudding and crab sausage then the broth which could've been divined from some magic spell. Our bowls were then topped with basil, mint, bird's eye chilis and sweet chili jam.

In the West the best bite of a meal is the first. Imagine that meal has just been presented to you and it's still warm. While you savor the first bite it never gets better and when the last bite comes it's usually the least enjoyed. The opposite is true with Vietnamese food where every bite gets better and better throughout the entire meal. When you eat a bowl of soup in Việt Nam for the first few bites you're adding various items like nước mắm, sweet chili jam, brightly colored bits of pickled shallots and carrots or a few extra bird's eye chilies. You make it to your taste which leads to the last spoonful in the bowl being the best. With the meal finished you then sit back and fondly remember that last, glorious bite. Happiness is fleeting but can be captured for a brief moment in a good bowl of soup.

Soon we were presented with our bowls of perfection. The first time I had this soup it expanded what I thought was possible from food and that initial joy was felt again. Vietnamese food nourishes not only the body but the soul and this dish like mì Quảng had become part of me. Thủy and I quickly became lost in our soup. After finishing we sat back in our little, wooden stools to savor that last, wonderful bite of bún bò Huế.

Thủy and I dutifully taught and finished our class to the tired but grateful thanks of her students and we returned to the Huế City railroad station for our return to

Đà Nẵng. On the train ride out of town I thought about how I could see myself living here someday. Huế City has that effect on you.

It was late Saturday morning and after an all-nighter at the computer lab I slept right through my neighborhood rooster alarm clock. Walking out to my balcony I saw chị Giang cleaning up from the morning's meal. Since chị Linh had also been long closed I figured I'd get some bún mắm. I cleaned up and headed out locking the door and gate behind me. Within a few meters I saw my friend and it seemed she had the same meal in mind.

"Chào em." I surprised her. "Anh xin lỗi em."

"Không sao anh. What are you doing here? Do you eat bún mắm?"

"Anh thích bún mắm but only once a week or so em. It's a special treat."

Thủy was surprised and asked a question to the woman behind the cart. "Dạ anh; she said you are the only westerner that has ever bought bún mắm from her. She was also surprised you liked it. You are also the only westerner I know that likes bún mắm. Even many Vietnamese do not like it."

"How many westerners do you know?"

"Only three but there will be more." There was that eye towards the future Thủy always had.

"The first time I tried bún mắm I didn't like it but then I was wandering around the city one morning and found this little place, Bún mắm Thanh, in an alley off of đường Ngô Gia Tự. The smell was so strong and so enticing and after that second bowl that's when I fell in love with it. Bún mắm for breakfast has become one of my favorite meals but only about once a week."

"That shop is very good. How did you order? I know they do not speak English and they would not understand your French."

She couldn't be serious. "Excusez-moi, s'il vous plaît?"

"Je parle français un tres peu. Anh Dũng has been teaching me and I can hear the difference in your accents. He said he can help you speak better."

Ouch. "I think anh Dũng's dry wit is rubbing off on you."

"He was not being funny anh. He was serious." After a pause she gave a light-hearted smile. "Like anh Dũng and me you speak the language from your home and family and I will respect that. How did you order your food?"

"It was confusing at first but then I just pointed to a bowl she had made and she made the same for me. Since I've been here I've learned not to choose what to eat when I go out but to look and see what the street carts have except for bún mắm. Sometimes I have an urge that this is the only food that will satisfy me."

Thủy was quite pleased to see that I also enjoyed this dish.

Bún mắm is not for the faint of heart. If mì Quảng is a seductive rain then bún mắm is a typhoon. While nước

Everything can be said in food

mắm, the most common version of Vietnamese fish sauce, has a silky, smooth texture and perfect-golden color hinting to its refined taste mắm nêm, the fish sauce used in bún mắm, is the very opposite.

Mắm nêm instead has a thickish, opaque, brownish color and a texture like thin-mud full of good sized chunks of anchovies that contributed their many tiny lives to create this witch's brew. And it's strong. Many times bún mắm carts congregate together in a vain attempt at controlling the smell. This led to an alley off of đường Trần Kế Xương, where such regular gatherings of bún mắm carts happened, to receive the infamous title of "Bún mắm alley." It's so strong pregnant women are told to avoid it. Really, really strong like able to double as paint stripper but to its fans like me it "Smells like hell but tastes like heaven." and I took to it like a duck to water after my second bowl.

We brought our bún mắm over to a couple of nearby plastic stools and ate in silence like always leaving time to appreciate that last, smelly bite when Thủy spoke. "Do you want to date a Vietnamese woman?"

Interesting question. "I would happily date any woman so long as we liked the same foods. Vietnamese food has become part of me so she would have to like the same."

Thủy smiled. "Why do you love our food so much?"

I had to think about her question. "I find the food comforting and can remember the first time I had bánh bao, mì Quảng, bún bò Huế, cao lầu, bún mắm and bún chả along with so many other dishes. They brought me so much happiness with their perfect mix of ingredients. Vietnamese food showed me food could be so much more than what I knew from living in the West. And when I tried nước mắm for the first time—"

"—you really like our nước mắm?"

"Life is not complete without nước mắm and mắm nêm and I couldn't be with anyone that didn't think the same. I'm flexible but not when it comes to fish sauce."

Thủy smiled with approval. "Maybe you will find someone like that if you are fortunate."

Her smile left her face when she saw her brother running towards us. Quickly he was face-to-face with Thủy and started screaming at her. That didn't fly with me and my wayward days in South Boston kicked in. With a push to his chest now I was in his face. He reeked of rice wine.

"Back off man! You got something loud to say point your mouth over here!" I also suggested he should go perform an act of self-copulation.

Thủy had to translate as his English wasn't very good and when he understood my words it seemed he was up for the challenge. I didn't want to fight, especially with my "immigration issue", but you shout at a woman like that we've got a problem. Thủy spoke a few words to him and he begrudgingly left.

I had to get in a parting shot. "And the horse you rode in on!"

"He walked here anh. No horse."

"Anh xin lỗi em. It's difficult to translate."

"Dạ anh; next time please let me handle my brother."

"He doesn't have the right to shout at you like that."

"Dạ anh Upton but I will deal with him at home. You still should not have raised your voice. It is better to deal with these matters in private."

"So I should just let him yell at you?"

"He is my younger brother and he will do as I say. Em Ngô has a sadness in him like—he hides from his sadness with too much rice wine which hurts him even more and I do not know how to help him."

I could see this was hard for her to talk about.

"I am very worried about my brother." She looked down the street to see if he was still in sight. "Em xin lỗi. Đi đó về." Thủy quickly walked down đường Lê Lợi and disappeared around the corner.

"Anh ơi!"

My friend was calling me from below my balcony. I happily headed downstairs locking the house and gate behind me.

"Chào em Thủy. Em khỏe không?"

"Em khỏe. Cám ơn anh. Would you like to eat dinner at my home tonight? My mother is there and will make us dinner then we can drink tea."

"Will your brother be there?"

"Không anh; he is fishing with a family in Hội An." That was good news as Ngô, coincidentally the same fisherman down by the banks of the Hàn River that dragged his nets across my path, did not like me one, little bit.

"Then I would really enjoy a meal at your home." Thủy was an excellent cook because she learned from an equally good one: her mother.

Chị Ngọc was about chị Phương's age and she would offer me tastes of amazing foods from daikon radish cooked in beef marrow and ginger to uniquely spiced and dried tiny, whole anchovies. Like Thủy she saw my love for the food of her ancestors and wanted to push that love as far as I could take. Her welcomed presence was always near when I visited her home which was also expected by our community as Thủy and I were young and single; although there was a language barrier that offered us some privacy.

"You know I can't say no to your mother's cooking."

She smiled. "I knew that anh."

We left my home and soon arrived at Thủy's as it was only a short walk away. It was a simple, three story brick and concrete building, similar to all our other neighbors, painted a light shade of green-blue. In the very small space between the front gate and front door Thủy and her mother had a small garden with a few vegetables. We went inside.

"Sit anh Upton and have some tea. I must help my mother prepare our meal."

Many of my favorite meals had been enjoyed at Thủy's home. While street foods offered a singular and spectacular dish a family meal followed a different path. A typical meal would start earlier in the day with chị Ngọc, sometimes with Thủy in tow, going to our local wet-market down the street that offered a fresh selection of fish, meat and vegetables. While some thoughts of what to cook that night were present what was being offered before her was what mattered. There was no need to cook a meal with subpar ingredients just because that's what she had thought of making earlier. First she picked the best ingredients then thought of something to create.

Today she found what was needed to make tonight's meal: fresh squid, duck eggs, water spinach and pumpkin. While not popular in the past pumpkin was becoming more common and offered a nice compliment to a meal. Chị Ngọc honored her traditions and knew how to be flexible. She returned home and later started preparing for tonight's meal.

First she cleans the fresh ingredients, then assesses their strengths and weaknesses to take full advantage of the fresh bounty before her. Off to the side is a primitive electric rice cooker that, thanks to her many years of experience, yields a perfect bowl of rice every time. Soon with a plan she starts by boiling the duck eggs then with the same water she boils large chunks of pumpkin. When done they are put off to the side in a covered dish to stay warm. She then cleans the squid by carefully removing the ink sack and cartilage, cutting into bite-size pieces then frying in oil and bird's eye chilies.

Next comes the nước mắm which is Thủy's job as her mother's hands are full. She starts by crushing, using a traditional mortar and pestle, garlic and bird's eye chilies into a fine pulp. Those flavorings are placed in a small bowl where sugar and the star of the night, nước mắm, will be added. She squeezes in a lime then adds about a half a cup of nước mắm base which at this point only contains anchovies and salt.

This flavor of the heavens started it's life just a few kilometers northwest of us in the ward of Hòa Hiệp Bắc which is nestled between the scenic Hải Vân Pass and Đà Nẵng Bay and was locally well-known for this treat. Countless tiny anchovies and salt are placed layer after layer in clay barrels to ferment for a few months or so. When finished what is yielded is the golden-amber nectar we love so much.

With the squid done chị Ngọc flash-cooks the water spinach in the same water used for the pumpkin. When finished the spinach is removed and placed in its own covered bowl. The water used for cooking the vegetables or treasured "pot liquor" is poured in a large bowl for all to enjoy.

Thủy sees her mother is almost finished cooking so she moves the family Super Cub next to the staircase and rolls out a bamboo mat, where we'll be sitting, that's large enough for all and the meal to come. First she places a large bowl of rice for refills in the center, next to it a smaller bowl of nước mắm and bowls of rice for each. Strangely there are four rice bowls instead of three. Then bowls of water spinach, pumpkin and squid soon arrive. Everyone sits on the floor and the meal begins.

First I start by adding some pumpkin and squid to the rice already in my bowl, then a bit of duck egg that had previously been soaked in nước mắm and stir. The pumpkin and duck egg yoke coat the rice which creates an added dimension to the dish. After a few trips back and forth with adding what's in front of me I find my way to the bottom of my rice bowl and know it's time for the soup.

Tradition is to finish a meal with the pot liquor which was lightly flavored from the vegetables it was cooked in and the nước mắm that is left in your rice bowl making a wonderful way to end your meal. You look at your clean bowl and smile as you lean back from your spot on the floor with a Super Cub as your backrest. Welcome to an everyday, family dinner in Việt Nam.

While growing up I was expected to help out cleaning up after a family meal, that was not the case here with men almost being removed by force from the kitchen as the women cleaned. As a westerner I felt guilty not helping but I saw that time after the meal as time Thủy and her mother spent talking and by their looks it was a pleasant discussion.

I spent my time waiting by looking at the family portraits on the wall. There was one of Thủy when she was a teenager in a white, student áo dài with her younger brother. Another is of a well-dressed man in his thirties standing by an equally aged and well-dressed chị Ngọc and a much younger Thủy. With cleanup from the meal finished Thủy joined me.

"I noticed you made four bowls of rice but there were only three of us. Did you expect your brother?"

"Không anh; sometimes I make an extra bowl of rice for my father by mistake but tonight I decided to leave it there. It brought back happy memories of him sitting with us for a meal."

The Beauty of Aqua

"What happened to your father?"

Thủy paused to recount that painful memory. "My father was out on the ocean fishing when his boat was lost. Other fishermen found his body the next day and later small pieces of his boat. We think soldiers were the cause."

"Anh xin lỗi em."

"Cảm ơn anh. Do you want to see his photograph?"

"I would."

I followed Thủy up the three flights of concrete stairs to a room in the back of her home. When we reached the threshold of that room she stopped. "Please wait here anh."

The room was small and dimly lit from the moonlight. The only furniture in it was a waist-height credenza topped with a family-altar adorned with fruit and a half-dozen photographs of departed loved ones all in light-blue backgrounds. There were also three tea cups filled with rice to hold sticks of incense. Moonlight streamed in from the open windows which cast a white light across the room only interrupted by the leaves of the lemon trees outside. Thủy walked up to the altar sitting on the credenza, removed a stick of incense from the side cabinet and lit it. She gently held the lit incense between her pressed hands, stood still for a few moments, placed the incense stick in the center tea cup and was finished.

"Please come in."

"What is this place?"

"It is our family-altar-room. It is for this altar to our ancestors."

"You pray to your ancestors?"

"Not exactly anh. For a moment we clear our minds and only think of them. When we do this we are reminded that we are not alone. That many came before us and hopefully many will come after us."

"Why the incense?"

"An incense stick burns brightly and quickly just like life itself. Seeing it and smelling it reminds us that as the incense will soon finish burning so will our lives."

On the altar I saw an aged photograph of the man I had previously seen downstairs with Thủy and her mother. I saw Thủy's eyes in his. He looked like a kind man. His portrait was in front of a light-blue background.

"Is that your father?"

As I pointed to the photograph I could see a tear forming in her right eye. "Dạ anh; that is my father. I loved him very much." She choked a bit on her words. "Sometimes when I make mì Quảng I will first bring it up here and leave it so my father will eat and know that he is remembered."

We left and sat down in the main room, me on one couch, Thủy on the other and her mother chaperoning us from the kitchen. Thủy poured two cups of tea and offered me candied ginger.

"Em Thủy, we've been working together for a while, which has been nice, but I've never seen you go on a date. I just guessed you had a boyfriend. Do you?"

"Không anh; no boyfriend."

"Why not em?" I could've said that better.

"You sound like my mother." She replied with a taunting voice.

"Anh xin lỗi em. I'm just surprised you're not seeing anyone. Any man would be fortunate to date you."

"Cám ơn anh. Many men in Việt Nam want their wives to stay home, cook meals, have children and care for them. I want children and to cook but I also enjoy translating which is important to the future of my city. As Đà Nẵng grows we will have many more westerners visit us and more translators will be needed. I want to help train them. This teaching is difficult but the effort can make a big impact. In Việt Nam there is a thought 'It is not the size of the pebble you toss into the still pond but the ripples that are created that matter.' One person can make a difference in a few peoples lives and in turn those people can help others. Also there are many beautiful women in Việt Nam and I am not one of them so finding someone I like has been difficult."

"Please don't say that em. Your beauty comes from both inside and out. I find you more beautiful than most women I see." I could've also said that better.

She smiled. "If you are going to date a Vietnamese woman you should not tell her that you are looking at other women. It would be bad."

It's always ominous when someone says that. I apologized for a second time. "Anh xin lỗi em. All I meant to say was that you're beautiful in an uncommon way. Em rất đẹp."

Thủy blushed and looked down to her tea. "Cảm ơn nhiều anh."

I was curious and cautiously asked my next question. "Maybe someday we could date?"

"Dating is different in Việt Nam. When a couple date it is with the goal of getting married and that would be a difficult promise for a westerner to keep. Could you live here for the rest of your life?"

That was an easy question to answer. "Dạ em; không sao."

She smiled. "How could you know that?"

"Because I can't live anyplace else. I was lost in the West and couldn't find much happiness. I didn't know if it was a problem with me or my life around me: it was both. I was then and at times am still unhappy but I've found more happiness here than I ever knew. Every bite of chị Linh's bánh canh and chị Giang's bún bò Huế puts a smile on my face and when I finish my meal I sit back in my little, plastic stool and feel like a king. Nothing else matters but enjoying the last, little burn in my mouth of chili and remembering that last, glorious bite. Because I'll never taste any single flavor as great as nước mắm. I'm in paradise with each great meal. I'll miss my life back West but this is where I want to stay"

I didn't know it but she already knew this. Thủy and I quickly became friends because we shared the same passions. If we'd never met we would still be chasing after our next great meal but we did. While there was a sense of physical attraction between us our own passions were stronger which made us good partners. We didn't want to push our relationship in a physical direction for fear of losing what we already had and in anticipation for what could be, which we found seductive. We were flirting when we ate and food was our language. Together we were greater than the sum of our parts.

Thủy smiled with approval. "But life here is hard. Much harder than the West."

"Dạ em; I know and I worry about the future but I guess all we can do is hope for the best. Hope we find a way out of our problems."

"Dạ anh; I know someday life here will be better. You have not seen it but my city has greatly changed over the last few years. I can see things that you can not. If you stay you will see what I see and you will have the same hope for the future."

Thủy lived much of her life in an active war zone which also cost her father his life but she wasn't bitter. With a strength given to her from the memories of her ancestors she could only see a brighter future. Her strength was amplified by being apart of a community that did the same because their goal was noble: to make a better place for their descendants. This thought had a circular strength because it instilled the same, noble goal in their children. When Thủy needed to be reminded of that strength all she had to do was to go to that special place in her home she showed me today.

"I see your hope for the future when you talk about our city and this is where I want to stay. A place where I've shared the happiest times in my life with my best friend dining on the streets of the city we love." I smiled with the memories of every great meal we ate together.

"Do you think of anything else besides food?"

"Dạ em but not when I'm eating."

"I have never met a westerner that liked our food so much."

"My friend Roy told me a life with good food is a life well-lived. Every meal I've had here has brought me joy. The mixture of flavors and textures are perfect and the spiciness just amplifies that perfection. It's no longer do I like the food here but can I live without it." I paused, "I'm not always happy yet I find happiness here in every great meal and I just want to be happy."

This struck a chord with Thủy. "Dạ anh; there are times I am also sad and I also find happiness in our food. I also want to be happy. Maybe you would like living here for the rest of your life." The conversation stopped for an awkward amount of time and I could see Thủy wanted to say something but was hesitant to do so. We sat in that uncomfortable silence until she finally spoke. "Em thích anh."

Did she just say what I think she said? She did. I smiled and without hesitation replied,. "Anh thích em." I felt a sweet release rush through my body when I spoke those words but I was a bit confused. "I'm glad that I could finally say I like you but what does it mean for us?"

"Think of our special friendship like a boat on a deep river with a strong current. We could try to guide it to one side of the shore or the other but that would take great effort. It is better to relax, enjoy the scenery and see where the river takes us. 'The future's not ours to see'."

The Beauty of Aqua

The smooth and dry pavement gripped my motorcycle's tires as I could see the edge of the cliff I was warned about in the far distance. Without concern and a pleasant breeze from the south I pulled back on the throttle and sped up adding to the thrill of the ride. I had plenty of time before I had to slow down.

8

When two fire roosters fall in love

Unlike calendars in the West the Vietnamese people also consult the lunar calendar which plays a large role in their lives. Twice a month, on the first and fifteenth of the lunar month, many would abstain from eating meat and today was one of those days. Across from me was chị Giang making bún chay with tofu, baby corn, spring onion and young jackfruit for breakfast. While it was good I was in the mood for something different so I decided to visit Thủy to ask her for a recommendation.

I rounded the corner and caught sight of her home. She was outside watering her plants in a formal áo dài. Countless yellow flowers had fallen overnight with the change of seasons from a nearby tree only accentuating the beauty of Thủy.

The Beauty of Aqua

"Chào buổi sáng em Thủy. Em áo dài đẹp. Em khỏe không?"

She smiled at the compliment. "Good morning anh Upton. You are very kind. I did not think I would see you until tonight."

"I wanted to ask you where I should eat? Chị Giang's bún chay is fine but I wanted something different."

"Something different is good. I know where we should go. Please follow me." She put down the water bucket in her hand and started walking towards the street. In Việt Nam when you want to eat you don't wait. Life's too short to delay what makes you feel good.

"Em ăn sáng không?"

"This place is special so I want to eat." We walked around the corner to Quán chay Hạ which was to no surprise almost full with many others also observing this day with no meat.

"Should we get some take-away?"

"Please wait here anh. I will speak to the shop owner." With that Thủy spoke to the owner who showed us to a very small room in view of the main dining area where we sat. There was a tiny, wooden table with two chairs and little room for anything else. On the wall was a shelf with a statue of Quán Thế Âm Bồ tát or Guanyin, the enlightened being of compassion, which was a common sight in vegetarian restaurants across the country as many of the shop owners were also practicing Buddhists.

Thủy was dressed in a formal, well-tailored, dark-blue áo dài with a long row of yellow flowers along the front with silken, white pants which was more formal than most days and she was stunning.

"Em áo dài rất đẹp. Special reason?"

Thủy gave a gentle smile like only she could. "Cảm ơn nhiều anh. After breakfast I am going to a pagoda in Sơn Trà." She was so beautiful. I couldn't take my eyes off of this most beautiful sight before me and this was the first time we'd dined in such a private place. Not good for a couple whose passions were great food and each other.

I had plenty of road before the side of the cliff I was warned about so I decided to enjoy the ride and worry about the edge later.

Thủy sat coyly, looked at me and asked. "So you think I am beautiful?"

While I had told her this before it was the first time she had asked me this question. "Em rất đẹp."

She was sitting perfectly upright yet looked at ease when she then asked. "What do you feel when you see me?"

I found her question arousing. "Em Thủy, should we be talking like this? I just worry about becoming too close."

"It is called tán tỉnh, flirting. We know the rules that we must follow and we follow them. Tán tỉnh is talking, enjoying each other's company and nothing more. When done in a place like this we are reminded of the rules we must follow and the rules of our community. That is why I asked the shop owner for this room. We are both in public and in private."

Flirting had sadly fallen out of favor in the West with many choosing to go directly to carnal pursuits. The 1960's was the birth of the sexual revolution and the end of flirting. This was a "sport", in verbal form, I was somewhat unfamiliar with but wanted to try. Before I could speak she gently placed her hand on mine that was resting on the table and this was the first time that had ever happened. I had longed for so long to hold her hand and that time was now here.

My voice became weak. "From that first moment we met I saw a beauty that I had never seen before. You stood with such grace and had the most gentle smile. Turning to me you radiated like the morning's first light and I basked in its warmth. Then you spoke my name and my heart melted just a bit. My hands slightly trembled and my pulse quickened. I loved that feeling and it happened again when we first ate together. I was mesmerized by the way you carefully put together every bite for the perfect taste because you loved what I loved. Every time we ate together that feeling came back and over time even stronger. You are the most beautiful woman I'll ever know in my life ever again."

Thủy sipped her tea, thought for a moment and softly spoke. "Cảm ơn nhiều anh. The first time we met you spoke Vietnamese and I was so happy. I could see that you had already fallen in love with my country. Then we ate on the street that day and I saw the same joy in you as I had. In that joy I saw your heart was born here. Every meal we ate on the street were some of the happiest moments of my life because we were sharing what was in our hearts. You could not see but every time we ate together my heart melted a little bit. I could only be with someone that loved what I loved." She paused, "Like bún mắm."

We laughed which was a welcomed stop from the fast ride we were on. Better let the engine cool down before we continue down the road.

―――――

Saturday afternoon was here and with Thủy and her mother back in her home village of Hội An for the day I had slipped into my old routine of having a bánh mì que on the banks of the Hàn River while reading a book. The fishing boats had long finished unloading their catch for the day when the sound of one, last straggler could be heard. The high-pitched whine coming from its engine was the all too familiar sound of a stuck starter solenoid. As the boat came closer I saw it was Thủy's brother and he looked like he'd been up all night and then some. If I stayed where I was he wouldn't see me which I did for awhile. Finally growing tired of watching his failed attempts to fix the problem I threw caution to the wind and headed down to his boat.

"Ngô." No relational pronouns for him. He neither spoke or looked at me. "Starter solenoid; it's stuck." The smell of rice wine was everywhere.

He put his tools down. "Go away." No relational pronouns for me either. I had no time for manners and jumped into the engine compartment with him.

"Hammer." I pointed to the one beside him with the hope he'd put it in my hand and not hit me with it. With hammer in hand I gave the starter solenoid a few, gentle taps on the case and the problem was fixed. "Next time that happens do the same and no problem." I went back on shore and looked at Ngô. "Next time you shout at your sister you and I will have a big problem. You understand?" He didn't but that didn't matter. I could tell he was a shot of rice wine away from hitting me. He was a violent man who only deserved our pity.

———

"Em ơi!"

I looked up to see Thủy walk out on to her balcony on that warm, early evening night.

"Xin chào anh Upton."

"Would you like to go downtown to the night-market off đường Phạm Hồng Thái?"

We always spent Friday nights together so I thought I might choose where we spent it for a change. There was silence from above but soon Thủy exited her home with her helmet on and pushing out the family Super Cub. She seemed to approve of my choice.

"Hop on anh." She liked to tease me with that which never got old for her and I now found cute.

"I forgot my helmet."

"Wait here." She quickly went back inside her home and returned. "Here anh." It was her mother's pink helmet.

"Không cảm ơn em. It's pink."

"Không sao anh. In Việt Nam the color pink was worn by warriors and can be seen as a color of strength." She paused and smiled. "But I will let you use mine and I will wear the pink one." She was teasing me again but thankfully let me off with little pain as her helmet was much like mine.

We switched and I got on. Before we pulled out I tapped on her shoulder. "I like it when we have matching helmets."

She leaned back and said with a smile. "Dạ anh; same-same em."

We found our way through the busy Friday night traffic full of bicycles and motorcycles to an equally busy night-market where we were lucky to find a place to park. While still early in the evening the market was crowded with workers celebrating the end of the work week in traditional Vietnamese form: with friends, great food and beer. They would soon leave for there homes to be replaced by, thanks to the wisdom of midday napping, the well-rested who would also do the same long into the night. While in my little community we had a few food carts open late at night, here there was shop after shop full of people eating and drinking beer on the sidewalk and in the alley. They were eating the food they loved with their friends and at that moment their little spot in this city by the sea became their paradise.

Much like the Lunar New Year celebrations, multi-colored lights were intermixed with warm, incandescent bulbs that hung across the street bathing us in its festive glow. All our favorites were here and a few shops that sold sweet desserts which was a treat.

"This night-market is like many night-markets in Sài Gòn." She paused, "Except the food in Đà Nẵng is better."

"You say that about everyplace."

"Because it is true."

"Bún bò Huế here is better than in Huế City or bún chả in Hà Nội?"

"I always enjoy those foods in those cities and they will many times be better where they were born and are respected. The people of Đà Nẵng are fortunate to have good food from both the land and the sea which helps us better appreciate the dishes we make. I can have good bún chả in Đà Nẵng but I do not know of good mì Quảng in Hà Nội."

"Dạ em; I doubt there's any good mì Quảng in Paris either." Thủy smiled because she saw another irreversible change in me I didn't.

With all those choices we still had the same dish we always had on Friday nights: bún bò Huế. Its fiery broth gave us fuel for the night and it was what we liked to have together at that time. Thủy brought me over to a cart serving what we desired. We ate in silence then sat back to savor that great meal that once again brought us closer together.

"Cảm ơn em. That was wonderful."

"Không có chi anh. Anh và em uống cà phê không?"

"Dạ em; anh uống cà phê."

We set out to a nearby cafe and I ordered our favorite nighttime coffees at the counter. When I turned Thủy was gone so I found a table with a view of the night-market before me. Our small table sat nestled between a few large planters and under an overgrown flame tree which still had a few flowers left on its stems.

She soon returned with something sweet. We sat and watched the world before us from that somewhat private spot.

"This is a favorite of mine: bánh tiramisu."

"Tiramisu in Đà Nẵng?"

"Dạ anh; we make the best tiramisu in Đà Nẵng."

"I think the Italians might disagree."

She smiled. "And they would be wrong. I thought you knew that anh?"

I did and while tiramisu wasn't created here it was the best I'd ever had. We sat with our cake and coffee watching the people in the night-market enjoying themselves which brought us joy.

I looked over to Thủy. "The flowers on that tree are beautiful."

She turned the conversation to our favorite sport. "If I was a flower what flower would I be anh Upton?"

I thought for a moment. "The peach blossom because you are beautiful, delicate and fragrant."

"Cảm ơn nhiều anh. That is kind of you but I see myself as a lotus flower."

I was intrigued. "Why em?"

"The lotus is a special flower. Its life starts in a pond when its mother sheds one of her many seeds to the muddy bottom below. The mud is very unpleasant and a place of suffering but without it the lotus could not live. Some seeds, with the protection of the mature plants around it, are fortunate to grow and a very few of those get to see the sunlight from the surface and show their beautiful flower. As that flower do you know what I see?"

"What do you see em?"

"I see the few others that were as fortunate as me to see the sunlight and they are my community. Like my nation we were born out of suffering and only through the strength of our community we too will show the world our beauty. That is why it is the national flower of my country. When I see myself as a lotus flower I not only see great beauty but with my community great strength."

"Em Thủy: are all lotus flowers beautiful?"

"Dạ anh."

"Then please remember that. You are a beautiful lotus flower that found her way to the surface of the pond and you are also beautiful."

She smiled. "Cảm ơn nhiều anh. I will try to remember that."

Saturdays were a welcome respite from the week's activities. It was late afternoon and I was again reading on my balcony, this time a novel by Graham Greene, when I heard a voice from below.

"Anh ơi!"

I looked down to see my good friend. "Chào em. Em khỏe không?"

"I am fine. Thank you anh Upton. Would you like to go to dinner with me tonight?"

We usually ate dinner together on Saturdays so I was confused. "I thought we were going to look for a new food stall tonight down at chợ Cồn?"

"Không anh; nice restaurant so please wear nice clothes." Until now these evening meals had been confined to street food and simpler restaurants and certainly not ones with a dress code.

"That sounds nice. What time em?"

"I will be here at eight."

"Late dinner?"

"Dạ anh; we will be out late tonight. Hẹn sớm gặp lại anh." With that she was gone.

Đà Nẵng gets hot. Really hot. That night it was still 30°C. I now understood what Roy meant when he described the heat here and Đà Nẵng wasn't as bad as Sài Gòn. It was nice to get dressed up for a change. The few times I was able to dress like that night were at university activities and this was the first time it was personal.

Beep. Beep. Beeeeeep.

I was being beckoned by the beeping of a Super Cub horn. While not uncommon on my street I knew it was calling for me so I grabbed my helmet and locked up the gate behind me.

Thủy radiated. First she'd washed her motorcycle which as a fellow rider I appreciated. Next was the most obvious: she was the most beautiful woman in the world. With poise and grace she sat on her Super Cub wearing a dark-red áo dài with silken, yellow pants. She radiated even more as I approached. With a smile she said, "Hop on anh." And patted the rear of the seat with her left hand. I got on.

"You know I don't like it when you do that?" I was taunting her.

She turned her head and with a smile said. "I knew that anh." She was taunting me.

We headed down đường Lê Lai and found our way to Nhà hàng Madame Lan on đường Bạch Đằng and Thủy parked the Super Cub. I could feel the sweat on my shirt.

"It's hot. My friend Roy was in Sài Gòn and told me about the heat there and they're hotter than us."

"Dạ anh; Đà Nẵng is cooler than Sài Gòn." And with a prideful smile said, "And we have better food. Please follow me." Every chance she could she showed what was in her heart and this made me happy.

This was one of the finest restaurants in a city that truly understood great food and I expected only the very best that night. We walked through the Hội An style gate to a large dance floor with a small band. Thủy spoke a few words to the maître d' and we were shown to a small room like the one at Quán chay Hạ but this was luxurious and had a view of the Hàn River. It was barely big enough for four people with a wrap-around, well-padded seat where we sat with that spectacular view. It was very romantic which was reason for concern. I wasn't worried about Thủy following the rules. It was me.

A waiter soon brought me a bia Larue and for both of us a tea tray with two cups.

"It's fine for me to have a beer when you're not?"

"No problem anh. I am driving tonight." The advantages of riding pillion, other than being so close to Thủy, showed themselves again.

We were presented with menus which were in Vietnamese. I tried to piece together little bits: "fish" here and "chicken" there. By the time I deciphered the fifth or sixth word Thủy had skillfully ordered for both of us so I handed my menu back to the waiter.

I looked over to the dance floor below to see a few couples dancing. The small band was gently playing off to the side. "Would you like to dance em Thủy?" With that I stood up and held out my hand which she took for only the second time. She stood up and we walked down to the dance floor. I stopped at the floor's edge and held out my left hand which she grasped with her right. I then gently placed my right hand on her left hip. It rested right at that magic point between the top of her silken pants and the tiny opening of her áo dài. Like bird's eye chilies a little goes a long way.

The áo dài is an apt metaphor for the country: seductive and respectful. It is a dress worn to all the most important events in life and something happens when a woman wears it. Her back becomes a bit straighter and her movements even more graceful. She understands that this dress, next to her country's flag, is its national symbol and must be respected.

The Beauty of Aqua

We returned to our seats and on cue our first course was served. All talking stopped.

The night started with oysters on the half shell with sweet chili jam and lemon. I had fond memories of dad and me sitting on the side of the dock at the marina enjoying this delicacy of the deep. They were presented on ice and dripping with the cool, sea water from whence they came. With the gentlest squeeze of lemon, slowly we let each oyster slide from its shell into us as it pleased and it still pulsed with freshness, was sweet with a salty brine and a tiny chew.

Next was a wonderful surprise: chip chip or littleneck clams. When I saw them I immediately smiled which Thủy returned. She knew this was a childhood favorite of mine and I was thankful she'd remembered. Everything that needed to be said was done with our gaze into each other and our smiles. Our littleneck clams, Cape Cod's favorite clam, were in a large, ceramic serving bowl and had been steamed with lemongrass with much of the broth still in the bowl. We ate the clams and drank the precious pot liquor they had kindly left behind.

The final course was no surprise. It was the one dish that was our dish when we wanted to express our feelings for each other: mì Quảng cá lóc which had been skillfully prepared and presented for our enjoyment.

We sat in silence after that great meal overlooking the Hàn River but this time it was different. We were fire roosters with the same passions and we enticed the other with the pleasure we found in those passions with that amazing view of the Hàn River. It was a special night.

I thought of anh Dũng's warnings as I was now losing sight of the road ahead in a hot-road mirage.

The rains had been on and mostly off for the last few weeks but that afternoon it was dry and the clouds hung heavily over Sơn Trà Mountain. I was on my balcony when I heard an odd sound.

Beep. Beep. Beeeeeep.

It was a horn but it wasn't one from the ubiquitous Super Cub. I looked down to see Thủy on a Honda CB Series much like my Super Hawk back West but newer. I grabbed my helmet and headed downstairs.

"Chào em. Xe máy đẹp."

She smiled. "And the driver?"

"Em rất đẹp. Where'd you get the motorcycle?"

"From a cousin anh."

In Việt Nam everyone that's close to your family is a cousin. Adopting family members into your clan has an advantage over only having those that are born into it: your family is always close and so are their motorcycles.

"So where we going?"

"We are going up to Sơn Trà Mountain and we will ride through the clouds."

I'd ridden in some beautiful places like around the dunes of Lower Cape Cod near sunset and through the Eastern Townships of the Province of Quebec at autumn's peak and this could be on par with them.

She with a smile tapped on the backseat. "Hop on anh." I "hopped on" as instructed.

This newer motorcycle had a much stronger engine than her family's Super Cub and made quick work of getting us out to the Sơn Trà Peninsula and up the mountain. Thủy handled this larger motorcycle well. We were about halfway up when we stopped at a small Buddhist pagoda on a hill with a stunning view of the East Vietnamese Sea. The pagoda was old with its walls painted in the traditional yellow-orange scheme found in similar places and a dog quietly slept on the steps leading to the Buddha hall. We dismounted and sat on a large, cool stone bench out front.

Thủy spoke softly out of reverence for this place. "When I was young my mother brought me here and we were taught about a place called the 'Pure land.' They said it was a place of happiness where there was no sadness or hunger but I did not understand."

"Understand what?"

"How can there be happiness without some sadness in our lives? When I am hungry I am also sometimes sad but after I eat I am happy. A place without hunger is a place without food and that is a place without happiness."

I thought about Matt sitting in a Buddhist pagoda in Thailand listening to monks trying to teach about happiness when all he needed to do was to sit next to Thủy and listen to that last sentence. A place without food, good food, is a place without happiness.

We remounted our motorcycle and headed up to the top of the mountain. After a steep climb we found our road enveloped in a cool, thick fog with the sounds of wild monkey calls in the distance and we soon were driving through the clouds.

Near the top was a dirt path to what would be best described as a derelict ghost town, not unlike those found throughout the Southwest deserts of the USA, except this one was not as old. It was the former medical evacuation site used by US troops during the American War. Most of the buildings laid in ruins having long been stripped of any valuables but the ghosts were still here. We followed the road to its edge. Before us was the best view in Đà Nẵng. The view allowed us to see from the East Vietnamese Sea to the Annamite Mountain Range that rose between us and Huế City. We dismounted and looked to the south.

"I am happy here because I can not only see my city but when I come up here I can also see it growing. Đà Nẵng is small but I can see someday it will not. It will be like the best cities in the world. This is what my ancestors worked so hard for and it will happen."

"It's beautiful here. You know what we should've brought: food."

Thủy smiled, reached into the leather saddlebag and removed two bánh mì que, handing one to me.

"You think of everything em Thủy. Cảm ơn em."

"Không sao anh. When I come here I always bring bánh mì que with me and I also brought one for you."

We leaned against our motorcycle and enjoyed the view of our city by the sea while enjoying our favorite bánh mì together. I was a foreigner from a foreign land but my heart like Thủy's would always be here. We finished our meal and left.

On the trip down I thought we were a little too close to the edge of the cliffside road but there was still plenty of room between us and the steep drop off below. Thankfully Thủy was driving.

"Anh ơi!"

It was Saturday night and Thủy and I were out to try the food carts that only came out on the weekends down at Cồn Market and that was her calling. Without a word I grabbed my helmet and headed downstairs locking the door and gate behind me.

Thủy's dress for these affairs was usually casual but tonight she had stepped-up her game wearing a favorite well-tailored, modern, dark-blue áo dài with silken, white pants. Again she had washed her motorcycle before coming here which was a nice touch. She radiated on her Super Cub that night. Life is not complete without seeing such a sight first hand. No photographer's lens could have captured her "je ne sais quoi."

"Em rất đẹp."

Thủy gave a gentle smile like only she could and with her left hand patted on the back seat. "Hop on anh."

Her taunts to me about riding pillion had long become sweet.

"Anh và em đi chợ Cồn."

"Không anh; we are going someplace special tonight."

Curious. We had no problems finding great meals within quận Hải Châu which surprised me when I saw Thủy heading over to the Sơn Trà Peninsula. I had to speak up to be heard over the sound of the engine.

"Where are we going?" Nothing.

We drove down đường Nguyễn Thị Định to a shop just past a wet-market and parked. The sign read: "Mì Quảng Bông." It was a typical and well-cared for family restaurant with metal benches running from side to side and stools for close to forty people which would have been impressive to see in this five by ten-meter dining space. Thủy ran to the shop owner when she saw her and gave her a big hug. This was more than a favorite place. It was special to her. She soon returned and sat across from me.

"My mother is best friends with that woman and my parents use to come here and have the best meals of their life. She is making us her best dish: mì Quảng cá lóc."

I'd already lost my heart to this dish of Quảng Nam and this version added snakehead fish. Thủy had told me it was a difficult fish to clean and cut correctly but when done right it became a sublime taste of perfection. Our bowls of warm soup and plates of cool salad greens soon arrived and we ate in complete silence. Time stopped and nothing else mattered. We were both lost in the perfection before us. After extracting the last of the precious broth from our bowls we sat back in our stools and savored what we had just experienced.

Our bowls were soon cleared from the table and Thủy spoke a few words to the shop owner. We were shown to a tiny, alcove room only big enough for two beside the kitchen. There was a small table with two wooden stools and the room was gently lit from above. We were served tea by the shop owner and left alone.

"Did you like your mì Quảng cá lóc anh Upton?"

"It was one of the best meals of my life. I grew up in a fishing village and that was some of the best fish I ever had. The cook is a magician."

"Không anh; no magic. She uses the best ingredients she can find and a recipe that has been in her family for generations but she is not a magician."

"Anh xin lỗi em. I meant she's a very good cook."

Thủy's English was outstanding but many times idioms couldn't be learned, they had to be experienced.

"Dạ anh; her mother use to cook mì Quảng cá lóc for my parents and after they finished their soup they would sit here and have tea. In my family it is special when a man and a woman share mì Quảng and tea." She paused and smiled. "Maybe someday I will tell you why."

Our conversation stopped for a bit and we sipped our hot tea. We were still caught in the afterglow of our meal.

"Cảm ơn nhiều em Thủy. I came here and you were kind and sweet to me and showed me the greatest meals of my life. I've never been happier."

Happiness can't be saved in a jar for a rainy day because of its short shelf life. It has to be found every day and we had found an endless supply of it in the best foods our city could offer. In my old life I had a hard time finding happiness because I was looking in all the wrong places yet here it was presented to me in a bowl three or four times a day. I understood what Thủy said up at the pagoda on Sơn Trà Mountain: there is no happiness in a place without food. It also meant the happiest place was the one with the best food and that was where we lived. We found our paradise with every great meal and needed little more than each other.

Thủy surprisingly leaned over to me and whispered in my ear "Em yêu anh."

I could of said it was just hearing those words that made that moment so pleasant but there was so much more. More than the great meal we just ate. More than the gentle breeze of the evening air. I could smell Thủy's hair as it brushed my face. Then I felt her moist breath on my ear that had just conveyed the sentiment of what she had just said. I loved her too.

"Anh yêu em."

My motorcycle was now flying down the road and I was having the ride of my life when I saw the sharp turn ahead. I should've been watching but wasn't and there was no time to brake. I knew it'd be tight but could still make the turn. I knew my peg might scrape on the pavement leaving me in an uncontrollable skid down the side of the cliff in front of me but still made the only choice a motorcyclist could: I hit the throttle hard and leaned into it.

The Beauty of Aqua

9

Unrest

The hot and quiet days of summer had left and the turbulent rainy season was here. While a break from the seemingly endless days of heat was welcomed in the exchange we had to accept the seemingly endless days, and sometimes weeks, of constant rain with occasional flooding. Like my neighbors I too adapted and went on with my life as close to normal as possible. After a morning bowl of bún bò Huế I walked down my water-logged street in a hard rain to Cafe 47. My friend and fellow community resident Alan had arrived earlier and was halfway through his coffee when I joined him under the cafe's canopy which offered us some protection from the rain. The cafe owner's dog "mì" came up to me like usual wanting to be petted.

"Morning Alan."

"Morning mate. Sleep well?"

"Well enough; thanks. The thunder woke me up and getting back to sleep on the mattresses here isn't easy."

"Awe you've got to get an import mattress from the West. The mattresses here are too hard."

"I'll survive. Maybe I'll even learn to like it."

He laughed at that thought. "You'd be the first from the West to do that."

Alan was part of a small group of Australian epidemiologists studying the health effects of the American War on the residents around the Province of Quảng Nam. Days could pass between receiving field reports so in those slow times he could be found here. While we weren't expatriated from our home countries we acted like it and had embraced Việt Nam's slower speed of life. Alan was most recently from New South Wales and had been in country for the last two years, first south of here in the Province of Quảng Ngãi, a place he enjoyed for her people, then Đà Nẵng.

"So mate; you know anything about statistics?"

Other than a freshman course I'd long forgotten I had nothing. "No but I've got a few students that do. Why?"

"Every month we send our reports to Canberra but it takes months to get the results back. If we had access to a computer lab we could really speed up the process."

"And I've got the only lab in town."

"So how about it?"

"It's free late at night. You get the software and I'll get someone to run it."

"Thanks mate."

"So have you found anything yet?"

"It's still early but yes, we have and it's bad."

"How bad?"

"Major upticks in cancer rates and birth defects."

"What's causing it?"

"Dioxins used during the war that were stored not far from here at the airport were leaked into the water supply."

"So what's the fix and how much?"

"Many, many millions of dollars that the Vietnamese don't have. The least expensive choice is building a water treatment plant, piping water to every home and on-site filtering of all water used on every farm."

"Australian dollars or US dollars?" My poor attempt at humor.

"First one then the other. Doesn't matter mate; they've got neither."

"So the farms too? That doesn't sound practical."

"Because it's not but the rice fields were one of the main targets."

I was surprised. "They sprayed dioxins on the rice fields?"

Alan sat back in his chair and looked at me as the bearer of a sad tale he'd told too many times before. "The Americans started spraying dioxins to clear out the leaves and ground cover so they could get a better shot but that wasn't enough so they started spraying it on the rice fields to as the Yanks would say 'kill 'em all and let God sort 'em out'." I could see Alan almost retching with the thought of that disturbing phrase uttered by some of the soldiers that fought here during the war but there was a truth to it when it came to the use of dioxins. He was one of the very few that understood what could await the people that lived here and that knowledge weighed heavily on him.

"Like giving the Native Americans blankets with smallpox the easiest way to kill off an enemy is to poison them and here rice is life."

It is not possible to express how important rice is to the Vietnamese people. You eat it when you're happy, sad, in the throes of passion and the pains of heartache. It is eaten with almost every meal and found in every pagoda and family-temple. It is also found on every family-altar as an offering to those that are no longer with us. In Việt Nam rice is the embodiment of life and the use of dioxins on her rice paddies was meant for the sole purpose of making that symbol of life into an agent of death.

"Can't fight without food. About inhumane as it gets."

"All war is inhumane Upton but the use of dioxins by your government was especially cruel because it will keep killing for a long time."

"Hey; I was born under the Crown like you." He was right because I was also an American thus I was also to blame for my country's poisoning of these people.

"Sorry mate; your accent just sounds more Boston than anything else."

Correct again. While my father had a proper Canadian-French accent from his home province of Quebec and the patois of Newfoundland I had neither which reminded me of my feelings of not belonging anywhere. At least I could order a "bia." Time to get off the subject.

"I'm sure I can find a student to help you."

"Thanks mate. What are you doing today?"

"Don't know yet. Like every other Saturday I'll hang out here for a little while waiting to see if any students come by wanting me to look at their code otherwise I'll head home and read."

"Still on Camus?"

"Still on Camus with Dylan mixed in."

"Thomas or Bob?"

"Bob."

"Interesting mix. Translator still good?"

"Still good. Thủy knows her stuff. I couldn't work without her."

"It's not getting personal is it?"

Thủy and I were long past "getting personal" but I couldn't tell Alan that. "No; we're just friends. Why?" I wondered if he'd heard something through our tight-knit community grape vine which was good for more than just weather reports.

"Just checking. Be careful mate. you don't want to leave anything behind if you know what I mean. It'd ruin her life if you got her pregnant and left."

"We're not that close and you're not the first one to tell me that. As you'd say 'no worries mate'."

The Beauty of Aqua

Another lie. Our passion for each other, expressed every time in our silent meals together on the streets of Đà Nẵng, had transcended the physical into something much deeper but retaining control of our obvious physical attraction for each other could be as difficult to withhold as a typhoon's largest waves. We were rarely alone in private, as expected by our community, which offered us some welcomed protection from the storms that raged with inside of us.

"You sure Upton?" Alan could see I was in deep.

"I'll be fine." I wasn't going to be fine. Thủy and I were caught in a state of great unrest.

"Falling in love here is different mate. When it happens it hits you like a ton of bricks dropped by the Almighty himself and being careful quickly gets forgotten."

"All we do is eat together." I wasn't at a place I could even comprehend what was going on in my life never mind talk about it. Time to change the subject again. "You want a bánh mì que?" I'd just eaten but it was the best I could come up with and it wasn't good enough.

"That's how it starts mate. Here if two people can share food from the same plate then it's a match made in heaven."

Right again. Every time Thủy and I ate together on the street we were in heaven. We were lost in paradise and on a busy street corner in the City of Đà Nẵng at the same time with our most personal and sensual pleasures celebrated in the view of all the public to see. We were in heaven and it had all the best street foods this city had to offer. I still wasn't at a place I could talk about my relationship with Thủy and tried again to change the subject.

"Don't you need to be in the office?" Still weak tea but again the best I could come up with.

Alan looked down to his watch. "I've got to go mate. You going out for bánh mì que this afternoon?"

He finally picked up on the hint about bánh mì que. "Yeah; I'll bring some by your place later."

"Thanks Upton."

I said with a smile. "'No worries mate'."

Alan laughed. "You still sound like you're from Boston."

With that he headed into the rainy street and I sat watching the same.

Like most mornings I enjoyed a few minutes alone on my balcony this time wet from the constant rains which were warm and pleasant. Next to chị Giang's house was the local Communist Party meeting hall. It served as a place for marriage receptions, student events and voting among other activities and it was the social hub of the neighborhood. Normally closed in the morning today was different. There was a small group of older women, "aunties", sitting on the front steps all with somber looks and something was of great concern to them. Before I could walk back inside from my balcony Thủy pulled up on her bicycle so I headed downstairs.

"Chào buổi sáng em. Em khỏe không?"

Thủy gave a gentle smile like only she could. "Xin chào buổi sáng anh. Em khỏe. Cảm ơn anh. Where would you like to eat breakfast?"

"The place we always go."

She smiled. "I knew that anh."

We started our walk down the street to chị Linh's home when I asked Thủy about the disturbance at the meeting hall. She went over and spoke to one of the women and soon returned. "She says that a young girl went missing last night. She might have runaway but her mother does not think she would do that. They are worried—" Thủy was visibly upset. "They are worried that she was taken by smugglers to China and sold as a bride."

I was shocked and sickened by the thought of such a horrible act. "I'd never heard of that."

"Dạ anh; there are many men and few women in China so sometimes they come to Việt Nam and take our young women to sell."

"I'm very sorry. What will happen if they're caught?"

"I am not sure but it would be bad."

It's always ominous when someone says that. "How bad?"

"Very bad. It is one of the worst crimes someone can commit. If the police find them they will punish them."

"How em?"

"Some things are better left unsaid. There is nothing we can do to help and should go."

We headed down đường Lê Lai and took our seats at chị Linh's house.

While chị Linh made her bánh canh with various accoutrements there was no need to say how we liked ours prepared. She knew everyone that came to her house for breakfast and knew how they liked their soup. Some with pork, with or without the bone, more noodles or more broth or in my case topped with Vietnamese ham.

She opened for breakfast at 6:30 and she closed when her soup pot was empty which was about an hour later. If you arrived when she opened her thick, hand-cut, rice noodles were still very firm and by closing had softened and swelled to twice their original size. Our goal was to get there at 7am for the perfect texture although the last bowl of soup out of her pot was always the best with the flavors melding into a harmonious symphony.

Our meals soon arrived and, as we always did, ate in silence. We finished, Thủy spoke to chị Linh for a moment and we left. I was curious.

"Chị Linh khỏe không?"

"Chị Linh khỏe."

"Chị Linh seemed like she had something important to tell you."

"She said I looked different."

"Different?"

"Dạ anh; it is not important."

"You can't leave me hanging like that. What's up em Thủy?"

"Chị Linh knows. She could see it on my face."

"See what?"

The Beauty of Aqua

"That I was in love with you and she could see you were in love with me."

"How em? We ate like always."

"When a Vietnamese woman dedicates herself to a man it shows on her face. We pay attention to our man, tend to his needs and we become protective of him."

"Protective?"

"Dạ anh; if another woman looks at you I am there to remind you not to look back. To protect you from making a poor choice."

"And if I do look back?"

"Like I said before if you are going to date a Vietnamese woman then you should not look at other women. It would be bad."

There's that disturbing phrase again. Truth be told I only had interest in one woman. "I only look at em."

Thủy said with a smile. "Good choice anh."

It was dark and raining out. Really, really, raining out. The sounds of bucket-sized raindrops pounded the street below and a healthy stream ran down đường Lê Lai. I expected Thủy over an hour ago for dinner but she didn't come by. Her brother's hostilities towards me over the last few months had gone from a deep, smoldering, angry ash pile to a raging, open fire fueled with his excessive drinking of home-brewed, rice wine. As with all fisherman I gave him a wide berth but that didn't seem to help lately. He would only see Thủy and I together over his, or Thủy's, dead body.

With my Vietnamese, standard-issue áo mưa, mine in a translucent bright-yellow, I made my way along đường Lê Lai that rainy night. A few bicycles braved the foul weather and a few street vendors were in place offering a warm, late meal in the pouring rain. Even đường Nguyễn Thị Minh Khai, normally bicycle tire to bicycle tire in traffic, was peaceful in the rain. I found my way to Thủy's home where that peace was broken. Two local police officers were outside her home talking to Thủy and her mother and the police only showed up when something bad happened. I stayed back about ten meters in the shadows to watch when Thủy saw me and approached.

"Anh Upton; please go home. You should not be here." Even in the dark night only lit by a single street light I could see the start of a bad black-eye. Someone punched Thủy and I had to know more.

"What happened?"

"My mother and I were in a fight with someone that was very drunk but now không sao. Chúc ngủ ngon anh."

She wanted me gone and that wasn't going to happen. I usually acquiesced to her requests but not that night. I could see on Thủy's face she was both drowning and not trying to fight the waves that were taking her under. She was frozen inside. "What was the fight about?" Nothing. Not a word out of her mouth. That blank stare was one of shock.

"No problem now. Không sao. Chúc ngủ ngon anh."

"Không không sao em. Who hit you?"

"No one anh."

"Where's 'no one' live?" I was going to pay mr. 'no one' a visit which left Thủy confused with my use of a double entendre so I clarified. "Someone hit you. Who?"

"My brother Ngô."

"Fantastic. Get his photograph ready to put up on the family-altar." Screw being deported. Screw going to jail. Ngô's tiny reign of terror was going to end 'by hook or by crook'."

"Không anh; please, you and I are part of the same community and our community can not be strong when we are violent. The police are looking for em Ngô and you must leave now. Fine anh?"

"Not until you tell me what the fight was about."

She didn't want to say but finally spoke. "The fight was about anh. My brother does not want us to see each other."

"I'm very sorry that our friendship has caused you so much pain. What can we do?"

"We only have one choice until em Ngô leaves Đà Nẵng: I will ask anh Dũng to assign you a new translator and we can not be seen together again until he leaves." Then came the worst part of what she said. "We can no longer dine on the street together. Em xin lỗi anh."

I was heartbroken. "I trust you em Thủy and if that's what you think is best then I'll stand by it. Chúc ngủ ngon em."

"Chúc ngủ ngon anh."

I didn't like walking away that night but Thủy was right: we had to have faith in our community for a resolution and not to the individual.

Unrest

The heavy rains from last night never stopped and I stood on my balcony watching chị Giang clean up from breakfast. I should've had something to eat but didn't. I wasn't hungry and that wasn't good. I loved the food of my city but would miss Thủy's radiating joy with those meals. I felt alone without my best friend and believed the same of her.

Wearing only a shirt and pants I stood in the pouring rain on my balcony hoping it would wash away a bit of my sorrow. It's hard to be sad in a place with so much happiness but it happens to us all and no one is alone in those feelings. Soon the rumble and then the sight of a Harley Davidson-sized motorcycle in a sea of bicycles and other much smaller motorcycles stopped in front of my home. It was anh Dũng and while usually on a Super Cub he was sometimes able to ride something bigger; this time much bigger.

"Em oi!"

"Xin chào anh. Một phút xin." I bolted down stairs locking up behind me.

"Good morning cháu Upton. You know why I am here. We should sit and have coffee."

I with anh Dũng walking his 1970's Ural motorcycle, with a tell-tale fire-red, hammer-and-sickle badge painted on the motorcycle's massive fuel tank, finally made our way down to Cafe 47. Because of our slow pace and the sight of this dark-green, Russian bear being walked between us the cafe owner had plenty of time to make and place our regular coffees at our regular seats. The mother serving us remembered anh Dũng's preferred coffee. Something that I found was common here with the best shops.

"I spoke to em Thủy this morning about last night." He paused and I could tell this was personal to him. "Cháu Upton; do you know how many translators I will soon need?"

"Không anh."

"Over thirty. Do you know how many I have? Eight. I only have eight translators for Đà Nẵng and Huế City to show the most important guests of my country what we have to offer them and through them the world. Chào Thủy and those are the very best I could find. They are our future and chào Ngô is not. The national flower of Việt Nam is the lotus where life starts in the mud and a fortunate few grow to see the light of the surface. Chào Thủy has worked very hard to see that sunlight and chào Ngô has not. He has trapped himself in the mud of suffering and refuses to look at the beauty of the light above him. Unless he changes himself he will never change."

"Are one of those seven free?"

"Không chào; all are working and chào Thủy is my only technical translator so you will not be able to lecture. Where seven of my translators failed she excelled and that is why she teaches others." He smiled with a warm thought. "Chào Thủy grew up poor and had little access to modern schools yet she, with the help of her grandfather from Hải Phòng, conquered every challenge she faced but one to be who she is. When I hear her speak

I can hear the voice and wisdom of her grandfather."

"But one challenge?"

"Vâng chào; she like her brother have a sadness in their lives that will not leave them. Where her brother can only drown his sadness in rice wine chào Thủy, one of those fortunate few lotus flowers that grew to the surface of the pond, looks for strength in her community, the memories of her ancestors and happiness in noble pursuits like the foods of our nation." He was caught in a quick memory from Thủy's past. "Her not-so-noble pursuit of motorcycles has also been a passion of hers but that is for another time." Back to the business at hand. "I have spoken to the city police and when chào Ngô is found they will arrest him. I am sorry but you must not be seen with chào Thủy in public until we can find em Ngô and convince him to move back to the family home in Hội An where he will be the problem of someone else." He paused then smiled. "Chào Thủy has shared with me the immense joy you together find in our foods and I am happy for you both."

Anh Dũng's knowledge of Thủy and her brother seemed more than what she would've told a boss. "You know a lot about chào Thủy and her brother."

"Vâng chào because em Ngô is my nephew and chào Thủy is my niece."

"Why didn't you say something before?"

"Would you have treated em Thủy differently if you knew?"

I thought about his question. "I think most people would."

The Beauty of Aqua

"That is why my niece and I do not discuss that we are related unless we must and I would ask the same of you."

"Không sao anh."

"Cảm ơn cháu." Anh Dũng stood up to leave. "You and cháu Thủy have teaching to do and I will try my best to get you two back to work as soon as I can. We have a thought in Việt Nam: 'No one stops the train.' The future of my country is much too important for anyone to stop her progress forward. I will try to resolve this quickly but you must be patient." He started to his motorcycle but stopped and looked back to me. "I see it chào. I see even in this troubling time you can still see a little happiness. Do not forget your community wants you to be happy and will help you when they can. I must go to Huế City this morning and will be back soon. Au revoir cháu Upton."

"Cháu xin lỗi anh. Anh có thể nhắc lại được không? Anh không biết nói tiếng Pháp giỏi lam." It took me two weeks to learn that line. Anh Dũng spoke flawless French but I still had to say it and he smiled acknowledging my retort.

"Very good cháu. A sense of humor in times like this is good to have." With that he mounted-up his Russian bear, rode out on to a rainy đường Lê Lợi and was gone.

It'd been a week since the fight with the rains never once slowing down. Ngô had been in a "cat and mouse" game with the local police, the cat, wisely playing it long waiting for Ngô, the rat, to tire out and resurface to then pick him up. Either way having him off the streets made our community a better and more quiet place. Thủy's black-eye had not unexpectedly closed up which was painful to see and think about.

Wearing sunglasses and a nón lá she'd walk by my house once or twice every morning in the pouring rain knowing that without a translator I'd be home. Where smiles and warm greetings were once exchanged she now didn't feel comfortable looking up to me on my second-floor balcony. I knew that this was for the benefit of all involved but it still hurt us both.

After she rounded the corner I headed down to Cafe 47 for coffee and a different view where I found Alan also enjoying the same. Without a word I was served my usual.

"Hello mate. Saw your little lady walking by. She tried to hide it but she had a pretty bad shiner. You didn't have something to do with it did you?"

I looked at Alan in silent disdain.

"I know you wouldn't do that mate. So who did?"

"Her brother."

"I heard about him and the rumor he hit her. Thanks for confirming it. Back in Queensland where I grew up we'd take him to the Outback where no one would ever see him again. What are you going to do?"

Alan was a big man like many Australians. His father was a championship boxer and at one time he had been in the Royal Australian Navy, first as a line officer and later a researcher. With years of experience he saw the danger Ngô was to all that were caught in his damaging wake.

"My friends in Southie, South Boston, would tell me to get him drunk and make a call to put him on a one-way tour of a local landfill but it's not quite at that point yet. Anh Dũng told me to lay low and stay away from Thủy until Ngô left town."

Alan laughed recalling an earlier conversation. "I told you you sounded like you're from Boston."

I wonder what gave me away. "Besides, I can't even jaywalk."

"Awe mate; the coppers aren't that hard even on us white guys. Everyone jaywalks here and a lot more."

Many in Việt Nam, sometimes wisely so, were flexible and saw laws not as hard-and-fast rules like us from the West. They saw them like "hints" on how to go about life. Many saw that it was better to be a good person before just being a good citizen. I had to agree with that sentiment as I too was "bending" the law.

"I can't because I've got 'immigration issues'." That admission peaked his curiosity.

"What's that mate?"

I trusted Alan and suspected he already knew what I was about to say. "I was born in Canada but was raised in the States near Boston. I'm also an American citizen. If the government finds out I'll get deported."

"I knew it!" Alan's quick burst of joy confirming his earlier belief was soon tampered. "Deported if you're lucky. You know they don't feed you in jail? Why'd you do it?"

"Because I was in a dead end in my life and this job opened up. I knew the risks and took a chance."

"You're right Upton, you took a risk. Keep crossing the street where it's marked. If you end up in jail I'll bring you some bánh mì que almost every day."

"Thanks 'mate'."

"So how long do they think it will take for the police to find Ngô?"

"Hard to say. They're waiting to catch him from whatever hole he drags himself out of. They want him to go to the family home in Hội An."

"Good mate. Better for all but the police down there. What are you doing in the meantime?"

"Nothing."

It was another Saturday morning and the rains had been hard and constant for the last few weeks. A lot even for Đà Nẵng. I spent the morning watching my neighbors come and go to dine on chị Giang's bún bò Huế but I had no appetite so all I did was watch. I sat on my balcony in the pouring rain caring for little. I was emotionally frozen and unable to move. Chị Giang was cleaning up when I saw a woman with a bicycle on the sidewalk quickly duck through my gate. It must of been one of chị Phương's friends over for tea which meant I'd soon be asked to say hello and a few other words in Vietnamese. I didn't mind as chị Phương was a sweet woman and this small gesture made her and her friends happy to see this foreigner from a foreign land embrace what they loved.

The Beauty of Aqua

"Em ơi!"

Right on cue but with little enthusiasm I headed downstairs and walked into the kitchen to see chị Phương talking to another woman I knew very well. She was slender, a bit shorter than me at about five and a half feet tall, wearing wire-rimmed glasses and a well-tailored, light-blue, modern áo dài, with shorter front and rear panels than the traditional form, with silken, white pants and a translucent, bright-blue áo mưa offering her some protection from the rains. She radiated with a special beauty. This was not only on physical appearances but the way she held herself, with poise and grace. In her right hand was a tattered, bamboo basket and a nón lá. Just outside the main room was her equally worn bicycle.

I smiled and when Thủy saw me she did the same.

"Xin chào anh. Anh khỏe không?"

"I am now."

"Good anh. Anh ăn sáng không?"

"Anh không ăn sáng." This admission was both displeasing to Thủy and to all Vietnamese people. When happy, sad or in doubt you must always eat.

"Why anh?"

"You know why."

"Dạ anh; em không ăn cơm." While me not eating was not good for a Vietnamese person not to want to eat something, especially with the foods they loved everywhere found right on the street, was a sin.

"Em không khéo. You need to eat."

"Dạ anh that is why I brought us food. Please have a seat and I will serve you."

With chị Phương filling in for chị Ngọc as our chaperone we three enjoyed the one dish Thủy made better than anyone: mì Quảng cá lóc. With chị Phương in the kitchen Thủy and I ate in silence. Being apart for the last two weeks only made that meal all the better. For that brief moment in time Thủy and I were back on the street dining where we were most comfortable. We basked in that wonderful meal which was not lost on chị Phương watching us with a smile from her seat in the kitchen.

"Cảm ơn nhiều em. You always make the best mì Quảng with your mother's next best."

"Không có chi anh."

We didn't need to express our love in words because we had done the same with Thủy making us this wonderful bowl of soup and with my gratitude of the same. She really did make the best mì Quảng and her mother unsurprisingly was first runner-up.

After our silent meal we moved to the two couches in my main room with cups of ginger tea, thanks to chị Phương, who continued her chaperoning duties from her seat in the kitchen.

"Em khỏe không?"

Thủy paused in thought. "Em không khỏe. Anh Dũng has told me to stay home and rest for the next two weeks and if em Ngô has not left Đà Nẵng then for my safety I will be sent to Huế City to teach. I love Huế City very much like you but also like you Đà Nẵng is my home. This is where I find happiness but—" She paused again. "Em Ngô and I have much sadness in our lives. His sadness became bad and stayed bad after our father died.

All he can do is fish for a few hours each day and drink rice wine. He refuses to look at what once brought him happiness." She paused a third and an awkward amount of time, shifted her posture towards me, stared right into my eyes and with a firm voice said. "That is why we should drink little beer and try to find happiness in every place we can. We must make sure we do not make the same choices my brother has made or we will be as sad as he is, or worse we will be—" She thought twice about her next word then looked down to her tea.

"Dạ em; you and I will make good choices."

Thủy again looked right into my eyes. "I see the same sadness I have in me also in you anh Upton and I see the joy on your face with every meal we eat together. Our sadness can make us weak but our passions and traditions can make us strong and together we can be even stronger. We are the fortunate few that rose from the mud of suffering to grow into a beautiful lotus flower and to see the sunlight."

"You're a beautiful lotus flower but not me."

"Anh Upton: are all lotus flowers beautiful?"

"Dạ em."

"Then please remember that. You are also a beautiful lotus flower that found his way to the surface of the pond in my country and you are also beautiful." The beauty of Aqua once again shined through the storm clouds above offering me some welcomed light.

"Cảm ơn nhiều em Thủy. I will try to remember that."

"Không sao anh. I must go before—"

"Speak of the devil where's your brother?"

"I do not think that my brother is the devil but that is not important right now. He has been seen by the Hàn River but the police have not found him."

"It's just an expression. I didn't mean he was the devil, just he's like—" That was a good place to stop.

"Dạ anh; I understand." Thủy stood and thanks to chị Phương was handed her basket with clean pots inside. "Hẹn sớm gặp lại anh Upton."

"Hẹn sớm gặp lại em Thủy."

It would only take another week for her brother to finally make his presence known.

Flashing red lights and a siren screamed down đường Nguyễn Thị Minh Khai. Then another. As every building here was brick and concrete it most likely wasn't a fire. I was up so I investigated.

The bright, flashing red lights of the ambulance and police lead to the one place I wished it hadn't. Like the night of the fight about a month ago I stood in the shadow of a jackfruit tree and in the rain. Soon two police officers came out carrying a body bag with someone inside. Time froze. My heart was shattered with the thought Ngô had come back to finish with Thủy what he'd started with the black-eye. I stood still and watched. Thankfully Thủy and her mother soon followed the officers. I suspected it was Ngô in the bag. I waited again in the shadows until I was spotted by Thủy. She spoke to her mother then came over.

The Beauty of Aqua

"Ngô?"

"Dạ anh; he hung himself from the staircase and he is dead." She cried. "This is why you and I must always remember what brings us joy like our passions and avoid what brings us sorrow. We must remember our ancestors every day in that special place in our home to give us the strength to see a better tomorrow. My brother did not do this and he is dead. He stopped living after our father died but we can not." Then with fervor she said. "We have work to do and lives to live. Chúc ngủ ngon anh."

It was morning and the rains were gone for now. Not that the most recent rains were too unpleasant but the sunshine was welcomed. Thủy and her mother had been in Hội An for a small funeral for Ngô and I continued my days in limbo when I heard the sweetest sound I could imagine. The one sound that would echo up from the street below to my balcony that always put a smile on my face and a sound that I hadn't heard in oh so long.

"Anh ơi!"

It was my best friend. My dining companion to the finest food carts the City of Đà Nẵng had to offer. It was Thủy. I looked over my balcony and with a great, big smile shouted "Chào buổi sáng em! Em khỏe không?"

She stood there in the street wearing a favorite well-tailored, dark-purple áo dài with silken, white pants and with a gentle smile replied, "Em khỏe. Cảm ơn anh."

Thủy was back! I flew downstairs and saw chị Phương in the main room cleaning up. I was about to say good morning when she brushed me towards the door because she knew I had something more important waiting for me outside. Following her lead I left.

Thủy's reflection radiated in the puddles before her on the street. Her beauty was not only on physical appearances but how she held herself that morning. I gently but firmly grabbed her hand and started pushing her down the street. "Em đi! Em đi! Em đi!"

"Where are we going anh Upton?" She already knew but wanted to hear it from me.

"Anh và em đi ăn sáng bánh canh! Đi! Đi! Đi!"

I was so excited to have our favorite soup that morning with my best friend and so was she. We ran down đường Lê Lai like children filled with joy on the first morning of the Lunar New Year and our perfect bowls of bánh canh would soon fill our minds with nothing else while we ate. We sat and chị Linh, smiled seeing us back together, served us where, as always, we ate in silence. Thủy was back and we were back together.

"Em đi uống cà phê không?"

"Dạ không cảm ơn anh. I must go home. Our neighbors are visiting us today to give us their pity."

In the West the word "pity" was derisive and I thought her use odd.

"Pity?"

"Dạ anh; pity is the feeling of compassion at someone's suffering. Do you not know that word?"

I didn't know if her uncle's dry humor was once again showing itself to me. "I know what 'pity' means. It's just not a nice word in the West."

"Why anh?"

"Because when you say it it sounds like you're looking down on someone that won't take care of themselves."

"Then you do not know what that word means. Maybe that is why there is so much sadness in the West? Please follow me to my home and I will show you."

Chị Linh and Thủy shared a few words and we set off for her home.

"Chị Linh khỏe không?"

"Chị Linh khỏe. She wanted to tell me she was happy to see us again. She also was unhappy that you did not visit her while we were apart and she said you should not do that again."

"Anh xin lỗi em. I can't do that."

"Why anh?"

"You know why."

"Dạ anh; I know why."

Chị Linh's was the one place where we always ate together and never apart. Her soup was that special to us having been part of our most special and passionate times together.

"Then next time you will have chị Giang's bún bò Huế. You need to eat anh. Promise me you will do this?" Thủy always had an eye on me and it wasn't just to keep me from making poor choices. She wanted to protect me like a Vietnamese woman does when she loves someone.

Thủy's home had our neighbors coming and going. Some with food and all with compassion. We went inside where I found a seat off to the side of the main room on a hard, wooden couch. I watched neighbor after neighbor greet Thủy and her mother and offer their condolences with no thought about the suffering Ngô had brought us, just compassion for the family. On a shelf near the front door was a large picture of Ngô in a light-blue background. Thủy had told me about how many of the fishermen in our community would borrow a nice shirt and jacket, for all to share, and have their pictures taken before each fishing season. This one was taken earlier this year. Thủy soon joined me.

"Will this photograph go on the family-altar?"

"Dạ anh; very soon."

"I can't say I liked your brother but I'm sorry about his death and your sadness."

"Thank you for your pity." She smiled and I understood what she was trying to explain to me earlier. Pity in Việt Nam is a word of compassion and not a poor attempt at the same rolled in scorn for the recipient.

She brought me over to a desk in the back of the main room, pulled out a large envelope and opened it to reveal a picture I did not want to see.

"See anh; this is mine." It was her funeral portrait in the tell-tale, light-blue background. I became sick to my stomach and Thủy could see the discomfort in my eyes. She tried to comfort me.

"We do this so when we die we will be remembered. When I see this picture I smile because I know a family member will remember me and make me mì Quảng on special days long after I have died. Do you like this photograph of me?"

Again I could feel myself starting to retch.

"Anh ăn cơm không?" When in doubt offer food.

"Không cảm ơn em."

She continued, "This is the way of my people. This picture and all our other traditions keep us strong. Even when my father died during the war we still followed our traditions." Then she surprised me. "I will take you to have your photograph taken so someday, a very long time from today, your photograph may also sit on a family-altar."

My family didn't have a family-altar. "Any thought to whose family-altar my photograph could sit?"

She smiled. "There is an old song in Việt Nam we like to sing that says 'Que será, será. Whatever will be, will be. The future's not ours to see.' Whatever will be, will be."

The rains were starting to be replaced with the cool of winter where many would don heavy jackets on the coldest days. My Newfie blood and pride wouldn't have that with the temperature now closer to late spring back there. The summers were really hot but that weather was very nice.

Thủy and her mother had breakfast together that morning with her agreeing to meet me afterwards outside my home promptly at eight which she did. While punctuality wasn't very common here it was with her which I appreciated. We went on to Cafe 47 where Alan was already having his morning coffee.

"Hello mate. How are you this morning?"

"Good; thanks Alan. How's life with you today?"

"Good mate. Good morning Thủy. Please sit."

"Cảm ơn anh Alan."

"Where's my invitation to sit?"

Alan laughed. "You're a man. You can sit in the corner for all I care."

I sat and retorted. "Thanks 'mate'."

He had a small stack of papers with him.

"You working from here now?"

"No; I just picked up the latest results from our last batch of health surveys."

"Please tell me it's good."

"Sorry mate, it isn't. We've found a few more cancer clusters but I haven't mapped them out yet. Thủy, could you take a look?"

"Can we do this later? It's too early in the morning to deal with that."

Thủy reached over and started to skim the pages of streets in the city and the reports of illness. She stopped on one page and all expression left her face. "What anh Alan?" She pointed to the top of the page. I could read some Vietnamese with difficulty but I knew the name of her street and the meaning of "ung thư." Her street was a hotspot for cancer. She showed Alan.

"I'm sorry Thủy. This is bad. You need to start drinking only bottled water and watering all your food in the same until I can get you a proper water filter but even then you'll still need to boil. You should only eat vegetables you grow in soil that we can make sure isn't contaminated. We sent some food samples back to Australia for testing and we got the results back a few weeks ago. No surprises but it's in the food." Alan cautiously spoke his next words. "It's also in the rice."

Thủy sat there without any expression on her face. "What is causing my people to be sick anh Alan?"

"We can't say publicly for sure but privately we know: the use of dioxins during the war."

"How do we remove that poison from our soil?"

"You can't without destroying much of the city. The best you could do is for the city to build a water treatment plant and pipe water to every home. Farmers would also have to replace much of their soil and also use filtered water."

"How much anh Alan?" Thủy asked for a price she knew the city couldn't afford.

"Too much. It's more money than Đà Nẵng will have for many, many years and by then the damage will be done."

Thủy choked on her next question. "How bad?"

"No one can tell but many more people, especially women, will die than were lost during the war."

"Women?"

"Breast cancer is one of the most common. It's treatable in the West but that's no comfort to those living here."

Without a word Thủy got up from her seat and started walking towards her home as Alan and I watched.

"Go get her mate. She needs you."

"Yeah; see you later."

"No worries."

I caught up to Thủy and she looked incapable of expressing any emotions which worried me. "Anh xin lỗi em Thủy."

She stopped but was shaking, shifted her posture towards me, stared right into my eyes and with a firm voice said, "When the French came and tried to take our land for themselves they were removed. When the Americans came and tried the same they were also removed but they poisoned our land. They poisoned our rice fields! We can remove an enemy from our land but not the poison they left behind in our soil. In our rice fields!" She paused, "When the Americans hear what anh Alan found will they help us?"

Now I was the bearer of a sad tale. "Không em; anh xin lỗi em. I'm sorry but they won't help."

I could see a tear forming in her eye. "Why anh?"

"When the war ended all the Americans wanted to do was forget it ever happened much like we forget our ancestors soon after they die. You are already dead and forgotten in the eyes of the American Government so there is no reason for them to help."

This truth both sickened and infuriated Thủy. "How can they do that! Every life has value!"

After General Westmoreland left as Commander, U.S. Military Assistance Command, Vietnam (MACV) he said to the enduring shame of every good American:

"The oriental doesn't put the same high price on life as does a westerner. Life is plentiful. Life is cheap in the Orient."

It was a disgusting comment that sadly some Americans believed. What I believed before coming here I now knew was not true: life is precious to the Vietnamese people and they show that when they remember those that have died every day in their home.

Sadly General Westmoreland's comments were accepted by much of the American public because of her overriding ethos: America can do no wrong. Anything we did to others they deserved and their problems are their problems and not ours.

Thủy continued her shaky walk back to her home.

"Anh xin lỗi em Thủy. There's nothing we can do."

"We can remember the dead. We can make sure that everyone in my city that dies from the poison in our soil is remembered because every life has value. We can tell the Americans about those that died from their acts. I must go home now." She immediately stopped. "What if I get cancer?"

All I could think was: "Please not Thủy." She had good reason to be concerned as even a minor case of cancer here meant almost certain death. If she got sick and died I would never recover. "If that happens I'll be here to help you."

"So you now think you will be able to stay?"

"'The future's not ours to see.' Since you're going home let's pick up some bánh mì que for your mother. We can have some too." When in doubt offer food.

Thủy wiped the tears from her cheeks and gave a small smile because she understood the joy this simple sandwich could bring.

"Do you think of anything else besides food?"

"Other than em?" I smiled. "On every street corner and with every street cart I see a chance for happiness."

"Same-same em. Let us buy some bánh mì que."

Winter was here and the turbulent unrest of the rainy season had finally left us. I was up on the rooftop garden of my house where I could see a few multi-colored light strings intertwined with warm, incandescent bulbs that had been hung up and down my street below in preparation for the upcoming Lunar New Year celebrations. The clear skies of the upcoming season were above me on that peaceful night. It was quiet until I had an unexpected guest.

"Xin chào anh. Did you not hear chị Phương calling you?" It was my friend and she was wearing a jacket and toque in the cool, 15°C night air and I was wearing a short sleeve shirt.

"Anh xin lỗi em. I was up here looking at the stars above. I'll miss the rains but I like seeing the stars again."

Thủy came over and sat next to me revealing a bia Larue and two glasses with ice.

"Really em?"

"Dạ anh; we can share one beer."

Which we did under that star-filled sky. We were together and we were happy. Nothing more was said between us because words couldn't express what we felt for each other on that beautiful night.

The Beauty of Aqua

Because of its subject material I'd been reading "The Quiet American" by Graham Greene when I'd tripped across this passage which I paraphrase: "I didn't care a damn.... I wanted Thủy, and my home had shifted its ground eight thousand miles... I had to find a way to stay." Thankfully that worry would soon be forgotten in a blurry haze of almost daily lunar new year parties and strong drink.

10

Aqua Vitae

One night a few months ago the rain started and I didn't think it would ever stop. First the large, white clouds rolled in from the south blocking out the almost full moon. They quickly lost their innocence then became angry. First a drop on the street, then another. Soon the pitter-patter of rain could be heard everywhere. Minutes later the droplets became many times their earlier size, exploded on the asphalt and filled my world with a loud, steady drone of a seemingly endless supply of water. And I watched that ballet of nature unfold in front of me from the comfort of my room there in Đà Nẵng.

The Beauty of Aqua

Like most sixteen-year-olds on Cape Cod in the 1970's I was expected to get a summer job. If you landed the right gig with good pay you could make enough over the season to maybe buy a used car or at least fix up an old motorcycle and if you worked at the beach you also got to meet some girls. My first choice was working the parking lot at Red River Beach on Nantucket Sound as you were able to use your post to find the best parties in our village but that fell through. Second was turning a wrench with dad but Roy's brother came down for the summer so that didn't pan out either. Sadly my last choice hired me. A failure of all three attempts at finding a job would've meant little money but the summer spent carefree on the beach and riding my then newly acquired motorcycle but that would not be happening. For I had landed one of the worst jobs possible: cashier at a miniature golf course.

Cape Cod miniature golf courses were an instruction guide on how to create a completely false narrative of Cape Cod and how to clean out the pockets of the tourists. Where this gentle peninsula had the dunes that could inspire the greatest paintings of Edward Hopper or give us the inspiring words crafted by Henry David Thoreau from his tiny, Outer Banks shack our mini-golf courses presented cheap and tawdry caricatures and attracted the same. We didn't get the well-heeled Boston "blue-bloods" or even couples looking for a pleasant distraction. We got all the rest: the loud and impatient and they were as happy to see us cashiers as much as a flat tire on a hot, summer day.

Almost everyone would ask for a discount and take it out on us when we had to say no. These places were as cheap as possible except for the price where the owners would charge a princely sum, especially on holiday weekends which was about the cost of a small lobster meal, to offer group after group of cranky children the pleasure of banging a golf ball along poorly planned plastic grass paths for twenty minutes or so with their parents regretting the choice that brought them there.

Only one condition could light that powder keg on fire: rain. To our guests the rain was the enemy of all that was pure and good. They would curse the sky with anger as they saw their few days on the Cape mostly being spent watching local TV in their dingy motel room. As the rain would increase so were the demands for refunds. Time after time: "Sorry; no refunds." The owner's presence would've been welcomed except he knew the safest place to be: down the street drinking his lunch. Those people were emotionally melting down in that Cape Cod summer rain and I was the brunt of their rage.

Việt Nam was different. Very different. The rain here was as sweet and gentle as her rice paddies. First was the damp, thick fog telling us it would soon rain which offered a welcomed cooling from the hot day. Then a few drops started offering more relief from the heat. Food carts saw that and set up their brightly colored tarps to shield diners. Then a steady drumbeat of drops but life still went on. Motorcycles showed a bit more caution leaving some to seek shelter under shop canopies to wait for a break in the weather. As the rain worsened life would slow but never stop. Then the rain finally receded and all that could be heard were the steady drops of water falling off the leaves of the lemon and jackfruit trees on our streets. The rain was over and our beautiful, little community had been washed clean.

To see the rains in Việt Nam is a wonderful experience and living there during the rainy season changes how you see a single drop of rain for the rest of your life. The rain is your friend and you welcome it every time you see it.

I remember a day a few months back when the rain had just slowed and soon would be gone for the next day or so leaving an intoxicating smell behind. I sat in my chair on my balcony enjoying the view when I heard the voice of my friend.

"Anh ơi!"

I looked over the rail to see Thủy soaked through her clothes with the biggest smile. "Why are you so happy? Did you find a new food cart?"

"Không anh. The rain; I love the rain. Please come down."

"Dạ em; một phút xin." I left locking the door and gate behind me. Thủy's beauty could be seen on her face. She didn't hide her emotions well and her happiness would infect all that could see her smile. That was the smile on her face.

"It's raining." An astute observation from me.

"Dạ anh; it is beautiful?"

"Dạ em; it's nice."

"Không anh; it is beautiful. Please follow me."

We walked down đường Lê Lai like it was a sunny day and we let the last of the rain wash over us without contest welcoming its showering of warm drops. While life had slowed it hadn't stopped. The bún mắm cart had their canopy in place protecting the cook and a few diners. Cafe 47 across the street from them had drawn their tables and chairs under the same.

Then I saw it: one by one other couples joined us in the last, gentle drops of rain. They had the same smile we had as they slowly walked from house to house sometimes stopping to greet a neighbor standing by the ever-present open, front door. We were wrapped in the intoxicating scent of the fresh rain and freshly lit incense and we wanted to appreciate every moment before it was gone. Thủy, like other Vietnamese people, didn't curse the rain. The rain was their friend that fed their crops which would later feed their families. She saw through the inconveniences of the rain and celebrated this water of life.

She could see my happiness in my calm smile. "You love the rain?"

"Dạ em Thủy; mưa rất đẹp. Anh yêu mưa."

She smiled too. "If you are going to live here then that is what you should think about our friend the rain."

We found joy in the same great foods, motorcycles, love of our city and now the rain. Good thing as it was needed to slow down the ever growing fire between us.

The Beauty of Aqua

The voice of anh Dũng cautioning me to drive slower in the rain could be heard but I didn't listen and my speeding motorcycle was now quickly losing traction. My back wheel came out from under me, I lost my lane and was coming ever closer to the edge of the cliff in front of me. Braking not an option I steered into the skid.

Christmas on Cape Cod in the 1960's was a precious sight to behold. The roads were quiet in our small village with the tourists long gone and the warm winds of summer had been replaced with a cold snap in the air and rough seas. Simple home after simple home along Main Street, each clad in light-grey, weather-worn cedar shake shingles and white trim, had candles in their windows and similar dark-green wreaths on their wooden-planked, front doors made of fresh evergreen stems and tied off with a large, red bow; in fact the larger the better. This lead to some neighbors competing with each other with some like Roy at the marina going as big as he could. Roy, like my family, wasn't a follower of any religion but saw the joy these festive reminders of the impending holiday brought us and he did his fair share to help out.

The Sunday after Thanksgiving dad and I would help him assemble a six-foot wide and one-foot thick wreath, with a ribbon big enough to tie down a small boat, and would help him hang it on the boat barn for all to see on the land and water. He made sure he was going to have the largest wreath, like every other year before, and in the process he brought joy to our community. When most of us saw those wreaths we didn't see token signs to a religious holiday, we saw a community celebrating a time when our families returned home.

A week before Christmas except for the last minute shopping trip or two life slowed. Like others, our favorite pizza shop run by a nice Greek family would also shut down for the week and no one complained. Our local, family-run supermarket made fresh donuts by the dozen in only one flavor: donut. As a child my parents would take my brother and me there where we'd watch, with joyful anticipation, as basket after basket of fresh, golden-brown donuts were scooped out of boiling-hot oil and dumped on to waiting cooling racks and they couldn't make them fast enough that time of year. With our treats in hand we'd also pick up some fresh apple cider, later to be warmed with a few cinnamon sticks before serving, and head home.

On one day each year, those treats were carefully laid out on our dining room table with my mother's best tablecloth, one of the few times it was ever used, and in sight of our carefully decorated and oversized Christmas tree that stretched from floor to ceiling. Our neighbors would stop by and visit my family throughout the afternoon. On that one day many in my community came together and we were never more united. In my community in Đà Nẵng I also had that same sense of childhood joy and camaraderie.

Tết or Tết Nguyên Đán, the Vietnamese Lunar New Year, is the most important holiday of the year in Việt Nam and is also a celebration of the family. While shrouded in many treasured rituals they don't serve to remind them intrinsically of a mythological event but to remind them of the times in the past that were spent as children with their beloved parents and grandparents.

Tết is similar to Thanksgiving with its vast amounts and selections of foods including a few like the sticky rice, mung bean and pork treat bánh tết that normally appear that time of year. It's similar to Christmas with the gathering of families and New Year's Eve with excessive amounts of alcohol. Instead of drinks made of fruit juice concentrate and distilled spirits here it was massive amounts of beer punctuated with shots of rượu đế.

Rượu đế is Vietnamese rice wine, using the term "wine" very loosely, which is a high octane, homemade spirit made from a sticky rice mash and usually distilled in ancient, hand-fashioned copper pots which many times could be found boiling away in the back of a rural Quảng Nam family barn next to the chickens.

Over the last week before the holiday the fisherman that normally congregated across from my home had been inviting me with a wave of a hand to join them in strong drink. I didn't join in often but they knew if I came it was with a case of bia Larue under my arm which they always appreciated and I would have expected nothing less from my brethren of the sea.

A quick trip down đường Lê Lai to my local, five-meter-wide, family-run, convenience store about six doors down I picked up the necessary party supplies and soon joined my friends.

With Tết coming soon we drank our beer and rượu đế. I happily watched my friends hold forth like only fisherman could do with the only pauses for shouts of "Một, hai, ba, vô!" Between glasses of beer we imbibed ourselves on that water of life.

The sweetness of the rainy season had passed making way for the cool, dry days of winter. Schools were out in preparation for Tết and my street was awash with neighbors visiting each other as the first day of Tết was in two days. Thủy had just arrived and we started our walk to her house when we saw chị Giang locking up the front gate to her home. Chị Giang was an older woman but it didn't show. She was dressed in a bright-yellow áo dài with a green and red dragon embroidered along the front panel and she looked beautiful.

"Chị ơi!" I called out to her. "Chị đẹp!" I was in the spirit of the holiday. Chị Giang giggled and then left. Soon after she turned to walk away I felt a slap against my shoulder and heard a quiet yet firm voice.

"Không anh!" It was Thủy. I had angered her and I had to find out what I did that was so wrong.

"What em?"

"When you are in the company of a Vietnamese woman you should not tell another woman she is beautiful. She might think you are unfaithful."

"So it's fine to say it if you're out of the room?" That was the most obtuse question I had ever asked in my entire life and I immediately saw my mistake the moment after I had uttered those horrible, horrible words. I was falling fast but was sure I could save myself. "I was just complimenting her on her dress. She's twenty years older than me. I think she does yoga." Swing and a miss.

"Do you find her attractive?"

"Kinda?" Strike two almost hitting the catcher behind me.

Thủy paused in shock to my response but calmly asked, "More attractive than me?"

Time to come back. "Không em; em rất đẹp."

"Then next time you feel like saying a woman is beautiful you should be looking at me." Thủy smiled and we continued to her home. "You are fortunate her husband did not hear your comment about her áo dài because he is a fisherman. There might have been an incident."

Having grown up around fisherman I was well-aware of their pension for "frontier justice" but I thought I'd ask for clarification. "What do you mean an 'incident'?"

"This is Việt Nam. When it is time you will see. I hope you are only watching."

We soon arrived at Thủy's home. Paper lanterns, lit by tiny candles, hung across the front from the second-floor balcony. Thủy's mother had set up a folding table on the front steps topped with a few dishes of favorite meals, fresh fruit, lit candles and incense.

"An offering to your ancestors?"

"Dạ anh; on special days we make our offering to our ancestors here by the street so they will see the food, eat and not be hungry."

Thủy found comfort in these rituals. She didn't have to see her ancestors just as phantoms dining on these offerings but this ritual as a way to protect her memories of those she loved and meant so much to her. I watched her look down on that table with a smile because it reminded her of those that were no longer here in life.

"Mother and I must visit my neighbors. Would you like to join us?"

"Không cảm ơn em. Anh đi đó về."

I knew on social calls like the one Thủy and her mother were about to go on I would be left to myself while the others chatted the night away. Thủy's invitation was made out of politeness.

"Dạ anh; hẹn sớm gặp lại anh."

"Hẹn sớm gặp lại em." With that I made my exit.

That night's Tết party started early. This one was thrown by the local Communist Party committee in front of their meeting hall across from my home and was quite well stocked. Cases and cases of beer including the most prized Heineken, buckets of large ice cubes and mountains of freshly caught tiger shrimp, thanks to our local fishermen, awaited us. Also a wall of speakers that could possibly be heard from a kilometer away and I was quickly dragged into the hurricane before me.

The beer flowed freely and the music was loud. Chị Giang was sitting next to me at our table when she grabbed my hand to dance which I welcomed. Almost on command a slow song came on and my partner closed up the gap between us. One song was enough for me so I returned to my table. Thủy had soon arrived from her house and might of seen us dancing. I had beer to drink but then heard her familiar voice.

"Anh ơi! We must go now."

Slurring my speech a bit I replied, "One more beer and we can go. My friends want me to drink." I raised my beer to the air, shouted, "Một, hai, ba, vô!" and finished my glass of Larue.

"They are fisherman and will be here all night. You will not. I will walk you to your house."

I waved goodbye to my neighbors. "Hẹn gặp lại fellas!"

I doubt they understood the last part but thanks to the large amounts of beer and rice wine I'd consumed that night I had been inhibited from communicating on a more meaningful level. Thủy took my hand to keep me steady as she walked me home with the colorful, holiday lights illuminating my street above us.

"'Hẹn gặp lại 'fellas'?"

"Dạ em; what should I have said?"

"I would tell you but I do not think you will remember it or much else in the morning." Thủy was clearly displeased with me.

"I never drink like this back home but we don't have Tết." We did have the Stanley Cup playoffs but I didn't think it was the right time to bring that up. I vaguely remember dancing in the street and singing the chorus from a song about Tết that I had heard no less than one hundred times a day out of every loudspeaker in Đà Nẵng for the last month. I drunkenly sang:

"Tết Tết Tết Tết đến rồi! Tết Tết Tết Tết đến rồi! Tết Tết Tết Tết đến rồi!"

Thủy regained control and set us back on track. "You should not drink so much beer."

Out of the blue I replied, "A Vietnamese man without a beer is not a man."

"Maybe you are becoming too Vietnamese."

With Thủy's help I made it home, barely managed to unlock the front gate and door and stagger to bed all the while hearing "Tết Tết Tết Tết đến rồi!" in my head.

I'm not one to pay too much attention to politics but I must say that night the local Communist Party had the best party.

I was awoken that morning by a rooster that seemed to have escaped as I could clearly hear his loud call going up and down my street. Not a welcomed sound as it was a late night for me and many of my neighbors but hopefully a couple of aspirin would help. Chị Phương usually left a pot of ginger tea on a warm, cast-iron trivet in the kitchen to which I enjoyed on my balcony that pleasant, winter morning and soon I heard a much too loud voice from below.

"Anh ơi!"

"Chào buổi sáng em. Em khỏe không?"

"Em khỏe. Anh khỏe không?

I muttered out a weak "Anh khỏe."

She nodded no and had a confident smirk on her face. "Anh không khỏe."

"I'll be right there." I headed downstairs where chị Phương was in the kitchen. She tapped her head and pointed to me. "Mal de tête cháu?"

She might of heard me last night and I replied with little enthusiasm. "Dạ chị."

Thủy was on the street waiting for me and asked, "Do you remember last night?"

"Kinda?" If you have to ask someone if they remembered the night before chances are they didn't.

"That is what I thought. Please come with me and I will help you feel better."

"How em?"

She smiled. "Bún bò Huế."

She was right but chị Giang was closed and the street in front of her home was still littered with the remnants of last night's party.

"Chị Giang is closed. Where are we going?"

"Dạ anh; she must be very tired from dancing with you last night although you were dancing very slow."

Thủy saw that. "Anh xin lỗi em."

"Dạ anh." She paused to let her dissatisfaction known but the thought of a favorite food quickly changed her demeanor. "There is a food shop near my home and their family from Huế City brought everything with them to make bún bò Huế."

Tết was tomorrow and Thủy was as happy as a child on Christmas Eve at the thought of authentic bún bò Huế and I understood why. In the West regional foods vary their flavors with a change of ingredients but in Việt Nam you can taste the mild differences right down to where the vegetables were grown and the slight variations in seasoning a cook from Huế City would use as opposed to one from Đà Nẵng. While bún bò Huế ở Đà Nẵng was excellent authentic bún bò Huế was still the best. Its spiciness was also an excellent treatment for a hangover.

"Dạ em; I need bún bò Huế."

She smiled. "I knew that anh."

On the way to our special breakfast Thủy chided me about my excessive drinking the night before so I offered her a compromise. "Ok em Thủy; no more than six beers tonight." As a Canadian by birth I thought my opening offer to relieve her concerns was generous but it seemed by the look on her face it wasn't. "Ba bia không?"

"Dạ anh; three beers and no rice wine. Then you should help your body heal with a month of no beer and only eating vegetables after Tết."

Vegetarian food here was excellent but its scent didn't inhabit my bedroom every morning. A month without my favorites from my street would be difficult but Thủy had my best interests in mind which I always welcomed. She wanted me to make good choices. "Dạ em but not today."

"Dạ anh." Again she was displeased with my willingness to have even three that night and again I appreciated her concern for me.

With the thoughts of bún bò Huế also running through my head I soon smiled. "This morning will be a good morning em."

The Beauty of Aqua

We made our way through an alley running along đường Nguyễn Thị Minh Khai and found our way to a little piece of Huế City in Đà Nẵng.

It was a typical neighborhood bún bò Huế shop as the family was from Huế City but today was special. Family of theirs from Huế City were visiting for the holiday and brought everything necessary to make authentic bún bò Huế. On the floor were the home's family along with a few lucky friends and neighbors. We all were soon served hot bowls of this ancient soup of joys born in Huế City. Similar to its younger cousin here in Đà Nẵng the differences were subtle but Thủy and I could both taste and appreciate them. I scooped on an extra helping of sweet chili jam with the hope its spiciness would assist the aspirin already at work which didn't escape Thủy's gaze.

"Anh khỏe không?"

"Anh khỏe."

She smiled. "Anh không khỏe but you will be soon."

Except for a few celebrations I wasn't one to drink to excess because the food of Đà Nẵng was all I needed to stay in a perpetual cycle of halcyonic days.

I woke on that first day of Tết to silence. Other than the occasional footsteps of someone passing in front of my home it was very quiet. Even the rooster that normally woke me up seemed to have been included in the festivities, no doubt later to be seen with rice or in a pot of mì Quảng gà. As instructed by Thủy I dressed well and headed downstairs. With chị Phương spending the day with her son my home was unusually quiet. I left locking up behind me and mirroring my community quietly walked to Thủy's house.

Home after home was filled with happiness that morning. Children were opening a few simple gifts and lucky, red envelopes. Grandparents watched these children, lost in their joy, with memories of their own past Tết holidays and when their grandparents once did the same with them. Mothers and grandmothers were busy making the most important meal of the year from recipes handed down to her from her ancestors.

Like her neighbors Thủy's home had a festive look. Strings of multi-colored lights were intermixed with warm, incandescent bulbs that hung across her street and they cast a pleasant light on that cloudy morning. Red lanterns were hung from her second-floor balcony and like her neighbors her front door was open inviting all to enter although this first day of Tết was meant for family. Thủy's mother treated me like one of her own and being included in today's meal was an honor.

The front room was decorated with red lanterns of varying sizes along with red, cardboard diamond panels with Chinese characters hoping for good health and good fortune. Thủy and her mother were in the kitchen discussing the meal ahead when I was seen.

"Chào cháu Upton."

"Xin chào chị Ngọc. Chị khỏe không?"

"Chị khỏe. Cảm ơn cháu."

Chị Ngọc both appreciated and expected good manners from all. Now a shop owner she studied Vietnamese History in Hà Nội and lectured in the same before the war had inserted itself into her world and Thủy was her lifelong student. Soon we sat and ate many of our favorites like mì Quảng and a few specialties like bánh tết. While meals like this were usually lavish and boisterous this feast was simpler than normal and subdued because of Ngô's recent exit. Two bowls of rice sat with us on the floor in memory of him and her father. A reminder that life is precious to the Vietnamese people. We soon finished our meal and Thủy and I moved to our regular after-meal seats, each of us on our own wooden couch, with her mother not far away. I respected chị Ngọc and her concern that we act in a way our community expected of us.

"Cảm ơn nhiều em for having me here."

"Không sao anh. My mother thinks of you like a son and with em Ngô not here seeing you enjoying her food makes her happy."

"She's the second best cook I know."

"Who is the best cook?"

"Do I have to say?"

Thủy smiled. "Không anh."

Our relationship had transcended to a place where we didn't need to say what we already knew. We rarely spoke words of affection for each other: we could see it every time we ate, in silence, the best meals of our lives in each other's eyes. Our love had been intoxicating and now we were drunk.

Aqua Vitae

As promised I was at Thủy's house right at ten in the morning. It was the third day of Tết when students visited their teachers and Thủy's mother was kind enough to host me at her home and provide light snacks for our visiting students. Any chance she got to cook she took and did it with close attention to detail. Her mother respected food and her results showed it.

For the next few hours students visited me and Thủy with thanks for our work and a small gift of appreciation. I regret not showing the same respect to my professors. What might seem like a throwback to a time gone by, simple acts of respect can go a long way to holding a community together. I felt honored that day by each of my students.

The last students left us and soon after one of Thủy's neighbors was at the door and looked upset. With compassion she listened and spoke to the woman. It was bad news. Thủy returned with tears in her eyes.

"What's wrong em?"

"My neighbor is sick. She has breast cancer and she will soon die. Anh Alan was right. There is cancer on my street."

"Can't her doctor help her?"

Thủy held back her tears. "Maybe in the West but not here anh. Do you see any place that could treat that woman?"

"Không em." Because there wasn't. The USA had the

luxury of building hospitals while the people of this country were still removing unexploded ordinance and dioxins from their soil. These people were not poor in culture, great foods or kindness but were in money and those that control the money control the game. "Can we do anything for her?"

"Dạ anh; our community will help her be comfortable, we will feed her the best food we can and we will arrange her funeral when she dies." Thủy paused, "We can remember her life. We will tell it to everyone we can including those that caused her cancer that her life had value."

I could tell this hung heavily with her and as a citizen of the country that was most likely responsible for her cancer it also hung heavily with me. "Em Thủy ăn cơm không." When in doubt offer food.

"Dạ anh; we need bún mắm."

If mì Quảng was a gentle glass of white wine bún mắm was a shot, or a few shots, of tequila and the moment called for strong and comforting food.

"Dạ em; anh thích bún mắm."

She smiled. "I knew that anh."

Different foods offered us different comforts: mì Quảng for thoughts of family and love, bún bò Huế for energy, cháo for comfort and bún mắm for a reminder that we were still alive.

We set out for that reminder after the difficult news and soon found it. We sat and ate in silence then took a moment to reflect upon our meal.

"I like bún mắm but it smells like hell."

"Dạ anh but it tastes like heaven."

"Dạ em; it does."

"When a young man would ask me on a first date and I liked him I would ask to eat bún mắm. If he did not like it then there was no second date."

"So how many passed the test?"

She smiled. "Only one. I can not be with anyone that does not like the same foods as me. A husband with a closed mind and a wife with an open one will make for an unhappy marriage."

"Anh thích bún mắm."

"That is why you had a second date with me."

She was right. In order of preferences for a spouse if she didn't like bún mắm I knew it would never work. The food of Đà Nẵng did that to you and if you let it happen without resistance it was spirituous.

"Anh ơi!"

I looked over my balcony to see Thủy outside my house standing in the early morning mist.

"Chào buổi sáng em Thủy. I'll be right down."

It had rained the night before leaving an array of puddles scattered across the street below. Before her was one of those puddles which reflected her graceful image back to me. Thủy radiated with beauty and the water only made that radiance greater. I quickly got dressed and went downstairs. Chị Phương was in the kitchen as usual preparing her breakfast. She looked up from the stove and smiled because she knew what Thủy meant to me. I continued my exit out to the street.

"Em rất đẹp."

"Cảm ơn anh. You always say that I am beautiful."

"Because it's always true."

"More beautiful than chị Giang?" A reminder of my previous faux pas.

"You are the most beautiful woman I know and your bún bò Huế is better than hers." She wasn't jealous; she just wanted to taunt me which I accepted as it was deserved.

"Do you think I need to practice yoga like chị Giang?"

While Thủy didn't do yoga she knew she looked like she did and I wasn't going to mess this one up. "Không em; you don't need to practice yoga." I wasn't going to step into that bear trap again.

With a smile she replied. "Cảm ơn anh."

"Anh và em đi ăn sáng bánh canh chị Linh không?"

She smiled with thoughts of chị Linh's thick and warm bánh canh for breakfast.

"Dạ anh; em thích bánh canh."

I returned her smile. "I knew that em."

That was our breakfast. With all due respect to chị Giang's bún bò Huế with its striking-red, bold broth and an array of textures chị Linh's bánh canh, while also spicy, was thick and gentle and always brought us comfort. As we walked we talked.

"We should work on your Vietnamese."

"Why em? I'm leaving soon and I'll be alone."

"'The future's not ours to see.' When we try to see the future and what is not there all we see are shadows. We only see fear and doubt."

"I worry I won't see you again after I leave."

"Then anh you should stop doing that because 'the future's not ours to see.' Almost one year ago if you were told that you would be here in Đà Nẵng would you have believed it?"

"No way."

"Why not anh Upton?"

"Because other than the war I didn't know anything about Việt Nam."

"But you are still here?"

"Because I had to move and my uncle just happened to have a teaching job here."

"You told me that changed your life in one week."

"It did."

"And change like that will happen again and again anh. There is still a chance you can stay."

I reached out and held her hand in mine. Time seemed to stop and nothing else mattered for that brief moment.

We quietly walked down đường Lê Lai letting us absorb the life around us. A woman was pushing a bicycle with fresh jackfruit. Children sitting by a food cart were eating bánh mì. An elderly couple were drinking coffee in their front room. I stopped.

"Em Thủy; you see them?" I gestured towards the couple.

"Dạ anh; I do. They are in love."

"How do you know?"

"Look at them. She is resting her hand on his hand. She is reminding him she is there for him. That is love."

When Matt told me that living abroad was life-changing I couldn't understand how deep those changes would be. One of them was what I thought love was and what love wasn't. Before I saw love as a conditional loan: "If you love me I will love you back." Now I saw love as a gift: "I love you." No conditions. What Thủy and I had was very deep: we were best friends first and I would miss my friend more than I could ever miss someone I only loved.

We took our regular seats and without a word from us chị Linh served us our bánh canh prepared to our preferences. She carefully made Thủy's bowl as we could see her looking for the perfect piece of fish. Mine was with fish and a few shavings of Vietnamese ham placed on top. We were served and ate in silence.

Before we left Thủy had a brief conversation with chị Linh then we walked up to Cafe 47 for our morning coffee. Like with chị Linh, without a word from us we were served our preferred drinks.

"Chị Linh khỏe không?"

"Dạ anh; chị Linh khỏe. She saw us holding hands. She could see we were in love and that made her happy."

Our carefully hidden and brief moments of holding each other's hands while eating was the extent of our physical relationship and we both kept it there. Our meals together and those moments unseen by others would bring us more lasting joy then any physical coupling could ever bring and it happened with every great meal.

Love based on friendship and similar passions will always be stronger than love based on physical attraction alone. When we ate chị Linh's bánh canh together we both found it intoxicating.

As my home was on the way to Thủy's home many times we'd walk home together. Thủy and I had a late class that night which lead to an even later than normal walk. We rounded the corner from đường Lê Lợi to đường Lê Lai near Cafe 47 when we heard shouting from a nearby home. There were two men, by the looks of them had been drinking, fighting in the street and one was clearly losing.

"Should we call the police?"

"Không anh; we should wait."

"Wait for what? To see if he'll need an ambulance or a hearse? That guy's getting kicked all over the street."

"See the woman standing in front of the house?"

"Dạ em."

"If she wanted the police to be here they would already be here. I think this is a private matter and that the two men fighting wish it remain private."

"In the West fighting in the street makes it public. What do you think started it?"

"I think that the man on the ground is the woman's husband and he might of been having an improper relationship with the other man's wife."

"Really em? What makes you think that?"

"Because if that was not the case the police would already be here. Also the mother and father that run Cafe 47 next door are former, high-ranking police officers. They are watching and are not calling the police." Thủy paused, "I think the wife is waiting for the other man to become tired before she asks him to leave."

Great; South Boston rules.

"So what's keeping the guy who's getting beaten up from calling the police after the fight is over assuming he's able to pick up a phone and talk."

"By his haircut he looks like he might be a military officer. If I am correct calling the police would mean a report going to his commanding officer explaining the reason for the fight, which would mean he could lose his job and future pension. I think the neighborhood has decided that a little pain for the husband now is better than a lot of pain for both husband and wife later. It could be much worse for that man on the ground anh."

"How em?"

"The other man could have been a fisherman like chị Giang's husband."

Ouch. We continued our walk down đường Lê Lai leaving the ongoing melee behind us.

"That poor guy will be in a lot of pain tomorrow."

"Then he will have learned his lesson."

"What's that em?"

Thủy stopped and looked right at me. "Never cheat on a Vietnamese woman. You should remember that anh Upton."

"Không sao em. I will try to remember that."

Thủy smiled. "Good anh. I would be sad if that was you 'getting kicked all over the street'."

We walked back to my house with Thủy continuing on to her home for the night leaving behind the two combatants to continue their brawl in their state of drunkenness.

About a week after the holiday Thủy and I took our first monthly trip to Huế City since Tết where I would speak technical words and she would translate them for the class. While tedious and exhausting it was also important work. Before these were day-trips but this time, due to a train breakdown, we found ourselves stuck in this city by the river for the night and neither of us had a complaint about our good fortune. Thủy would be spending it with friends and I at a nearby hotel. This gave us a chance to explore the most magical city in Việt Nam which included eating a few small meals throughout the day and into the night.

We found a tea cart by the Perfume River where we sat and enjoyed the cool, night air.

"Anh thích Huế."

"More than Đà Nẵng?"

"Không em; Đà Nẵng is still my favorite but Huế is different, it's special."

She smiled. "How anh?"

"Đà Nẵng is old but feels young with all its growth and Huế City is old but also feels old, very old. There's no rush to build tall buildings or faster roads. No rush to do anything. Just sit and watch the rain with a warm bowl of bún bò Huế. The first time I came here I felt something I couldn't describe and still can't. I want to explore every part of this place. I could live here."

"Dạ anh; Huế is special. My home is Đà Nẵng but much of what I cherish came from this special city. Maybe someday we can buy a home here." Thủy blushed and looked down to her tea. We both had unspoken thoughts of marriage and the joys it could bring but had never said them out loud before.

I smiled. "Dạ em; we can buy a home here."

By instinct we discretely held hands and enjoyed our tea by the side of the Perfume River as brightly lit longboats passed before us. We finished our tea and I walked Thủy back to her friend's home before I needed to return to my hotel. The night was cooler than Đà Nẵng and a fine coat of evening dew covered our path. There was a sadness that seem to be with us in the dark. We talked along the way.

"I feel sad."

"Why anh?"

"I feel like there are a lot of sad people here."

"It is the ghosts. We are walking on their graves and they want to be remembered."

I looked down to see ordinary slabs of concrete. "Walking on their graves?"

"Dạ anh; there was much fighting here during the American war and there were times when our only choice was to bury the dead under the sidewalks. It is said that you can not walk more than a few meters in Huế City without stepping on someone's grave. Many of them had no family to remember their death-anniversary so they wander the streets at night begging to be remembered."

This thought struck me with a profound sadness. I'd seen how Thủy and her mother had lovingly tended to their family-altar and remembered every death-anniversary. With each remembrance they were reminded that someday their photograph would also be on their descendants' family-altar and they would also be remembered. Be it with a favorite meal or the simple lighting of incense the dead were not forgotten. This gave Thủy a strength I didn't have but longed for. Then I saw a source of my sadness: because I, like most westerners, will soon be forgotten after we die never to be remembered again by our descendants except in their times of fear and doubt.

"Every year they have the 'day of the wandering souls' to try to remember them but it is not the same as having a family member care for their memory in their own home."

"My family has no altar to our ancestors. A month after I die I'll be like the ghosts around us: alone and forgotten."

Thủy's eyes teared up. "Em xin lỗi anh. That is very sad. No one should be forgotten because every life has value." Thủy paused, "Maybe someday you will meet a nice Vietnamese woman, marry her and when your life ends you will be remembered."

"Maybe I've already met someone."

Thủy smiled. "'Que será, será'."

I replied, "Whatever will be, will be."

"Dạ anh; 'Whatever will be, will be'."

As I walked Thủy back to her friend's home we could both feel the sadness from the thought of those lost and lonely ghosts in the dense, nighttime fog that held their lives.

The days of winter would soon come to a close like my time here. I knew that if I wanted to marry Thủy I first had to ask her mother for permission. We had little hope of obtaining a marriage license but if she said no that would be a moot point. While she was always very kind to me I didn't know if that kindness would extend to including me in her family. I respected her and would abide by her decision because she wanted to make the best choice for Thủy, their family and our community.

I asked Lời, a good friend originally from Kon Tum and fellow lecturer but over at the law school, to act as my translator since we couldn't have Thủy here. When he came to my house we made our way to Thủy's home when we were sure her mother would be there and Thủy away. We arrived and I took a minute to compose myself.

"Thanks for helping out em Lời."

"No problem Mr. Upton. Are you ready?"

"As much as I'll ever be. Let's go in."

We announced ourselves and were invited in. Chị Ngọc didn't seem surprised I wasn't using her daughter as my translator. I spoke and Lời dutifully translated.

"Chị Ngọc; I love your daughter very much, she loves

me and I ask your permission to marry her. If you give me your permission I will then ask Thủy to marry me."

"Thank you cháu Upton for asking me first to marry my daughter. As you have seen I watch over my daughter carefully and only want what is best for her. You have been kind and close friends while respecting what our community expects from both of you. This makes me very happy but I have one concern."

"What is that chị Ngọc?"

"My daughter loves her country very much and this is her home. If you ask her to move to the West with you she will follow but I know in her heart she would be sad. Con Thủy sometimes has much sadness in her life that can cause her not to see the happiness around her. When you eat together I see she is happy which makes me happy. If you marry you must promise that she will always live here in her country even if you can not stay. It would be better for her if you lived apart than if she left her home. I worry if she did not live in Việt Nam her sadness would overwhelm her and cause her not to be able to return here in life. If you agree then you have my permission to marry."

"Thank you chị Ngọc. She has told me of her sadness and I too have the same. When we together eat the foods we love, for that brief moment, we are without concern and are happy. I promise not to ask her to move to the West with me because I know if she left Việt Nam she would be sad. Same-same cháu."

She smiled and left the room. I asked Lời why but he

didn't know. She soon returned and handed me a light gold necklace attached to an engagement ring.

"When em Thủy was a small child she would put this ring on and think about the day she would someday wear it. She has a special beauty about her which some do not see but you do. Please take this with my permission."

"Cảm ơn nhiều chị."

She held my hands in hers. "Welcome to our family."

With permission and ring in hand Lời and I thanked her and left. While Thủy and I still needed a marriage license that didn't matter. I was in a state of pure euphoria.

"Em ơi!"

It was anh Dũng here for his monthly visit and sadly this would be our last one before I left Việt Nam.

"Xin chào anh Dũng." I headed down and invited him inside where we sat and had tea.

"Your pronunciation is getting better. Have you also been working on your French?"

"Again with my French anh? Mon Dieu."

"What did you say cháu?"

"Anyways. I'm scheduled to leave soon but there's still work to do and because of Tết got delayed. Can you get me a new visa?"

"Không cháu; my government is very strict on issuing new visas like yours."

"Please anh Dũng. Is there anything you can do?"

"This must be important work. What is it?"

"I need to finish reviewing some of the code of my students."

"Really cháu? That sounds like weak tea to me."

"Dạ anh; really."

"I am not sure cháu."

I paused, "Không anh; it's not about my students. It's em Thủy. I love her and she loves me. I want to ask her to marry me."

"I suspected as much. Where would you get married? I do not think the city will issue a marriage license to a foreigner."

"First things first anh. I still have to ask em Thủy and she still needs to say yes."

"Have you spoken to anyone else about this?"

"Dạ anh; her mother. I first asked for her permission with the help of a student."

"What did she say?"

I pulled out the light, gold chain and ring chị Ngọc gave me from around my neck and showed it to him. This seemed to please him.

"Going to her first showed a sign of respect that will be remembered. As for the visa I should be able to get you a one month extension. Let us say it is for 'medical reasons' but the marriage license will be very difficult to obtain. Are you sure you want this? Life is not easy here. There are many things we do not have—"

"—like great food on every street corner or neighbors you know or simply happiness?"

Anh Dũng smiled. "You and I are different from

many others because we have both experienced life in the West and here in Việt Nam. Maybe we understand that happiness is family, friends and good food and not trying to feed an endless desire for more material items that only weigh us down."

Anh Dũng thought for a moment. "Speak of this to no one but cháu Thủy. I will get you a visa extension but after that you must return to Canada to receive a new one. Understand cháu?"

"Dạ anh; cảm ơn nhiều anh."

We left my home, walked out to the street and anh Dũng got on his motorcycle. "I see a difference in you. I see you found happiness with my people and that makes me happy." With that he headed down the street and was gone.

"Anh ơi!"

I leaned over my balcony to see Thủy on her Super Cub and she looked happy.

"Dạ em; một phút xin." And with that I headed out. Over the last few weeks our dining habits had turned from exploring on foot the treats of every nearby neighborhood to going to Thủy's favorite places all around the city. When she was working day tours for the Foreign Ministry she wasn't allowed to express a preference for a favorite restaurant which she clearly had as seen throughout our travels and tonight would be no different.

"Chào em. Em khỏe không?"

"Em khỏe. Cảm ơn anh."

Thủy was well-dressed in a short, dark-red áo dài with embroidered peach blossoms and silken, white pants. Again her Super Cub had been freshly washed which as a fellow motorcycle rider I appreciated. I got on.

"What are we having tonight?"

"Bún riêu cua." A favorite of ours.

"Anh thích bún riêu cua."

She smiled. "I knew that anh."

We found our way to the ward of Thọ Quang on the far side of Sơn Trà Peninsula to a street-side food shop, "Quán Ba", on the sidewalk in front of a bright, yellow-orange wall on the side of đường Nguyễn Phan Vinh just north of there. We sat and Thủy ordered our meals. She removed a pair of chopsticks from a metal basket on our table and carefully wiped them with a small piece of paper serving as a napkin. When finished she wrapped the tips in the same paper placing them in front of me. She cleaned a pair for herself and did the same with our spoons.

Bún riêu cua ở Đà Nẵng is another gift from the sea that's both well-executed and enjoyed by almost all in the City of Đà Nẵng. This soup is a maverick with the table-side addition of one special, most beloved or highly scorned ingredient depending on who you ask. The stock starts with lightly stir-fried tomatoes, to bring out their sweetness, then to no surprise nước mắm is added. Water follows and is left to boil when the onions join in. After simmering for a bit the star of the night arrives: gạch cua or crab patties made of minced crab and pork with eggs binding their two worlds together and more nước mắm. They are then scooped in with some tamarind and mắm nêm into the hot stock to cook for the prerequisite time.

While mắm nêm, the thick, opaque, dark-brown, extra-chunky witch's brew of fermented anchovies is usually not a problem when mixed in before serving it can decidedly be one when sitting in open jars on your table. There is no common ground here: you either love mắm nêm or you don't and if you don't then you have my sympathies. It's an acquired taste like the finest scotch whiskeys. If you don't like it that means more for us that do.

Thủy and I reached for the spoon that would make our meal ready to eat when our hands touched. It was like Adam and Eve touching the apple from the tree of forbidden fruit. Mắm nêm is that good. A heap of this witch's brew was added to each of our bowls. Those perfect bowls of bún riêu cua eaten in silence on a little, plastic table with traffic flowing by us was our garden of Eden. When finished we sat back in our little, plastic stools and felt like we were in paradise.

"Cảm ơn nhiều em. That was wonderful and their mắm nêm was good." This pleased Thủy as with every time I expressed joy in the treasures she shared with me.

"Không có chi anh. The best bún riêu cua is in our city and this is my favorite shop." Any playful ribbing about Thủy's pride in the food of Đà Nẵng were long gone. We'd both had long been sucked into this city's culinary vortex and were enjoying every bit of the ride;

all I could do was agree. We sat in silence for a moment and felt a warm breeze from the south.

"Em uống cà phê không?"

"Dạ không cảm ơn anh. The beach is very close. We should go there."

In little time we found ourselves with a nighttime view of the East Vietnamese Sea and Sơn Trà Mountain in all their beauty. Unlike the gentle waves of summer, tonight the sight of whitecaps reached across the horizon. We walked within a few meters of the high-tide mark and stood silent in the beauty of this special place. Unlike summer with its crowds of tourists we were alone on that winter night.

"This place reminds me of the beauty of my favorite beach in the West. When I was a child my mother would bring me there and we would take long walks together. Those long walks made us both happy. The sight and sound of the waves were comforting. I found the same comfort here and my good life here made it all the better. I found the happiness I was looking for and know why my happiness never lasted."

"Why anh?"

"Because happiness can't be saved like words in a book, it has to be lived every day which I do in every great meal."

"Dạ anh; I have seen a change in you. You found happiness in my country and I am happy for you. That is why I became a translator. I want people all over the world to see what you see in our city."

Anh Dũng warned me that falling in love with a

Vietnamese woman was like falling off a cliff and the same could be said of my city by the sea. I fell in love with Đà Nẵng and only wanted to stay within her warm embrace. No matter where I would find myself in the future this would always be my home.

"Em Thủy; there are many things I love about you but the most is that you are at your best when you follow your passions. Those passions you shared with me every day, with every meal, changed me for the better."

"It was through the lessons of my ancestors I was able to help you change but you changed yourself."

"Dạ em; and they would be pleased with you."

I had the ring and this was the perfect place to ask the question. I was pretty sure I knew her answer but also knew either way we'd still be good friends. When you truly love someone all you want is for them to be loved, be it from you or another. I was both intoxicated by the sea before us and Thủy. "Would you marry me em Thủy? I don't know how, when or where but please marry me?" Thủy looked both pleased and unsurprised.

"You must first ask my mother for permission to marry me. It is our way. If she says yes then I will say yes." At that moment I pulled out the light, gold chain from around my neck and showed her the ring. Thủy held her hands to her face and cried. "That is my mother's ring! How did you get it?"

"She gave it to me to give to you when I asked her permission to marry you. If she hadn't approved I wouldn't have asked."

"Are you sure you want to marry me? Where will we

get married?"

"Dạ em; I'm sure I want to marry you and that's what matters. We'll figure out the rest later."

"What about a marriage license?"

"I spoke to anh Dũng and he'll try to help us but no promises."

"Then all we can do is wait. 'The future's not ours to see'."

"Speaking of which how about bánh canh for breakfast tomorrow?"

Thủy smiled. "Do you think of anything other than food?"

"Dạ em; I think about you."

She walked over to the ocean's edge with its soft, wet and gentle sand to rest her feet in its waves. Thủy, "Aqua", was in her element which reminded me of one of her greatest strengths: to be as flexible as the water. That night we shared a kiss, an intoxicating kiss, for the first time.

The Beauty of Aqua

11

Last Days

Thủy and I were on our last walk from our university. With only a week left before I had to leave Việt Nam I said goodbye to my students and turned my keys over to security. I was no longer a teacher.

Every time I had my breakfast bún bò Huế at chị Giang's I was always greeted with a smile and that smile continued as she watched me enjoy what she had just made. It wasn't that she liked me, per se, it was because she knew I appreciated what she had worked so hard to create. She saw the fruits of her labors in the expressions of joy on my face with every bite. There is happiness in doing what you are good at and watching others appreciate what you just made. That's what teaching here brought to me.

"Do you know where you're working next?"

"Dạ anh; I am to wait for the next teacher like you and translate for him."

"Good luck with that em." I could say nothing more.

"My mother and I are going to our home village in Hội An. We are having the ten-year-death-anniversary of my grandfather and I will visit the grave of my brother. Will you join us?"

"You've told me a lot about your village and I'm glad I can finally go. When do we leave?"

"This Friday. My mother will rent a car and we will leave at seven in the morning then eat breakfast in Hội An."

"I'll be awake. The neighborhood rooster will make sure of that."

"Dạ anh; I am woken up by the same rooster too. He will soon be someone's meal." I laughed to myself thinking back to before: "and another will replace him."

"Please pack a bag for three days and bring a nice shirt and pants."

"Three days em?"

"Because we will be there for three days and you will need three changes of clothes. Is that not obvious?"

I once again thought anh Dũng's sense of dry humor was rubbing off on her.

"I meant what are we doing there for three days?"

"Pig."

"We're doing a pig?"

"Phrasing anh. We are cooking a pig and it takes one day to cook. It is very good."

A whole pig along with our favorite foods should make for a meal or party not to be forgotten. I smiled and said, "Dạ em; anh thích heo."

She smiled back, "I knew that anh."

Friday was here and thanks to our rooster I'd been up and ready for awhile. Downstairs I saw chị Phương happily making her breakfast when she saw my bag in hand.

"Em đi Hội An ba ngày." As I held up three fingers signaling how long I'd be gone she once again giggled at my poor use of her native language. I could still only string a few dozen words together, many of them foods, and while my pronunciation was only barely understood at least I didn't starve or go without "bia." With that I made my way to Thủy's home.

Outside was a late model Toyota Hiace big enough for Thủy, her mother, three cousins, me, the driver and enough food for everyone in the van for the entire day and then some. Thủy was bringing out a basket full of bánh nậm.

"Em Thủy, why all the food?"

"For the trip to Hội An. We will get hungry."

"It's less than an hour away and you have enough food for the entire day."

"Dạ anh; this is Việt Nam: we eat anytime and everywhere. I thought you knew that?"

I did and it was one of the most endearing traits of the people of this country. Whether they ate in the morning, in the afternoon, in the evening, late at night, on a train, on the floor of a Buddhist pagoda, in the back of an ox-cart or rear seat of a Honda Super Cub the Vietnamese people had the greatest food in the world and they ate it everywhere. Where many places lifted their flags with patriotic pride the people of Đà Nẵng did the same with a bowl of mì Quảng and they were going to eat it wherever they darn well pleased.

I started looking carefully at the bánh nậm in her hands and she knew what I was thinking.

Bánh nậm is a happy, little, soft, flat, rice dumpling filled with ground pork and shrimp then carefully seasoned with shallots, garlic, annatto oil and, of course, nước mắm. After steaming in banana leaves it's served with nước chấm: a gentle fish sauce that's lighter and sweeter than nước mắm. This soft treat has a texture similar to gnocchi but the rest is pure Vietnamese. In the past I'd enjoyed having a few for lunch with my bún mắm from a cart on my street which would induce a pleasant state conducive with my forthcoming afternoon naps.

Thủy asked, "Anh ăn bánh nậm không?"

"When? Now, on the drive to Hội An or after we get there?"

She smiled "Dạ anh." And I enjoyed that bánh nậm all three times.

Thủy's family home in Hội An was typical for the area and very different from the city. While three-story brick and concrete, five-meter-wide buildings covered the landscape of Đà Nẵng many of the homes in Thủy's village were made of bamboo and on stilts lifting them about two meters off the ground. A necessity due to the annual floods. We left the van and brought our wealth of provisions from home inside.

"You like my home anh Upton?"

There was one large room with bamboo leaf curtains acting as dividers. Inside the bamboo walls had taken on a light-caramel color from a nearby stove and the floors were worn from many years of use. The ceiling above revealed the bamboo-beam supporting the house in a much darker shade of brown. A family-altar was in the far corner. It was home. I paused and closed my eyes. From Thủy's stories about growing up here I could feel the memories and see the lives that had come and gone in this place so special to her.

"Anh ăn cơm không?" When in doubt offer food.

I smiled and opened my eyes. "Your home is as beautiful as you." It was as beautiful as Thủy because this was her home and the place she grew up. This was where she was born, where she learned to walk and where she ate her family meals. A place I once had but now only existed in my memories.

"I am happy you like my home. Please follow me." Thủy brought me over to the family-altar. It was much simpler than her's in Đà Nẵng being hung on the wall and built of a few simple pieces of reclaimed wood. It held three photographs all in tell-tale, light-blue backgrounds.

She pointed to the photograph on the left. "This is a picture of my grandfather and why we are here today. He was born in the North and is why my accent sometimes sounds like I was also born there. When I was a small child the other children at my school would tease me but I did not care. It was not their accent but it is the accent I hear when I hear my grandfather say to me 'I love you child.' and 'you will be fine'."

I remember when my grandparents came down to Cape Cod from Canada for my mother's and their daughter's funeral. It was a long drive for them and I, only twelve years old, patiently waited by the front door for their arrival. They finally came late that night and I ran as fast as I could to greet them. My grandfather gave me a hug that could've lasted forever and with his kind voice said. "I love you grandson. You will be fine."

Thủy continued. "This is my grandmother. She died soon after my grandfather died. She had a sadness inside of her and many said she was too sad to live and stopped living. She taught me how to make mì Quảng cá lóc using fish from the nearby stream and I will make that tonight to honor both my grandparents." Thủy paused and the smile left her face. These altars are meant to be an irenic place to remember our ancestors but some pains never go away; they can only be respected. She pointed to another funeral portrait. "This is my father and I miss him very much." She paused choking on her words. "We remember him in our home in the city and in our home here. He and my grandfather built this house for his new family and was very proud of it."

"Anh xin lỗi em Thủy."

"Không sao anh. He lives in my heart and I smile

Last days

when I light incense in this special place in my home. That is where I remember the times of happiness." Thủy then looked out the window to the stream behind the house.

"We should go anh. We need to catch dinner."

"Catch dinner?"

"Dạ anh; we need to catch some cá lóc for dinner. I know you know how to fish so please follow me."

It was my first fishing trip since I'd come here and catching a 'cá lóc' or snakehead fish would be a bit of a challenge. Rumor had it that it was a really mean fish that could leave the water and walk across a mud paddy. It fought to the bitter end and could hit you with a nasty bite if cornered. Thankfully this creature wasn't found in North America.

Thủy handed me a bamboo fishing pole, net and club. A club big enough to take down a small tuna.

"We need a club this big?"

"Dạ anh; không sao. You will catch the fish and I will club him. I do not want you to get dirty."

Ouch. I had been out in George's Bank and had clubbed and cleaned my fair share of bluefish and tuna and I wasn't going to take that challenge laying down.

"That is kind of em Thủy but I can club the fish and you can catch them. I don't want you to get hurt and I've done this before." That should've showed her but it didn't and I'd soon find out why.

She smiled. "Cảm ơn anh. You can club the cá lóc and I will fish from the river bank like a woman should do."

The Beauty of Aqua

I remembered that bear trap I'd previously avoided with my comments about chị Giang but now felt it was close by.

We soon found ourselves a good spot to catch our evening meal. Thủy was well-versed in fishing for the snakehead and quickly caught one. I scooped it up in the net which it almost ripped through trying to get free or its revenge on me. I took a hearty swing which my friend in the net seemed to sense, throwing its body out of the way of my club and that's when the bear trap snapped. I lost my balance and found myself covered head-to-toe in mud. Thủy came to my assistance quickly vanquishing my attacker then looked down to me.

"Anh khỏe không? Do you want me to go back up on the river bank and watch you try again?"

She knew my answer but her lesson required that I ask for her help. "Maybe I should catch the fish and let you club it."

She smiled. "Good choice anh. Please go on the river bank and I will club the fish."

My humiliation was complete. With Thủy's help I was able to catch a few and she with great skill finished them off each time with a single blow. It seemed she didn't want them to suffer by giving them the least painful end and for me to not suffer by having me safely on the river bank.

We soon caught what we needed and Thủy cleaned them as well as I'd ever seen someone clean a fish before. We returned to her house so I could clean up and change into something with a little less mud.

Last days

"There is a shower behind my house. The sun has heated the water and it will be warm."

I retrieved a fresh change of clothes and headed out back to the shower which was secluded away from the gaze of the road. There was an old fifty-five-gallon drum with traces of yellow lettering similar to every other possession owned by the US Army hinting that her father had repurposed it in to its current use. The only markings on it I could read were "2,4,5-T." I showered, cleaned myself up and dressed well for the night's ceremony.

Thủy was preparing the mì Quảng stock for our special meal ahead when she looked over to me. "Anh đẹp. You clean up well."

"Cảm ơn nhiều em."

While waiting for Thủy to finish cooking I took the time to lightly dust and remove any traces of previously burnt incense from the family-altar. It was a custom that I had recently started with chị Phương's family-altar since she sometimes had a difficult time walking up to the third-floor. When finished cleaning I lit a stick of incense, held it between my pressed palms and remained still for a moment. I found comfort in these simple acts. While I didn't fully understand what these altars meant I knew it was important to those I cared about so that was enough for me to always show respect in that special place. Unbeknownst to me my respect didn't go unnoticed by the family and friends within viewing distance.

On the kitchen table were a few dishes for tonight's "đám giỗ" or death-ceremony and meal. There was a tray

The Beauty of Aqua

of bright-yellow jackfruit and bananas, light-red and green papaya and deep-purple dragon fruit; all with their own rich smells. Another tray had bánh tết, bánh chưng and bánh nậm that we brought with us from the city and the most important dish of the night: Thủy's mì Quảng cá lóc which she had moved from the pot to a serving bowl. All favorites of her grandparents.

She was at peace because she was again "in her element" like many Vietnamese women are when they cook. With every step Thủy made sure that her soup not only met with her family's expectations but to those of her ancestors.

"Anh ơi!" Thủy called me over to the kitchen table. "Please take this tray and place it on the table by the front steps. Then please take the others." Like many Vietnamese women Thủy had no problem giving instructions, especially to men, when work had to be done. She finished her meal preparations then disappeared.

As instructed I moved the trays over to the table just outside the house. Tradition was to place these dishes outside and light incense so her ancestors would know she had taken the time to make them a meal that would bring them happiness. After the incense finished burning the food was brought back inside, placed on a table next to the family-altar where Thủy's mother read a few words from a yellowed piece of paper that must of been in the family for many years. Thủy was respectfully dressed in a well-tailored, dark-blue áo dài with silken, white pants. The food was then moved to the floor in front of us

Last days

where we sat and ate remembering those that came before us with every bite. Thủy's mì Quảng cá lóc, this offering to her grandparents, was the best bowl of mì Quảng I ever had.

After our meal we shared the hammock on the front porch and listened to the night. The early evening twilight was here and we were at peace.

"Cảm ơn nhiều em. That was the best bowl of soup in my life."

"Why anh?"

"If I could choose my last meal your mì Quảng cá lóc would be it. It was even better than what we had at Mì Quảng Bông. I sat there on the floor and from your stories I could see the lessons from your grandmother in my bowl. I'll never forget that bowl of soup for as long as I live. Cảm ơn nhiều em."

When a man and a woman can find great joy, never mind ecstasy, from the same meal it is a match made in heaven and, at that very moment, no man or woman could be closer. We didn't have to say we loved each other because we knew it in our hearts. I was in love with a woman that made the best bowl of mì Quảng in my life and I was truly fortunate.

The next day was spent mostly in a hammock on the front porch watching Thủy, her mother and a few women from the village making their preparations to cook a whole pig in a pit in the front yard. They carefully wrapped our dinner-to-be in dozens of large banana

The Beauty of Aqua

leaves after seasoning with traditional flavors. I wanted to help but knew it would be best to stay out of their way which I did from the comfort of my hammock. While a bit similar to a typical Cape Cod clambake I was useless for the task at hand. A bucket of ice and beer sat below my resting spot and I spent the day napping on and off which would be helpful for the party that night. Later that day the pig was finished cooking and its smell was seductive.

Soon that smell acted as an invitation for the community to join us which they did. While there was no shortage of beer many were kind enough to bring even more. Last night's ceremony was meant to be for family but tonight was for the community to join us in this remembrance of Thủy's grandfather and grandmother. Where the night before had a somber tone with personal stories of the departed this night would definitely not be quiet.

A few large, folding tables leaned against the bamboo home and were full of every dish you could imagine from around the Province of Quảng Nam with our friend the pig as tonight's star. Close to forty people were there eating and drinking. While not only sharing stories of Thủy's grandparents they were also sharing stories from their own lineage. Buckets of ice and bowls of nước mắm and nước chấm were on every little, plastic table with local children helping out by quickly refilling both as needed. Multi-colored lights intertwined with warm, incandescent bulbs used for Tết were hung above us.

Thủy walked out with a large platter of freshly made bánh xèo or "sizzle cake" with the same nước chấm dipping sauce as the bánh nậm which was cleaned off before she could put the tray down. Thủy excelled above most in a few dishes including that one which was evident by the speed in which it was quickly finished by those lucky enough to get some.

Then there was the beer. An ever-present staple of every Vietnamese celebration and I was happy to see there was plenty of my cherished Larue. While I couldn't understand what was being said I could tell everyone was happy. Partly from being with their community, partly from the amazing food Thủy, her mother and the community made and of course the continually flowing beer. This went on for hours well into the night.

After much food and drink I found it was time to take a break and walk. Everyplace in the world has its own unique 'nooks and crannies' that are one to themselves and that part of Hội An was no different. Where Đà Nẵng was a city being reborn nothing like that could be found here. The dirt road beneath my feet might've been here unchanged for hundreds of years. Old growth trees enshrouded my path blocking out much of the moonlight above but there was something ahead lighting the way forward. I approached and saw an old man sitting on a rock. He looked at me and said, "Hello child."

"Do you speak English?"

"I am speaking to you and you can hear me." The man before me was in his eighties wearing farmer's clothes and holding on to a cane with a red rag tied around the top. He appeared to be at peace and content to be where he was at that moment.

"You're English is very good. Where'd you learn it from?"

"I learned from others." He shifted his position on the rock. "Why are you here on this path child?"

"I was just at a death-ceremony for a friend's grandfather down the road."

"I know that family well. Con Thủy is your friend."

"She is. Were you there? I don't remember seeing you."

"You did not see me but I was there. I saw you at the family-altar." He adjusted his seat again. "There is a story in my country about a young scholar. One day when he was a foreigner in a foreign land he met a special woman also from a distant land. They fell in love and he begged her to show him her home. She said it was very far away and time went by much slower than where that traveller was from. If he went with her he would lose everything from his life before they met. He went and they stayed together but he missed the place from where he came. She told him that if he left he could not return to that slow-land but the traveller longed for his previous life. He left and returned to the land of his birth which now seemed foreign and where all traces of his previous life had disappeared. He walked away never to be seen again."

"What happened to the traveller uncle?" Calling someone "uncle" is seen as a way to show respect to an older man that is close to you and your family. He wasn't my uncle but at that moment he felt like he was.

"It does not matter what happened to the traveller but about his choice to return to the land of his birth."

"He was sad because he missed his old life."

"And he was told there were only memories there but he still went anyways. He gave up a life of joy in that slow-land for something that he knew was already gone. When you find a new place that you love you will not be at peace until you let go of the past."

"How do you let go of the past uncle?"

"By remembering it but not being attached to it. Remembering means celebrating the past and attachment is wishing for its return. The first will bring you happiness and the second will bring you sadness." He stood up with the help of his cane. "Please tell con Thủy I love her and she will be fine."

With that the old man walked away into the night. I wanted to follow him into the dark but didn't.

It was early in the morning and I had once again been awoken by the call of a neighborhood rooster. There was a pot of ginger tea on a still warm, cast-iron trivet in the kitchen, to which I helped myself to a cup, then walked out to the front porch to enjoy the early sunrise. Thủy must of heard me from her side of the small home and soon joined me also with a cup of tea in hand.

"Xin chào buổi sáng anh. Did you sleep well?"

"Chào buổi sáng em. Dạ; cảm ơn em." I thought about my conversation with the old man. "I met an old man on the path behind your home last night. He said he knew your family well and knew we were friends. He told me I have to celebrate the past and not be attached to it."

"Dạ anh; the old man gave you good advice."

"He asked me to tell you he loved you and you will be fine."

"Do you remember his name? What did he look like?"

"He didn't say his name but he used a cane with a red rag tied around it."

Thủy warmly smiled. "That was my grandfather anh. He came to you to help you with your pain. My grandfather understood what happiness was and lit the path he found with the hope others would find their way too."

"Không em; your grandfather is dead. It couldn't have been him."

"He is alive in my memories of him and with the stories I told you about his life he is now alive in you. He wants you to be happy."

I thought about what she said. Thủy had told me so many stories about the good times she had spent with her grandfather and those stories in deed had become part of me; a good part of me. "Vâng em."

Thủy looked at me with a smile. "My grandfather was from the North and that is what he would have said too. See anh, he is now part of you."

"If so then that part of me is saying I'm hungry. Anh và em đi ăn sáng không?" I already knew her answer to my question. Breakfast was our favorite meal of the day because after a good bowl of soup you were awake, refreshed and had the entire day to remember that last, glorious bite that made you smile.

"Dạ anh; anh và em đi ăn cao lầu." Within a flash she already knew what she wanted. Thủy's English was outstanding but when it came to eating many times she defaulted to her native language. That's how deep the food traditions run here. The problem was we were in farm country and I didn't know anyone who was cooking cao lầu but I suspected she had someplace in mind and it'd be good.

"Where'd you want to go?"

Thủy had one special smile and a gleam in her eyes when she thought of the most enjoyable meals of her life. "Chợ Hội An. My grandmother use to have an áo dài shop there and when I was little she would take me to a friend's cao lầu stall." She had that gleam in her eyes. "It is very good."

Throughout the last year Thủy and I had been on the greatest culinary adventures of my life. We ate bún chả in the Old Quarter of Hà Nội, bún bò Huế in chợ Đông Ba in Huế City and mì Quảng in Đà Nẵng. These places not only served the best foods but reminded her of some of the best times of her life.

"Wait here anh and I will get the family motorcycle." Thủy ducked underneath her home and returned pushing a well-worn but original Russian Minsk motorcycle. I remember seeing them on the news during the recent Soviet-Afghan War where many times the driver could be seen with a rocket launcher strapped to his back. Another war relic like the water tank for the shower but this one was "liberated" from the other side. I was impressed.

"Your motorcycle?"

"Dạ anh; this is the motorcycle my grandfather taught me to ride on. I have spent many, many hours riding the small roads around my village." She had a smile from those memories and I understood why. I too spent much of my youth riding on the trails and beaches of Cape Cod and found peace in that solitude. I also sometimes found excitement.

We mounted-up and left. Thủy was driving slower and more cautiously than normal while everyone but those on bicycles were passing us and I had to know the reason why. I spoke up so she could hear me over the whine of the two-stroke engine spinning below us.

"Why are we going so slow?"

She leaned back and loudly said, "Police."

"But what about everyone passing us?"

"The police do not know them. The police know me and my motorcycle. They know me well."

Thủy later explained that she could be difficult to deal with as a teenager and riding offered her an outlet for her frustrations. Occasionally during her many hours of riding on the small roads around her village she'd challenged herself with a hard ride and in return attracted the attention of the local police. Sometimes she stopped to talk with them and sometimes she didn't, a choice not uncommon to other motorcyclists including myself. I could imagine this diminutive rider taking jump after jump scrambling to get away with the sounds of sirens in the distance like a hard-core racer up Pike's Peak. She drove a motorcycle like she conducted herself, cooked and walked: with skill and grace.

In my youth I too chose a couple of times to run but that was me on 400 pounds and two wheels versus about 4,000 pounds, including the weight of the driver, and four wheels. Hardly fair to the police back home but here it was motorcycle versus motorcycle and the police were top-notch riders. She was every bit as good as them and they knew it.

Now she was a responsible member of the Party and a respected translator for the Ministry of Foreign Affairs but that still didn't stop them from once in awhile stopping her to talk about the "good old days" which she now handled like the upstanding member of society she had become.

We found a spot to park near the market on đường Bạch Đằng along the Thú Bồn River. It was early and the stalls inside of Hội An Market were still closed. The morning sun had just passed the horizon and its warmth was welcomed after our ride. Women lined the street selling the catch of the day that was retrieved just a few hours earlier. Thủy took my arm in hers and guided us over to a simple food stall on the southeast side of the market much like those in chợ Đông Ba in Huế City. She caught sight of the woman she was looking for behind a small, plastic table and steaming pot of soup.

"Chị ơi!" The woman recognized Thủy and called her over. We sat and after a few words between them we were served. Before us was a simple bowl of cao lầu. Not as fancy as other places but was still very inviting. Thủy motioned to my bowl. "Kính mời anh." She dived into her soup and without another word would be gone until she was finished. With every bite I could see Thủy remembering when she was a child and for that moment her grandmother was sitting next to her in this special place. Her invitation was for me to join her in this moment of bliss which I happily did.

After finishing our soup and Thủy said goodbye to her friend. We walked towards the shops on the west side of the market stepping around the vendors setup on the ground around us.

Chợ Hội An or Hội An Market was a collection of orange-yellow brick and concrete dry goods shops some over one-hundred years old. While there was building almost everywhere in Đà Nẵng there was no desire to do the same here. It was a throwback to a slower time and was as peaceful as the expression on Thủy's face.

"Did you like your soup?"

"Anh thích, cảm ơn em. It was like chị Giang's cao lầu she makes on Sunday mornings."

"Dạ anh; I know that but the woman that made our cao lầu is not as attractive as chị Giang."

There's that bear trap again. "I only look at you and no one else."

Thủy smiled. "Good choice anh."

We meandered from alley to alley to absorb this ancient collection of shops selling dried foods like rice and wheat and others selling clothing. Thủy looked over to an áo dài shop ahead of us with an old woman setting up for the morning. Thủy called out to her. "Chị ơi!" The woman turned and smiled. "That was my grandmother's áo dài shop and that woman was her friend for many years. This is the only woman I go to when I want a new dress." The shop owner welcomed us in and gave Thủy a big hug. The two immediately started a conversation I had no hope of following. This wasn't the first time this had happened and I'd found it was best to find something to keep my attention until she was finished which wasn't a problem here.

The simple and very old, four-meter-wide shop was painted an orange-yellow like its neighbors and reached back to the alley behind us. The walls were also painted a matching orange-yellow color and there were four tightly packed rows of every imaginable color of bright, silken fabric running from front to back with two rows down the middle leaving little room to move. The old, wooden shelves were stained from age and the annual floods. On my side was every shade of red, orange and yellow surrounding me leaving only a narrow path out. On the other wall was an array of blues, greens and purple, silken fabric. All for a single purpose: to make the iconic áo dài.

Thủy soon joined me in that cramped space which was both comfortable and not. She started looking at the red bundles of fabric and pulled out one with embroidered orange and yellow flowers. After inspecting it she held it up in front of her. "Anh thích không?"

I said the first thought that came to me. "The fabric is beautiful but not as beautiful as you." Thủy's real beauty came from within and anything she thought looked good on her only accentuated her beauty.

"Cảm ơn anh. Which one do you like?"

"I like the colors here: the reds, oranges and yellows. They remind me of you."

"Why anh?"

I whispered in her ear. "Because I'm in love with a fire rooster." She smiled and we left. We rarely spoke such words out loud because we said them silently every time we ate the same, great meals together. When you see that special person in your life enjoying the same, great food that also brings you joy, you are happy for them and they are happy for you. That is a love without words.

"I enjoyed visiting my grandmother's shop when I was a child."

"Everyone likes seeing their grandmother."

"Dạ anh but also because of the fabrics here. Every time I walked in I felt like I was walking through a rainbow and I would find many beautiful colors and patterns. The áo dài is very important to my country and my grandmother helped protect that custom. I think of her every time I put one on and I think about the traditions behind that dress." Thủy knew that every time she put an áo dài on she wasn't only representing herself or her family but also her ancestors and what they held dear to their hearts.

We spent the next few hours wandering the back alleys taking in this very old and slow place when we once again became hungry.

"Em ăn cơm không?" I knew the answer but still had to ask. Thủy again had that look in her eyes like with breakfast.

"Anh và em đi ăn bánh mì Phương." She quickly took my arm in hers and we headed down the street. In Đà Nẵng we never walked arm-and-arm but Thủy seemed more comfortable here which made me happy.

We returned back to Thủy's home where she and her mother took the Minsk to visit friends leaving me to spend much of the rest of the day napping on and off in the hammock on the front porch.

Later that afternoon I was woken by the smells of something good cooking from inside. Thủy and her mother had grilled some of the pork they'd put aside before our guest of honor was placed in his pit to make bún thịt nướng ở Đà Nẵng: charcoal grilled pork with cold rice noodles, fresh salad greens, mint, basil, bean sprouts, spring rolls and, of course, nước mắm and finally topped with roasted peanuts. And bún heo, a pork and rice noodle soup with a rich, warm broth that offered us a nice contrast. We feasted on those and various treats leftover from the celebration the night before. It created the perfect conditions for a pleasant afternoon nap.

The sun had set and the evening twilight was here where I once again found myself in the hammock appreciating this old and quiet place when I was called.

"Anh ơi!" It was Thủy.

The Beauty of Aqua

"We are leaving soon. Are you ready?"

"I forgot about tonight. Where're we going again?"

"To the old town in Hội An to watch the lanterns on the river. It is time to go." I saw Thủy and her mother getting their helmets on which caused me to think.

"How are we getting there?"

"On the Minsk. It is too far to walk."

"But there's three of us?"

"Dạ anh; you can ride in the middle."

Before coming here I'd never seen a man ride pillion on a motorcycle with a woman driving and I certainly wasn't excited about being in seat two out of three on this trip. I was about to say something when I knew my objections would be quietly dismissed. Matt's advice about "living like a local" were again haunting me. There was only one response I could give: "Dạ em."

The ride was a strange experience in a long line of strange experiences I had over the last year. We arrived in the old town of Hội An and parked the Minsk. The three of us quietly walked through the streets in the cool, night air. Thủy's mother soon left us telling Thủy she was going home with a friend so we could stay out late.

Hội An was beautiful during the day and stunning at night. Almost every shop had brightly colored lanterns hanging from their second-floor balconies. The soft candlelight from those lanterns accented the orange-yellow walls found throughout that very old village.

The nearby Thú Bồn River was filled with lanterns illuminated by tea candles floating in the darkness. Thủy and I walked arm-in-arm along the river bank with the full moon gently lighting the path ahead.

"Lighting these lanterns reminds us of our ancestors. We like to think when they see the light from the lanterns they will know they are remembered."

"Do you think they see them?"

"Maybe anh. I think there is more in the sky above and around us on this land than can be explained by only what we have been taught. I know my ancestors live in my heart and maybe someplace else where they are happy." Thủy motioned to a nearby child selling lanterns. "We should light a lantern for our ancestors." We paid the child for our lanterns which we lit and walked over to the river bank. "Think of your ancestors and place your lantern in the river." With that our lanterns were set adrift.

"Who did you think of anh?"

I smiled. "My mother and brother. Em?"

"My family that I remember every day in my home."

We continued our walk along the river bank watching hundreds of multi-colored lanterns float by us each with the hope that their ancestors would be reminded they weren't forgotten. It was a magical night. We had been transported to—I stopped.

"Anh khỏe không?"

I now understood what the old man told me. "This is the slow-land the old man told me about last night."

"What anh?" Thủy was confused.

I stood still and looked around me at this ancient and beautiful place, this slow-land: I was the traveller and Thủy the woman from the slow-land.

We continued our walk along the Thú Bồn River back to the old city where we saw a lantern shop on đường Nguyễn Hoàng that caught our eye. There was a beautiful white, bamboo-paper lantern with a rooster in a fiery red, orange and yellow. We stood there to appreciate it.

"Do you like that lantern anh Upton?"

"Dạ em but it's too big to take it with me."

"Không sao anh. I will hold it for you and you can have it when you come back."

According to anh Dũng my visa required I return to the West with no promise of return to Việt Nam and nothing had changed but this wasn't the time to bring up that unpleasant subject.

"Cảm ơn em. Hang it in your home because it's as beautiful as you." To me Thủy was the most beautiful woman in the world and I was going to remind her of that every day.

I was awoken the next morning by a neighborhood rooster but by his call I think it might of been a different one from the day before. It was our last morning in Hội An before we returned to Đà Nẵng. I headed out to the front porch like before to watch the sunrise where I saw Thủy sitting. She was well-dressed with some flowers and a box of incense.

"Chào buổi sáng em. Em khỏe không?"

She gave a lukewarm response. "Em khỏe." She wasn't fine.

"Em không khỏe."

Last days

"I will be fine. I must go visit my brother before we leave today. Will anh please come with me?" This was the first time she'd returned to her village to visit the grave of her brother since the funeral.

"Dạ em; không sao."

We took a short walk to the far side of the property where there was a small, family graveyard. In Việt Nam you keep your family close to you in both life and death. Thủy walked across the uneven ground and reverently approached her brother's grave. It was the only new addition to this place compared to the mostly very old graves that surrounded us. It sat next to their father's grave.

On the headstone was a relief of a boat anchor, traditional for fisherman both here and back West, Ngô's name, year of birth, date of his death and his "Buddhist name." This was a tradition where adherents would receive a name that was either reflective of their talents or given with the hope the same could be nurtured in them. Ngô's Buddhist name was "Phổ Minh" or one who freely shares his knowledge with others. Like many here Thủy's family weren't practicing Buddhists but would go to a local pagoda on high holidays.

Thủy placed the flowers on the grave and lit two sticks of incense, handing one to me, and we stood quietly for a moment. I could see her doing her best to hold back her tears. After their father died Thủy and her brother had a turbulent yet loving relationship which made her loss difficult. We soon left.

The Beauty of Aqua

I could see that the last few days had taken their toll on her both physically and emotionally so I suggested we sneak away to a little cafe I saw down the street before we returned to Đà Nẵng. Thủy wasn't doing well. We soon found the cafe and ordered. She looked down to her tea with an empty look in her eyes.

"Em khỏe không?" I asked with concern.

"Em khỏe." She paused. "I am fine but have some sadness. This will pass."

"How do you know?"

"Because it always does and it always will. I will eat a good bowl of soup and I will be happy again."

"Dạ em; I also find happiness in a good bowl of soup but sometimes it's not enough. I'm happy here but I'm tired of trying to be happy." The weight of leaving Việt Nam had been taking its toll on me.

Thủy spoke her next words without looking up. "One time I was very sad and that sadness would not leave me. Five years ago after we had the same ceremony for my grandfather all I could think about was how my grandfather, grandmother and father were gone. My mother has the same sadness inside of her as we have inside of us. She knew how I felt but there was nothing she could do to help. I always felt better—" She started choking on her next words. "I always felt free when I rode my motorcycle so I rode to the Hải Vân Pass but—but I was so sad I could barely breath when I—" She started to cry. "—when I saw a fuel truck coming towards me I crossed the center of the road, steered in to its path and let go of my handlebars. I wanted to die." Tears were

Last days

now streaming down her face.

The long shadows of the setting sun were getting longer on that warm, Cape Cod summer evening and Matt and I were finishing our ride. For the last few weeks we'd been rebuilding the transmission on my Super Hawk and we talked; a lot. Matt had recently resurfaced after going missing for a couple of years and we had just gotten his motorcycle out of mothballs. He was there for me when mom and Beall died and it was good to have him back. I'd confided in him that I was starting to become tired of living and thankfully he listened. I suspected he already knew.

It was late when we finished our ride so he let me spend the night on an old sofa in his garage. The next morning his home was empty and what few items he owned and his motorcycle were gone. I smiled because I knew this was what made him happy and this time he'd soon be back.

Seeing it was time to go I pushed my Super Hawk out and reached into the leather saddlebag to get my gloves when I found a book wrapped in newspaper. I opened it and read the note:

"Upton, Every life has a story and this is yours.
Matt."

In that journal book were the personal stories Matt had written down from my friends and how my life had made their lives better. Matt wanted me to see that my life had value.

I was again torn apart when I thought about Thủy dying.

"What happened?"

"I closed my eyes to let fate decide if I should live or die. Then I heard my grandfather's voice say: 'I love you child. You will be fine.' I woke up on the side of the road. I was hurt, my motorcycle was badly damaged but I was alive. Sitting there I thought about what my grandfather would want me to do and I saw the answer." She paused, shifted her posture towards me, stared right into my eyes and with a firm voice said, "That I, and you anh Upton, must every day take joy in our fight for happiness and we must always revolt against our sadness. When our sadness seems too great we must follow those passions that bring us joy and avoid what takes us away from the same. There are others that have struggled with a sadness like ours and more will come. My grandfather understood what happiness was and lit the path he found with the hope others would find their way too. When we do the same our descendants will thank us every time they see our photographs on their family-altar."

Where many western philosophies touted the biographies of "great men" as guides for life the Vietnamese instead remember not those that were well-known to many but those that were well-known to them: their family. It is not abstract stories of joy and sadness that move them but the same from the most important people in their lives. This was what made them mighty but that was Thủy's path in life and not mine.

"I'm from the West. My picture won't be on anyone's family-altar. Being remembered is not my fate."

"You now believe in fate?"

"It's just what's obvious. I will have to leave here soon and might not be allowed to come back. We might not see each other again."

"'Que será, será. Whatever will be, will be. The future's not ours to see'."

I smiled. "Em và anh không ăn sáng. Em và anh đi ăn bánh canh không?" When in doubt offer food and we hadn't eaten breakfast.

Thủy smiled. "Dạ anh; em thích bánh canh."

I smiled. "I knew that em."

We'd seen a bánh canh cart on the way to the cafe that looked enticing so we started our walk back.

"We should work on your Vietnamese language."

"Why em? I'm leaving soon and I'll be alone."

"Please do not close that door anh. 'Que será, será'."

"'Whatever will be, will be'."

For the last year Thủy had not only been my voice as my translator but also my teacher to helping me understand what and what was not happiness. She gained strength every time she stood in front of her family-altar, lit a stick of incense and remembered her ancestors with the smell of the incense helping reinforce those memories. This was her tradition and sadly not one obtainable to us in the West.

The Beauty of Aqua

12

Exit

"Yết đế, yết đế, Ba la yết đế. Ba la tăng yết đế Bồ đề tát bà ha."

It was very late in the evening and a heavy fog had encompassed Đà Nẵng. The far-off sounds of a Buddhist nun chanting with an occasional, single ring from her pagoda's bell echoed throughout our quiet streets. A few lights leftover from Tết were left on which cast my street in a faint, multi-color glow. I sat quietly on a little, plastic stool outside of my home thinking about how I would have to leave here in three short days when I heard a familiar voice.

"Hello child."

I was surprised to once again see the old man from Hội An. This time he was wearing a traditional men's brown áo dài with white pants and a white cloth wrapped in a circle around the top of his head. The clothing older men wore to funerals.

"Hello uncle. What are you doing here?"

"I also live here with my family." With the help of his cane he sat down on a little, plastic stool next to me. "When we first met I asked you why you were on the path you were on but you did not answer my question."

"I told you I'd just come from a death-ceremony."

"I was not asking about the footpath where we met but the path your life had taken you from the West to my country."

"I'm here by chance. It's not a path I chose."

"But you did choose the path you are on. We all choose the path we are on if we know it or not. You chose to come here. Why child?"

I had to think. "Because I was unhappy and thought I might find some happiness here."

"Why are you sad?"

"My father and I will never live together again. My mother and brother are dead. I've lost my family home and my friends."

"Why else are you sad?"

"Because I will lose the good life I have here. Because I will miss Thủy. Because I have to leave here." I could feel my pulse getting faster.

"Are you sure child? Could it be something else? Look deep and tell me your sadness."

Exit

I had to admit to my and everyone's greatest fear. A fear so terrifying we as human beings do everything we can to forget it exists. We drown out that fear with superstition, excessive consumption, constant distractions and intoxicants. "I'm afraid that I'll be forgotten after I die. I'm afraid I will be abandoned." The admission of that was relieving.

"How will staying here change that child?"

"Because you remember your ancestors."

"When we remember our ancestors we find great comfort and strength but you will not be at peace until you travel to one more, far-off land. A place where there is no time, a place with no happiness or sadness, a place that is void and without form. Go there and then you will be at peace child."

"How do I get there uncle?"

The old man stood up with the help of his cane with its red rag tied around the top. "Did you tell con Thủy that I loved her and she will be fine?"

"Yes uncle; I did. She smiled when I told her your message."

"Thank you child. Good night."

"Hẹn gặp lại chú."

He paused, "Yes child. I will see you again." With that the old man walked down the street and around the corner.

After being here for the last year I'd found myself waking early like many others. Since I was no longer teaching I sat on my balcony on that beautiful morning engaged in a favorite past-time: watching the world unfold from my perch while drinking a glass of coffee. Soon a small pebble gently tapped my leg and I heard a giggle from below.

"Anh ơi!"

It was Thủy and she radiated more than usual. I headed downstairs to greet her.

"Chào buổi sáng. Em khỏe không?"

Her face had already answered my question. "I am very fine. Cảm ơn anh."

"Why are you so happy?"

"Because my grandfather visited me last night and he wanted me to tell you 'I love you child. You will be fine'."

I smiled. "Cảm ơn em Thủy."

While we hadn't received our marriage license it seemed the memories of her ancestors didn't care and had welcomed me into their family. Where I once felt alone that feeling was nowhere to be found on that day.

"Em ăn bánh canh không?"

"Dạ anh; em thích bánh canh."

I smiled. "I knew that em."

We walked down to chị Linh's home for one of our last meals together.

"I'll miss chị Linh's soup when I leave."

"Now is not the time to talk about that anh Upton. 'The future's not ours to see.' It is better to enjoy your soup now and worry about the future when it comes. I think we will be fine."

Exit

"What makes you think that?"

"Because my grandfather told me so. I have faith in the lessons of my ancestors and our community."

She was right. She could see things I could not.

"Dạ em; no more talk about the future."

We sat and without a word we were served and ate. Chị Linh smiled when she again saw us briefly holding hands.

I spent the rest of the morning packing up much of my life for my return to the West. Later while finishing my daily nap I was once again beckoned from below.

"Cháu ơi!"

I looked down from my balcony to see anh Dũng. He looked happy.

"Cháu uống cà phê không?"

"Dạ anh; một phút xin." I headed downstairs locking the house and gate behind me.

"Xin chào buổi trưa anh Dũng."

"Chào buổi trưa cháu. Good cháu, you remembered to lock your gate. I have many papers for you to sign before you leave. Maybe we should drink some coffee?"

"Dạ anh; let's go down to Cafe 47.

"Very well cháu. I will drive." With that we got on his Super Cub and headed down the street.

Anh Dũng spoke to the cafe owner and told her I was leaving. She said it made her happy that I enjoyed her coffee so much and so often.

That was a common theme here. I found that when I went to a food cart for the first time the owner was happy to see a westerner enjoying what she made. The second time there was even more joy because she knew I wanted what she was cooking. In the case of chị Giang, where I ate three or four breakfasts a week, it became personal. She knew exactly how I liked my bún bò Huế ở Đà Nẵng and started preparing it the moment she saw me walking towards her home. All I had to do was to sit quietly and wait a few moments for my bowl of nirvana to arrive. Her food made me very happy which also made her very happy.

We sat close to the cafe under a banana tree for some shade.

"This is paperwork from my government that I need you to sign before you leave if you please."

"It's in Vietnamese anh. I can't read it."

"No problem cháu. Just sign where you see your name if you please."

I went ahead and signed. Anh Dũng's obligations to his employer, the Vietnamese Government, had never gotten in the way of our friendship. Maybe because we had the same values and the same hope for a better country.

"What did I just sign?"

He held up the top stack of papers. "These are to acknowledge that your contract with the university is finished and you agree with their performance review."

"Performance review?"

Exit

Anh Dũng showed me another form. "Let me finish if you please. This is stating that if you are offered another position at the university you agree to return."

"That'd be great but I don't know if they'll have me back. Maybe if I could read the performance review I just signed."

Anh Dũng pulled out yet another form. "This is an offer for you to teach for two years which you have just accepted. Congratulations cháu."

"But you said teachers could only get a one year visa. How can I teach for two years?"

"Again, let me finish if you please. This is a completed visa application for your return."

"And it's already approved? How did that happen without my passport or signature?"

"There were people in your community that wanted to help you so those issues were overlooked. Anh Dũng leaned towards me. "It is better to be a good person and not just a good citizen."

"How long is the visa for?"

"Two years. You are still required to return to Canada but you will be able to come back to Việt Nam."

"How did I qualify for a two year visa?"

He put the papers down and smiled. "Because you are the spouse of a Vietnamese citizen."

"Không anh."

"You will be tomorrow. Again, congratulations cháu. This is your approved application to marry cháu Thủy. You need to be at Đà Nẵng city hall tomorrow afternoon when they open. Do not be late."

The wet pavement under my motorcycle had now turned to gravel and I couldn't stop. With the frequent warnings of danger ahead long gone I rode full throttle over the side of the cliff in front of me and couldn't be happier.

"I can't believe you were able to do this for me. Cảm ơn nhiều anh Dũng."

"You are welcome cháu. You need to have faith in your community and when you do you will see that many things are possible. It is very difficult for westerners to understand never mind adapt to Vietnamese culture but you did. You have shown respect for our culture and that has been noticed by everyone around you."

"I've enjoyed living here and I like my neighbors."

"And they like you too."

I thought about his response. "How would you know?"

"I was asked to make sure you were safe so I talked to your neighbors about you on a regular basis. Please understand we had your best interests in mind." Anh Dũng once again was looking out for me just like my uncle would.

"Cảm ơn anh."

"You should go now and tell em Thủy. Would you like a ride?"

"Dạ không cảm ơn anh. I'll walk."

"I will see you tomorrow for your marriage reception and the next day to take you to the airport."

The all too happy news anh Dũng brought me still had that difficult ending that was almost here. I soon arrived at Thủy's home and looked up to her room on the second-floor.

"Em ơi!"

Thủy walked out on the balcony wearing a white áo dài with lotus flowers along the front with silken, white pants.

"Em rất đẹp."

She gave a gentle smile like only she could. "Cảm ơn anh."

"May I come in em?"

"Dạ anh; please come in."

I walked in and greeted her mother. "Xin chào buổi trưa chị Ngọc."

"Chào buổi trưa cháu Upton."

Thủy soon joined us with chị Ngọc leaving us alone and I removed the marriage license from my pocket. "Will you translate this for me?"

She read the paper and started to cry. "It is our marriage license!"

"Dạ em; so will you still marry me?"

"Of course I will! We must tell my mother." Thủy looked over to the kitchen. "Mẹ ơi!"

"Dạ con."

Thủy ran over to her mother, showed her the marriage license and then both came back. Thủy and her mother exchanged a few words. "My mother is happy you will be part of our family and knows that your mother died. She understands your pain and hopes that you can think of her as your second mother."

I was touched by this act of kindness. Thủy's mother had always been kind to me and we shared an appreciation of the same, great foods. Plus she was the second best cook I knew.

"Cảm ơn mẹ hai."

She smiled. "Không có chi con."

Following tradition the next day Thủy and I spent the morning apart at our respective homes. She told me she'd start the day by cleaning and decorating her family-altar in preparation for our wedding-ceremony. Then she would help the women in the neighborhood cook for our meal for that evening's festivities.

On that day of our wedding I sat on my balcony in nervous anticipation when I saw a beautiful and calming site: Thủy had just rounded the corner wearing her wedding áo dài. The dress was the same bright-red shade as the flag of her country with a bright-yellow ribbon, also in the same shade as the flag, that ran along the top seam. Accenting that perfection, she was wearing the traditional circular headwear in the same bright-red color of her dress and carrying a bright red, orange and yellow bouquet of flowers. She looked like what every Vietnamese bride dreamt of: to be the most beautiful woman in the world. I rushed downstairs and to the street to greet my bride. "Chào em. Em rất đẹp."

We noticed chị Giang across the street in front of her home in a formal áo dài in preparation for this afternoon's reception. She looked at us with approval.

Thủy smiled and saw an opportunity to see if I'd remembered my previous lesson concerning our friend.

"Cảm ơn anh. More beautiful than chị Giang?"

I had this one covered. "You are the most beautiful woman in the world." I said it because it was true. Then I whispered in her ear, "Anh yêu mì Quảng cá lóc em Thủy."

She smiled with approval. "I knew that anh. Please follow me."

Thủy and I took the short walk up to đường Nguyễn Thị Minh Khai where a brightly colored pedicab awaited to take us to city hall. We soon arrived with Thủy's mother leading the way. After some confusion we were directed by a city official to a small and simple room complete with the required government-issued table with chairs and flag. We signed the necessary forms, a city employee spoke a few words to us, none of which I understood, and we were married. We returned to our pedicab to complete the most important task of the day: to ask Thủy's ancestors for their blessing on our marriage.

My first night here in my city by the sea an old woman stopped to stare at this westerner on her street. I was a foreigner in a foreign land. While anh Dũng taught me a few numbers he also taught me how to show respect to the people of this country. He could not have been more correct on the importance of the use of pronouns in Vietnamese culture. When I saw myself as part of a community in Việt Nam the idea of not saying "anh" and "chị" became unthinkable and every time I remembered to use those pronouns I was accepted a little bit more into my community. As my community saw my respect for them they opened their hearts and lives to me. Our community was preparing to celebrate our wedding that evening but first we needed to return to Thủy's home.

Our small procession of family and friends made its way upstairs to Thủy's family-altar-room for a brief ceremony and to make an offering to her ancestors along with asking for their blessing on our marriage.

The room was small and brightly lit from the afternoon sun. The only furniture in it was a waist-height credenza topped with a family-altar with a half-dozen photographs of departed loved ones all in light-blue backgrounds. Thủy and I carried some freshly prepared food and fruit stopping to place them on the altar. Bright light streamed in from the open windows highlighting the smoke from the burning incense. Its smell intermixed with the dishes of food and lemon blossoms from just outside the tightly packed room. Thủy also respectfully placed on the family-altar a small statue of a rooster ablaze in a fiery red, orange and yellow. We stood in silence in front of the altar with our palms pressed together, holding a stick of incense for a minute or so while a family friend spoke a few words to solemnize our marriage. We were now husband and wife.

"The rooster is for us?"

"Dạ anh; we are both fire roosters. It is a reminder of our passion for many things including each other."

"And a reminder to always follow our passions?"

Thủy smiled and meekly replied, "Dạ anh; it is also a symbol of our hope that we remain together to at least the year of the metal rooster."

"When is that?"

"Many, many years from now."

During the ceremony I had noticed photographs from my photo album of my mother and brother on the family-altar but waited to ask Thủy about them. "Why are those photographs there?"

"We are now family and your mother's and brother's photographs are here so their lives will be remembered every day because their lives had value."

I felt a great sense of relief hearing how Thủy would help us protect the good memories of my family that were no longer here in life. When my mother and brother died the funerals were fast and we went right to work on burying our pain. First with a few days of expressing a profound sense of sadness and the rest of our lives living in denial of those same, dark feelings. But now the memories of those family members that had died return to us in this well-cared for place. Their photographs reassure us that we carry their strength inside of us but only when we remember them. While food had been a large part of my life here I now understood that every great meal I ate was made possible by the ancestors of those who first cooked it. In every great bowl of bánh canh, bún bò Huế or mì Quảng cá lóc were the lessons from the ancestors of the chef. She not only cooks for her family but the food must also be worthy of those who gave her those traditions. By eating the food we earlier place on the family-altar we again remember whence we came.

I finally understood an overriding ethos of this country: the people of Việt Nam must always labor on because that is what their ancestors would want from them. They remember that lesson every day by memorializing these ancestors in this special place in their homes.

This family-altar to their departed loved ones also reminds them that someday their photograph will also sit on that same altar and be cared for in the same, loving manner. That their photograph will someday serve as a reminder to their descendants not to give up trying to move forward in their lives and to always labor on no matter how difficult their lives had become. This tradition only required a person to believe in the value of their life and the lives of their ancestors and hopefully descendants. It's also a reminder that when we remember our ancestors we are never alone.

Then everything stopped and I could hear nothing. I was frozen-solid as I stood in front of our family-altar and I had a cathartic response to this one, singular thought: someday my photograph and Thủy's will also be on this same altar. Someday my picture and Thủy's will be the ones giving strength to our descendants so we must also always try to move forward in life for those yet to come. To remind me why I needed to never give up I only needed to look to the photographs on what is now our family-altar. Dad was right "When you remember your family you're never alone."

Thủy walked up behind me and put her hand on my shoulder. "You understand."

I paused, "How do you know?"

"Because it shows on your face. When life is lived from experience and not just knowledge it shows on a person."

"I thought about your photograph and my photograph on our altar."

"Someday our photographs will be there and they will be cared for by our descendants just like we do today. That way we will not be forgotten. There is a Vietnamese thought that says a person dies twice: the first time we die is when our bodies no longer have life. The second time we die is when we are forgotten by our ancestors. The lessons of our lives will be remembered long after our bodies cease to have life because of our traditions. This is what makes us strong in times of peace and in times of war. This is the way of the Vietnamese people."

A tear rolled down my cheek. Thủy gently brushed it aside and showed me the teardrop on her hand. "This is how I know you understand."

We returned to my home for our daily nap which would also be helpful for the night that was ahead.

After our nap and some quiet time we crossed the street to chị Giang's home where our wedding reception had started earlier. Our happy, little place in the world was illuminated with long strings of warm incandescent bulbs that had been hung across đường Lê Lai. The front of chị Giang's home was decorated with a large collection of multi-colored lights and bright-red, paper lanterns, also used during the Tết holiday, that were hung from her second-floor balcony. Nothing is wasted here.

The chrome-plated tables and chairs were polished and the street had been freshly washed down. Our neighbors greeted us with loud applause and cases of beer. Lots and lots of beer. There was already the start of a scattered rainbow of discarded Larue and Huda cans to which I know we'd be asked to contribute to that ever-growing collection below our feet. The sounds of the party could be heard throughout our street including the shouting of "Một, hai, ba, vô!" and "Một trăm!" or "Bottom's up!" signaling that there would be a long and happy night of drinking ahead.

Then came the food. It started with large plates of sticky rice topped with crushed peanuts, salt and sugar; large squares of bánh chưng and pyramids of bánh gio, both variations of sticky rice filled with pork and mung beans and seasoned with spring onion and, of course, nước mắm. Then plate after plate of fresh tiger shrimp with chili sauce followed by carefully prepared plates of fish, pork, duck and chicken. All the smells of those wonderful foods intertwined with the many bowls of nước chấm on every table creating a fog that added to the happiness of the night.

It was a party for the ages. I understood little beyond "Một, hai, ba, vô!" and the food but I felt at home because I was with my community. Thủy and I along with her mother sat at the head table and were served course after course. It was a feast fit for a Vietnamese emperor and it felt like our community was in paradise.

Thanks to Thủy's mother we were able to sneak away from the festivities that would be going on for many more hours. Thủy returned to her home and I unlocked the front gate and door to mine. Chị Phương wasn't there but had left a note in Vietnamese on the kitchen table. Thủy soon arrived at my home with a basket in hand.

"Xin chào anh Upton."

"Chào em Thủy. Em khỏe không?"

"Em khỏe."

"Em Thủy rất đẹp."

"Cảm ơn anh. You always say that—"

"—because it's always true."

Thủy smiled and I showed her the note from the kitchen table. "It says that chị Phương will not be home tonight." We again smiled to each other then I asked her about the basket she was holding.

"What's that em?"

"Something special. Please go upstairs and wait."

I went upstairs to my bedroom and again awaited in nervous anticipation. There were the sounds of a gas burner igniting and then cooking. Soon I heard her gentle footsteps coming up the stairs. What I saw was breathtaking. Thủy changed into the most beautiful áo dài I'd ever seen. From shoulders to feet she was covered in a fiery-red silk with orange highlights and silken, yellow pants. With all the grace that she had been taught since childhood she walked over to me and sat down. Before me was a bowl of soup with a plate of salad greens and a pot of tea. It was mì Quảng, the most beloved dish of the Province of Quảng Nam.

"I made you mì Quảng cá lóc and tea. It is tradition in my family for a wife to serve this meal to her husband on their first night as a married couple. This is a special moment." She then whispered in my ear: "Thương nhau múc bát chè xanh, Làm tô mì Quảng mời anh xơi cho cùng."

"What does that mean?"

She smiled and said, "I will translate later."

We listened to the sounds of the party below and shared the mì Quảng and tea Thủy made for us as husband and wife.

It was about five in the morning and a nearby rooster was happy to announce the new day. I walked over to my balcony as Thủy continued to sleep. Chị Giang was almost finished setting up her food cart for the morning. The smell from her fifty-liter stock pot of bún bò Huế brewing below entered our room which Thủy noticed in her half-awake state. "Bún bò không?"

I smiled. "Dạ em; em ăn bún bò không?"

"Em ăn bánh canh xin." She rolled over away from the balcony to finish her sleep.

Thủy and I had our favorite foods for different times because picking one favorite meal was like picking a favorite child. On special days we ate mì Quảng cá lóc because it was a long-time tradition in Thủy's family. When we were out late at night we ate bún bò Huế with its spiciness that made the rest of the night more enjoyable and breakfast together was bánh canh.

"Anh xin lỗi em. Không bánh canh. Chị Linh isn't here. She had to go to her home village in Kon Tum for her father's death-anniversary."

"Em thích Kon Tum. It is very peaceful there and the coffee is very good. There is something special there I want to show you. We will go there when you come back." Thủy rose from our bed and put on her robe. "We can eat bánh canh on đường Ba Đình. We should go." It was clear that Thủy had breakfast on her mind. As she dressed we talked.

"I'll miss you em Thủy."

"I will be with you everywhere you go when you remember me and remember our good times together."

"I'll miss the food too."

"I know anh Upton. All you have eaten in the last year is food from here. It will be difficult for you to adjust. Many Vietnamese have the same problem."

"I'm not Vietnamese."

"Your body was not born here but your heart was. When people see your heart that is what they will see. This is where your heart and your stomach will always be. It will be difficult for you to adjust to western food but you will endure until you return. How long do you think you will be gone?"

"Not long, about a month. While I wait for my new visa I'll visit my father and my village."

We left my home and entered the alley off of đường Ba Đình for one last time. We sat by the bánh canh cart and ordered our breakfast. Thủy cleaned our spoons wrapping them in the paper she used to clean them. This would be the last time we would dine together on the street and our sadness could be seen on our faces.

As I was taking one last look around the alley with its food carts that had brought me so many wonderful meals I once again caught sight of the bakery owner on her balcony. I tapped Thủy on her shoulder and motioned towards the bakery. The two previous times I saw this older and very beautiful woman, with her angelic smile, her eyes were gazed across the horizon but this time was different. Now she was looking at us with her reassuring smile as to say "everything will be fine."

Thủy smiled and the woman returned to her home. "We will be fine." Thủy paused choking on her words. "We will be fine if we remember what gives us strength in our darkest moments. With that we can survive any storm. That woman has seen many hardships but she still has a beautiful smile on her face and in her heart. It is what is expected by her, and our, ancestors." We ate in silence and started our walk back.

"We should first go to my home to visit my—our family-altar so our ancestors will be remembered."

The family-altar. A place I first saw with sadness is now a place of comfort. Until recently I had suppressed many of the memories of my mother and brother because every good memory was haunted by the bad ones but not in this place. On our altar their photographs sit where they can be remembered for the good they did while they were here and to serve as a reminder that their lives had value. With every incense stick I light and see my family's photographs I'm reminded that my photo, and

Thủy's, will also someday be on that same altar and given the same great care.

We arrived at Thủy's home and walked upstairs.

The room was small and brightly lit from the early-morning sun. We walked over to the waist-height credenza topped with a family-alter adorned with fruit that Thủy's mother had placed there earlier. On it were a half-dozen photographs of departed loved ones all in light-blue backgrounds and the pictures of my mother and brother. Bright light streamed in from the open windows along with the smell of lemon blossoms from just outside the room. Thủy removed two incense sticks from the side cupboard, lit them and handed one to me. Without a word we placed the incense between our pressed palms and remained still for a moment.

"I will remember your family when I remember mine."

"Cảm ơn em Thủy."

"Không sao anh. I am your friend and your wife. I do this for us." Thủy paused, her voice trembled a bit and her eyes teared up. "We should go now. Em yêu anh."

I reached over and wiped a tear from her cheek and showed it to her. "This is how I know you love me." We left the family-altar-room and headed downstairs.

"Here anh, this is for you when you get hungry."

"Anh thích xôi. Cảm ơn em."

She smiled. "I knew that anh."

Thủy had earlier picked up some sticky rice with crushed peanuts, sugar and salt she'd purchased from around the corner by a local grammar school. One of my favorites and the first meal I had when I came here so long ago. A simple dish served to children and beloved by most adults. It was a dish that opened my eyes to how something very simple could be very delicious.

We left Thủy's home and took one last walk back to mine. "You said that you wanted to stay married until the year of the metal rooster. When's that em?"

"Many, many years from now."

"That sounds like a lofty goal."

"It is not because we are best friends first and best friends are loyal to each other. We met in the year of the ox whose quality is loyalty to family. I believe you will be loyal to me and I promise the same to you."

"I never doubted that so long as you don't have to make a choice between me and our city."

Thủy smiled. "There is room in my heart for both of you."

"Would you like to visit my village someday?"

"Dạ anh; very much. I would like to visit were you were a child."

"I can't show you that because my family's home has been torn down."

"I would like to see your village and meet your friends. I want to hear about your life there and your family's lives. When we visit the places where you have good memories of your mother and brother for that moment they will be with us. Their memories will bring us comfort. We will visit their graves, light incense, stand quietly and think good thoughts about them so they will be remembered. Someday our children will do the same for us." She paused for an awkward moment. "Your village is Harwich, Massachusetts in America?"

I didn't know what to say. If I told her the truth I feared she would be in trouble but still spoke. "How did you know?"

"In your family photographs I saw a sign with the name of your village and found it in an atlas."

"I was born in Canada but I was raised in America. I was told not to say where I was from. I was afraid that you'd get in trouble for knowing and I'd be deported."

"I understand but now that we are married there can be no more secrets between us."

"Anh xin lỗi em. Is it fine that I am from America?"

"What matters is that you gave your heart to my country and I know you can never take it back. My country is now part of you. That is what matters."

When I came to Việt Nam I thought I knew who I was. What I thought was static and unchangeable was not. Matt was right about how living abroad is life-changing and living here made those changes for the better. How I looked at everything from the past and present had changed. As for the future I was reminded of Thủy sweetly singing "Que será, será." She was right; "the future's not ours to see." She was also right when she said happiness can always be found in a good bowl of soup.

I also became part of a beautiful community. I didn't speak their language but did show respect to their—our, customs and they soon welcomed me into their homes. These were people with few possessions but were always happy to share their family meal with me and every time that happened I felt honored.

Matt's thoughts on "living with less leads to a happier life", while denigrated in the West, was celebrated here and a lesson that also became part of me. The Vietnamese people have many fewer possessions than most westerners and seem to be happier without that burden.

We returned to my home for one last time where anh Dũng was waiting to take us to the airport. I said goodbye to chị Phương and thanked her, tossed my bags into the back of anh Dũng's UAZ and we started to head to the airport when chị Phương stopped us, spoke to anh Dũng for a moment and we left.

"Chị Phương khỏe không?"

"Chị Phương is fine. She said that she wants to move in with her son and asked if you and cháu Thủy were interested in renting her house when you come back. She said you should have a place big enough for children."

"I just got married yesterday."

"Part of your job as a husband is to have children. No better time than the present."

I laughed. "Em Thủy and I will talk about that when I come back."

"I do not think you can have children by just talking."

"You've always had that dry sense of humor. So what did you tell her about the house?"

"I said that you would be happy to rent her home and would take care of her family-altar."

"I'd be glad to do that but she's not taking it with her?"

"Không cháu; her home has been in her family for generations. The family-altar must be cared for every day because many of her family were born and died in that house. That is where their memories are."

"I promise I will."

"She would not have asked you to rent her house if she doubted that. She has seen how you have embraced our culture and respects you for it. The Vietnamese people take great pride in their culture and enjoy seeing others enjoy what we hold close to our hearts."

"I try to embrace that which is good. There are a lot of lessons I've learned from living here."

"Like what cháu?"

"Like not to look at another woman when you're with your girlfriend." I then felt a slap against my shoulder from Thủy and anh Dũng gave out a hearty laugh.

"Vâng cháu; when either driving a motorcycle or when you are with a Vietnamese woman it is better to keep your eyes strait forward to avoid an accident."

"It only takes once to learn that lesson."

At the airport anh Dũng and Thủy accompanied me through immigrations for the required exit-stamp on my passport officially marking my departure from Việt Nam.

Anh Dũng and Thủy spoke a few words then Thủy left us walking ahead towards departures.

"Here is a letter to present to the Vietnamese mission in Montreal requesting they issue you a new visa. It should insure that there are no problems. Do not lose this letter and do not wait too long to use it. You have family here waiting for your return."

He was right. I had family waiting for me here. Family, a simple yet comfortable home, doing the work I was good at and a bowl of soup was more than enough for me to be happy yet it took an eight-thousand mile move to learn that.

"Cảm ơn nhiều anh Dũng."

"Con Upton; I am no longer anh Dũng to you. Please call me chú Dũng." He smiled and continued. "Are you going back to America or staying in Canada?" I said nothing. "It was something I should have discussed with you but I forgot."

"You don't seem like the kind of person that would forget something like that."

"Vâng con; I am not."

I smiled. "Cảm ơn chú."

"You are welcome con Upton. Does em Thủy know where you are from?"

"She asked me about it this morning. She saw a photograph of a sign at the edge of my village with its name and looked it up in an atlas. I said she was right."

"What did she say?"

"She said that I gave my heart to this country and she knew I could never take it back. That's all that mattered."

"The people of Đà Nẵng have a long history of welcoming those who respect their city and removing those that do not. You are welcome here." He paused and smiled. "You are also welcomed in my family. I am very happy for both you and my niece."

"Cảm ơn nhiều chú."

Exit

"When you return to Montreal please thank anh François for the maple syrup and tell him I wish him well."

I thought about what he just said. "I never mentioned my uncle's name."

"That is correct con. You did not."

I smiled again.

Chú Dũng looked at the clock on the wall. "It is time for you to leave."

"Hẹn gặp lại chú."

"Bon voyage con Upton." He turned to leave then looked back. "Remember your uncle will be looking out for you." With that he was gone.

Thủy was waiting by the boarding ramp next to my plane. I paused before approaching her to appreciate one, last look at my wife and best friend. She was dressed in a favorite áo dài and radiated. I finally walked towards her. "I will miss you em Thủy."

She silently breathed and had tears in her eyes. "I will have some sadness without you anh Upton."

I pulled from my carry-on bag a book wrapped in newspaper and handed it to Thủy. She opened it and read the note:

"Thủy, Every life has a story and this is yours.
Upton."

In that journal book were the stories from our lives and the happiness we found together in our meals on the streets of the City of Đà Nẵng. She smiled when she read those stories.

"See you soon anh Upton."

"Hẹn sớm gặp lại em Thủy."

We kissed goodbye. While not long or deeply passionate it was a kiss that would never be forgotten. I turned and boarded my plane back to the West but I would soon return to Thủy.

Postscript

Places mentioned

Chị Giang's bún bò Huế
Quán Thảo
135 đường Trí Trạch, Phước Mỹ, Sơn Trà
Open mornings. Thảo's bún bò Huế is pure happiness. Her husband is also a fisherman.

Chị Linh's bánh canh
Unnamed
Corner of đường Nguyễn Công Sáu and đường An Cư 4, Phước Mỹ, Sơn Trà
Bé is a very sweet woman and makes one of the world's greatest soups from 6:30am to 7:30am in her main room every day.

Cafe 47 and the home of "bún" and "mì"
Ca Fe 49
49 đường Loseby, Phước Mỹ, Sơn Trà
The owners are really retired, high-ranking police officers and very kind people.

Bánh mì que cart
Unnamed
Corner of đường Loseby and đường Võ Nghĩa, Phước Mỹ, Sơn Trà
Summer afternoons only. The same woman sells bánh mì ốp la in the mornings year round at the corner of đường Nguyễn Công Sáu and đường Trí Trạch.

Postscript

Mì Quảng Bông's mì Quảng cá lóc
Quán Dung Mỳ Quảng
99 đường Nguyễn Thị Định, An Hải Bắc, Sơn Trà
Open all day. To me they have the best mì Quảng cá lóc in all Đà Nẵng and it's run by a kind family.

Quán chay Hạ
Nhà hàng Nén
Lô 20 đường Mỹ Đa Tây 2, Khuê Mỹ, Ngũ Hành Sơn
Much of the food written about in this novel was inspired by my work with the owner of this fine restaurant and her sister. Their love of the food of Đà Nẵng knows no bounds.

Quán Ba
Quán Hải
Near 58 đường Nguyễn Phan Vinh, Thọ Quang, Sơn Trà
Open nights. A popular and favorite place for bún riêu cua ở Đà Nẵng. If you want a bia Larue they'll happily get you one from across the street.

Bún mắm cart
Bún mắm Bé Hà
130 đường Bùi Hữu Nghĩa, Phước Mỹ, Sơn Trà
Chị Bé was always happy to see this westerner enjoying her bún mắm.

Sticky rice by grammar school
unnamed
đường Hoàng Bích Sơn and đường Phạm Thiều, Phước Mỹ, Sơn Trà
Served every school morning from 6:30am to 7am.

Xôi gà Bà Hồng
Quán Xôi gà Bà Hoa
37A Nguyễn Thị Minh Khai, Thạch Thang, Hải Châu
A favorite place for sticky rice and chicken among many and especially with students.

Bún mắm Thanh
Quán Bún mắm Vân
23/14 Trần Kế Xương, Hải Châu
One of the most crowed bún mắm shops in the city for a good reason.

Bar-B-Shed
Bar-B-Barn
3300 Sources Blvd, Dollard-Des Ormeaux, Montréal, Quebec H9B 1Z7, Canada
Serving some of Montréal's best barbeque for over fifty years.

Upton's bedroom and balcony
Conical Hats Homestay, third-floor, old building
Corner of đường Nguyễn Công Sáu and đường Trí Trạch, Phước Mỹ, Sơn Trà

This novel would not have been possible without that room and balcony or the family that lived there. Their family-altar-room, next to my room, was the inspiration for the one in Thủy's home. It is a good place for a writer to work and stay.

Their daughter and her love of everyday life in Việt Nam was the inspiration for me to write this novel and to which I will always be in her debt.

Also her mother's nước mắm is still the best I've ever had. That and her kindness will never be forgotten.

Postscript

Glossary

Anh	Older man to a younger person
Chị	Older woman to a younger person
Cháu	A much younger person to an older person
Em	Younger person to an older person
Con	Child
Chú	Uncle
Mẹ	Mother

dạ ("ya")	yes (South)
vâng	yes (North)
không	no
chào / xin chào	hello
xin / xin vui lòng	please
cảm ơn	thank you
cảm ơn nhiều	thank you very much
dạ không cám ơn	no thank you [to an older person]
không cám ơn	same but to a younger person
xin lỗi	[I am] sorry
không sao	similar to "no problem"
chào buổi sáng	good morning
chào buổi trưa	good afternoon
chúc ngủ ngon	good night
đường	street
thích	like
hẹn gặp lại	see you again or see you later
hẹn sớm gặp lại	see you soon
đi đó về	[I] leave
xe máy	motorcycle
cà phê	coffee
đẹp	beautiful

Postscript

rất đẹp	very beautiful
ăn	eat
cơm	rice
uống	drink
đi	go
kính mời	"welcome" and used as an invitation to eat or drink (South)
rồi	Changes present to past tense

không có gì (North), không có chi (South)
Nothing. Similar to "You're welcome."

"[Anh | Em] khỏe không?"
                similar to "Are you OK [fine]?"
"Một phút xin."   "One minute please."
"Cảm ơn anh."
Younger person thanking an older man
"Cảm ơn em."
Older person thanking a younger person.
"Anh xin lỗi em."
Older man apologizing to a younger person
"Em xin lỗi anh."
Younger person apologizing to an older man
"Em thích bánh canh."
Younger person telling an older person they like bánh canh.
"Em thích bánh canh không."
Older person asking a younger person if they like bánh canh.
"Anh và em đi ăn sáng bánh canh chị Linh không?"
A question asking if the older man and [và] younger person would like to go [đi] and have [eat] for breakfast

325

[ăn sáng] chị Linh's bánh canh.

"Anh và em đi uống cà phê không?"

A question asking if the older man and younger person would like to go and have coffee.

"Em thích anh."   Younger person likes older man.

"Anh thích em."   Older man likes younger person.

"Em yêu anh."   Younger person loves older man.

"Anh yêu em."   Older man loves younger person.

"Yết đế, yết đế, Ba la yết đế. Ba la tăng yết đế Bồ đề tát bà ha."

"Gone, gone, beyond gone. Completely beyond gone towards enlightenment." - The Heart of the Perfection of Wisdom Sūtra

Bibliography

Denial of Death (1973) Earnest Becker
An Outline of Psycho-Analysis (1949) Sigmund Freud
Motivation and Personality (1954) Abraham Maslow
The Myth of Sisyphus (1955) Albert Camus
Being and Nothingness: An Essay on Phenomenological Ontology (1943) Jean-Paul Sartre
Outlines of Mahayana Buddhism (1907) Daisetz Teitaro Suzuki
The End of Belonging (2010) Greg Madison
Economic and Philosophic Manuscripts of 1844 (1844) Karl Marx
The Jungle (1906) Upton Sinclair
Network (1976) Paddy Chayefsky
The Quiet American (1955) Graham Greene
Hamlet (1.5.167-8), Hamlet to Horatio (1599) William Shakespeare
The Associated Press Stylebook and Briefing on Media Law (1977) Norm Goldstein
Vietnamese Food with Helen's Recipes (2014) Helen Lê
"*Que Será, Será (Whatever Will Be, Will Be)*" (1956) Jay Livingston and Ray Evans
"*Archer: The Rock*" (2010) Adam Reed and Boswell Crocker
"*Rick and Morty: Mortynight Run*" (2015) Dan Harmon and Justin Roiland
"*BoJack Horseman: Out at Sea*" (2015) Raphael Bob-Waksberg

Gratias

This novel is dedicated to the people of the great city of Đà Nẵng. Thank you for showing this westerner how to live a good life.

"It's difficult to do but every day it gets a little easier. The hard part is that you have to do it every day, but it does get easier."
"OK."
Thank you BoJack.

"With that I headed downstairs locking the front door and gate behind me like anh Dũng always told me to do. He was just looking out for me."
I remembered to lock the gate just like you always told me to do. Thank you for welcoming into your home and your family. The lessons you taught me and your sense of humor will never be forgotten.

Thank you George for always being there for me. You're a wonderful son.

Postscript

Thank you em Thủy for your kindness and all the time we spent together. You have the sweetest laugh. Also thank you for allowing me to use your ovens which allowed me to follow my passion for baking.

Thank you em Summer for showing the best food in the city of Đà Nẵng. That food was my drug and you were my dealer. Working with you was always a joy.

About the author

Brian Beeler was born in Boston, Massachusetts and raised on Cape Cod where his interest in motorcycles began. At seventeen years old he enlisted in the United States Coast Guard Reserves (Tango 107) and at eighteen became a non-commissioned officer in the same. He was a Machinery Technician (MK) assigned to the Coast Guard's venerated 44' Motorized Lifeboat, the USCG Cutter Bittersweet (WLB 389) and USCG Group Woods Hole, where he worked with his father, serving his career in and around the North Atlantic Ocean.

He is a life-long photojournalist and videographer with numerous international credits. As part of that work he lived in the City of Đà Nẵng for two years where his love of Vietnamese food was born.

He was also a computer programmer and network engineer.

In 2013 he was diagnosed with stage-four squamous cell carcinoma of the right mandible which almost cost him his life and is thankful for the good people at Boston Medical Center and Boston University. And also to Dr. Monica Gobran, DMD who is a true bodhisattva.

Brian has intermittently suffered with depression throughout his life which he now uses for inspiration.

Postscript

Stay up to date about book two "Return to Aqua" at: twitter.com/TheBeautyofAqua

Business inquiries may be sent to: TheBeautyofAqua@gmail.com

This is a work of fiction. Names, characters, businesses, incidents, et al are either the products of the author's imagination or used in a fictitious manner. Any resemblance to actual persons, living or dead, or actual events is purely coincidental.

"Buy the ticket, take the ride...and if it occasionally gets a little heavier than what you had in mind, well...maybe chalk it up to a forced consciousness expansion: Tune in, freak out, get beaten."
- Hunter S. Thompson

Return to Aqua

1. Foreigner in a foreign land
2. Return to Aqua
3. Happiness
4. Welcome to our family
5. Life goes on until it doesn't
6. 1945
7. Far-off land
8. Kon Tum
9. More unrest
10. Aqua non vitae
11. Recovery
12. Rebirth
13. The offer
14. City by the river
15. Another new life
16. Lonely ghosts
17. Exit

Postscript

The Beauty of Aqua Series

The Beauty of Aqua
Return to Aqua
Year of the Water Cat
Exit

www.ingramcontent.com/pod-product-compliance
Lightning Source LLC
Chambersburg PA
CBHW060148050426
42446CB00013B/2719